JERVIS ON THE OFFICE AND DUTIES OF CORONERS

with Forms and Precedents

FOURTH SUPPLEMENT TO THE
ELEVENTH EDITION

by

PAUL MATTHEWS, B.C.L., LL.D.
Solicitor, Withers;
Visiting Professor, King's College London;
Deputy Coroner for the City of London

and

JOHN FOREMAN, M.B., B.S., PH.D., F.I.BIOL., D.SC.,
Fellow of University College London;
Professor of Immunopharmacology, University College
London Medical School

Consultant Editors

J.D.K. Burton, C.B.E., M.B., B.S., F.F.A.R.C.S.,
Barrister-at-Law;
H.M. Coroner for Greater London, Western District

D.R. Chambers, M.A., M.B., B.S., LL.B., F.I.BIOL.,
Barrister-at-Law;
H.M. Coroner for the City of London;
formerly H.M. Coroner for Greater London, Inner North District

LONDON
Sweet & Maxwell
1998

Published by
Sweet & Maxwell Limited,
of 100 Avenue Road,
London NW3 3PF
(http://www.smlawpub.co.uk)
Typeset by Interactive Sciences Ltd,
Gloucester
Printed and bound in Great Britain
by Butler & Tanner Ltd, Frome and London

No natural forests were destroyed to make this product: only farmed timber was used and replanted.

A CIP catalogue reference for this book is available from the British Library

ISBN MAIN WORK 0 421 44970 5
ISBN FOURTH SUPPLEMENT 0 421 626801

HOW TO USE THIS SUPPLEMENT

This is the Fourth (Cumulative) Supplement to the Eleventh Edition of *Jervis on Coroners*, and has been compiled according to the structure of the main volume. The Third Supplement should now be discarded.

At the beginning of the supplementary coverage for each Chapter the mini Table of Contents from the Main Volume has been included. Where a heading on this Table of Contents has been marked with a square pointer then there is relevant information in the Supplement to which you should refer. Material that is new to the Cumulative Supplement is indicated by a black square. Material which has been included from the previous supplements is marked by a white square.

Within each Chapter, updating information is referenced to the relevant paragraph in the main volume.

TABLE OF CASES

NOTE: References to newspaper reports may relate to news items as well as law reports.

TABLE OF STATUTES

NOTE: Bold references indicate that the relevant statutory material has been reproduced in the text.

TABLE OF STATUTORY INSTRUMENTS

NOTE: Bold references indicate that the relevant statutory material has been reproduced in the text.

Chapter 1

GENERAL INTRODUCTION

The Inquest into Death

1–07 In *R. v. North Humberside Coroner, ex p. Jamieson* [1995] Q.B. 1, the Court of Appeal held (at 23G–24A) that:

> "An inquest is a fact-finding inquiry conducted by a coroner, with or without a jury, to establish reliable answers to four important but limited factual questions. The first of these relates to the identity of the deceased, the second to the place of his death, the third to the time of death. In most cases these questions are not hard to answer but in a minority of cases the answer may be problematical. The fourth question, and that to which evidence and inquiry are most often and most closely directed, relates to how the deceased came by his death . . . . It is noteworthy that the task is not to ascertain how the deceased died, which might raise general and far-reaching issues, but 'how . . . the deceased came by his death', a more limited question directed to the means by which the deceased came by his death".

And again (at 24B),

> "It is not the function of a coroner or his jury to determine, or appear to determine, any question of criminal or civil liability, to apportion guilt or attribute blame."

These passages (*inter alia*) were cited with approval by the Northern Ireland Court of Appeal in *Ministry of Defence's Application*, unreported, June 17, 1994, and by Kay J. in *R. v. Birmingham and Solihull Coroner, ex p. Benton*, unreported, July 31, 1997. See also *Hay v. Devon Coroner*, unreported, February 10, 1997, C.A., and *Re Bradley's Application*, unreported, August 29, 1996, H.Ct. of N.I. (Kerr J.).

Functions

1–08 Whilst it is the inquest's function to inquire "how" the deceased came by his death, and this includes matters directly causative of death, it is not its function to inquire into the underlying responsibility for every circumstance which might have contributed to the death: *R. v. East Sussex Coroner, ex p. Homberg* (1994) 158 J.P. 357, D.C.

On the other hand, in *R. v. North Humberside Coroner, ex p. Jamieson* [1995] Q.B. 1, the Court of Appeal, whilst accepting the need for limits to the coroner's inquiry, emphasised the duty of the inquisitor within those limits:

> "It is the duty of the coroner as the public official responsible for the conduct of inquests, whether he is sitting with a jury or without, to ensure that the relevant facts are fully, fairly and fearlessly investigated. He is bound to recognise the acute public concern rightly aroused where deaths occur in custody. He must ensure that the relevant facts are exposed to public scrutiny, particularly if there is evidence of foul play, abuse or inhumanity. He fails in his duty if his investigation is superficial, slipshod or perfunctory. But the responsibility is his. He must set the bounds of the inquiry" (at 26B-C).

This was followed by the Divisional Court in *R. v. Birmingham Coroner, ex p. Cotton* (1995) 160 J.P. 123.

In *Re Clegg* (1996) 161 J.P. 521, D.C., Phillips L.J. said that:

> "the purpose of an inquest is not to identify individual fault on the part of those involved. On the contrary it is expressly not concerned with that question. It is much more important that it identifies any deficiencies of the system and ensures that steps are recommended to deal with those deficiencies."

The function of the inquest as an inquiry into violent or unnatural death will acquire even greater significance if the European Convention on Human Rights is incorporated into English law. Article 2(1) of the Convention provides that:

> "Everyone's right to life shall be protected by law. No one shall be deprived of his life intentionally save in the execution of a sentence of a court following his conviction of a crime for which this penalty is provided by law."

In *McCann v. United Kingdom* (1996) 21 E.H.R.R. 97, the European Court of Human Rights noted that the protection conferred by Article 2(1):

> "would be ineffective, in practice, if there existed no procedure for reviewing the lawfulness of the use of lethal force by State authorities. The obligation to protect the right to life under this provision, read in conjunction with the State's general duty under Article 1 of the Convention to 'secure to everyone within their jurisdiction the rights and freedoms defined in [the] Convention', requires by implication that there should be some form of effective official investigation when individuals have been killed as a result of the use of force by, *inter alios*, agents of the State" (para. 161).

In that case, which concerned the shooting of three terrorists by the British army in Gibraltar, an inquest was held there into the deaths. Allegations were made to the ECHR that there had been violations of Article 2 by reason of, *inter alia*, shortcomings in the inquest process. The allegations were left unconsidered on the basis that, *in fact*, "a thorough, impartial and careful examination of the circumstances surrounding the killings" had taken place. But it shows that the conduct of the inquest into a death *can* fall within Article 2. If the Convention becomes part of English law (as is the current Lord Chancellor's proposal), that Article, and the case law dealing with it, may be or become relevant in argument before the coroner, and subsequently on review of his decisions in the High Court.

Footnote 27: See also *R. v. South Glamorgan Coroner, ex p. Basoodeo Sujeeum* [1993] C.O.D. 366, D.C. (no need for inquest when cause of death known to be natural, even though hospital had admitted negligence in treatment).

Other functions

Other inquiries:

Footnote 43: For "Chap. 18", read "para. 15–29". 1–11

Chapter 2

CLASSIFICATION AND APPOINTMENT OF CORONERS

Appointment

2–13 Since the Local Government (Wales) Act 1994, Sched. 16, para. 82, came into force, coroners in Wales are to be appointed for the *whole* of Wales, although assigned to a particular district. The "relevant council" is the council of a "Welsh principal area" (see ss. 1–2 of the 1994 Act), *i.e.* either that in which the coroner's district wholly lies, or such one of two or more such areas in which it lies as the Secretary of State may designate (as to which see the Coroners' Districts (Designation of Relevant Councils) (Wales) Order 1996). As a consequence of various changes to local government in England under the Local Government Act 1992, a number of amendments have been made to provisions in the Coroners Act 1988, to ensure continuing consistency. Thus new subsections (1) and (1A) have been inserted in section 1 of the 1988 Act, by the Local Government Reorganisation (Amendment of Coroners Act 1988) Regulations 1996, made under sections 19 and 26 of the 1992 Act. The only significant changes are to provide for the case of a coroner's district being constituted by an order under section 17 of the 1992 Act and lying in each of two or more non-metropolitan counties (when the "relevant council" will be designated in the section 17 order), and for the case of the remainder of a non-metropolitan county after a section 17 order has constituted part of it either the whole or part of a coroner's district (when the "relevant council" will be the non-metropolitan county concerned).

Number of coroner's districts

2–15 In respect of Wales, after the coming into force of the Local Government (Wales) Act 1994, Sched. 16, para. 82, provision is made by a new section 4A of the Coroners Act 1988. However, the role of the Secretary of State is greater, and that of the local government authorities smaller, than under section 4. Various amalgamations and alterations were made, together with transitional provisions, by the Coroners' Districts (Wales) Order 1996, made under s.4A(1), (7), and printed in Appendix 2.

Footnotes 44,46: See the Kent (Coroners' Districts) (Amendment) Order 1996, the Cornwall (Coroners' Districts) Amendment Order 1996 and the North Yorkshire (Coroners' Districts) Order 1997, all printed in Appendix 2. **2–15**

Powers of the Secretary of State

Footnote 56: For "para 2–10", read "para 2–13". **2–16**

The impact of local government reorganisation

The Local Government Act 1992 established the Local Government Commission, for the purpose of conducting reviews of local government areas in England and making recommendations to the Secretary of State as to structural, boundary or electoral changes. The Secretary of State has power under section 17 of the Act to give effect to all or any of the recommendations by order, and has power under section 19 of the Act to make regulations supplementing such an order. Both powers are exercisable by statutory instrument under section 26. Section 17 does not refer to coroners, though section 17(3)(h) refers to "the abolition or establishment, or the restriction or extension, of the jurisdiction of any public body in or over any part of any area affected by the order." Section 19(2)(d)(i), on the other hand, refers to "the functions or areas of jurisdiction . . . of . . . any . . . coroner . . . " However, it is to be noted that the orders so far made all refer to section 17, but none of them to section 19. These include the Avon (Coroners) Order 1996 (S.I. 1996 No. 656), the Cleveland (Coroners) Order 1996 (S.I. 1996 No. 657), the Humberside (Coroners) Order 1996 (S.I. 1996 No. 658), the York and North Yorkshire (Coroners) Order 1996 (S.I. 1996 No. 659), the Humberside (Coroners) (Amendment) Order 1996 (S.I. 1996 No. 787), the East Sussex (Coroners) Order 1997 (S.I. 1997 No. 488), the Hampshire (Coroners) Order 1997 (S.I. 1997 No. 489), the Leicestershire (Coroners) Order 1997 (S.I. 1997 No. 490), the Staffordshire (Coroners) Order 1997 (S.I. 1997 No. 492), the Wiltshire (Coroners) Order 1997 (S.I. 1997 No. 493), the Bedfordshire (Coroners) Order 1997 (S.I. 1997 No. 494), the Buckinghamshire (Coroners) Order 1997 (S.I. 1997 No. 495), the Derbyshire (Coroners) Order 1997 (S.I. 1997 No. 496), the Dorset (Coroners) Order 1997 (S.I. 1997 No. 497), and the Durham (Coroners) Order 1997 (S.I. 1997 No. 498), all printed in Appendix 2. For the purpose of enabling compensation to be paid to any coroner who suffers a loss or reduction of remuneration in consequence of an order made under the 1992 Act, s.17, or indeed through the equivalent Welsh provisions in the Local Government (Wales) Act 1994, the Local Government Reorganisation (Compensation for Loss of Remuneration) Regulations 1995 have been extended, by the Local Government Reorganisation (Compensation for Loss of Remuneration) (Amendment) Regulations 1996 (S.I. 1996 No. 660), to coroners, treating them for this purpose as if they were employed by the relevant council. **2–18A**

Assignment to a District

2–21 After the coming into force of the Local Government (Wales) Act 1994, Sched. 16, para. 82, a coroner appointed for a district in Wales is treated as a coroner for the whole of Wales: see section 4A(8) of the Coroners Act 1988.

Qualification for appointment

2–25 But it should be noted that the Courts and Legal Services Act 1990, section 75, Sched. 11, prevents a *full-time* coroner from providing legal services or acting as arbitrator for personal reward. However, this does not prevent a coroner providing other services (*e.g.* medical).

Disqualifications

Statutory Disqualifications

2–26 After the coming into force of the Local Government (Wales) Act 1994, Sched. 16, para. 82, there is a similar prohibition on the appointment of a present or former councillor of a Welsh principal area to be coroner of a district wholly or partly within that area: section 2(2A) of the Coroners Act 1988.

Acts inconsistent with the office of coroner

2–27 *Footnote 94*: *R. v. Inner West London Coroner, ex p. Perks* is now reported, *sub nom. R. v. Inner West London Coroner, ex p. Lockwood Croft*, at (1993) 157 J.P. 985, D.C. The decision of the Divisional Court was, however, reversed on the facts by the Court of Appeal, *sub nom. ex p. Dallaglio and Lockwood Croft* [1994] 4 All E.R. 139, who held that a coroner (a) who described a deceased's mother as "unhinged", and (b) in relation to whom there was a real possibility (though not a probability) of unconscious influence against her and other deceaseds' relatives in the particular case, satisfied the test for apparent bias. See also *R. v. South Yorkshire Coroner, ex p. Stringer* (1993) 158 J.P. 453, D.C. (fact that coroner appointed and paid by local authority did not demonstrate apparent bias in favour of local authority), *Matthews v. Hunter* [1993] 2 N.Z.L.R. 683 (outspoken criticism did not amount to an appearance of partiality), *R. v. East Sussex Coroner, ex p. Homberg* (1994) 158 J.P. 357, D.C. (coroner's caustic public comments on lawyers representing deceased's families were regrettable but did not undermine public confidence in the proceedings), and *Re Sutherland* [1994] 2 N.Z.L.R. 242 (coroner wrong to preside over inquest into death of former client and personal friend, particularly as mental state of deceased was in question). In the criminal context, see also *R. v. Wilson, The Times*, February 24, 1995, C.A. (jury included wife of prison officer at prison where Defendant remanded: held, real danger of bias).

In 1995 the Solicitors Disciplinary Tribunal found a solicitor coroner to have been guilty of unbefitting conduct. He had opened and adjourned an inquest on a deceased who (unknown to him) had been employed by one of his clients. Having discovered this, the solicitor arranged for the inquest to be transferred to another coroner. This inquest was, for unconnected reasons, quashed and a further inquest held before another coroner. At *this* inquest the solicitor appeared to represent the interests of his client, the deceased's employer. The Tribunal held that "his knowledge of the matter had not been expunged by the order quashing the first inquest and he had acted in the same matter as both coroner and advocate for an interested party [*sic*]. Such behaviour was reprehensible. The conflict of interest was clear." However, as there were mitigating factors the Tribunal merely reprimanded the solicitor and ordered him to pay a contribution towards costs.

The Law Society's *Guide to the Professional Conduct of Solicitors* (7th ed., 1996), says (para. 15.06(e)):

"Coroners

(e) A solicitor who is a coroner or deputy or assistant deputy coroner should not appear on behalf of a client before a coroner's court for the area or district for which he or she is appointed. Nor should such a solicitor (or any partner or employee of the solicitor) act professionally in any civil or criminal proceedings resulting from a death where the solicitor has held an inquest into the circumstances of such death. Further, since the coroner acts in a judicial capacity, such a solicitor must make arrangements for another person to carry out an inquest into the death of a person where it might be thought that some bias could arise out of his or her personal or professional connection with the deceased, or with a near relative of the deceased."

At the words "capable of acting impartially", add new footnote. 2–27

Footnote 94a: "His successor should start all over again. He is not bound by anything the first coroner decided in relation to the inquiry, for example as to who is to be regarded as a 'properly interested person': *R. v. South London Coroner, ex p. Driscoll* (1993) 159 J.P. 45, D.C."

In *Re Sutherland* [1994] 2 N.Z.L.R. 242 the High Court of New Zealand quashed an inquest verdict and ordered a new inquest where (*inter alia*) the coroner had identified the body of the deceased and had provided a written statement of identification to herself. Barker A.C.J. said: 2–28

> "Moreover, by the act of formally identifying the deceased's body, she gave evidence before herself, something which no judicial officer should contemplate."

It is undesirable for the coroner to discuss with the media any aspect of current inquest proceedings : *R. v. Inner West London Coroner, ex p. Dallaglio and Lockwood Croft* [1994] 4 All E.R. 139, C.A. (coroner's decision not to resume inquest quashed for apparent bias after coroner described deceased's mother as "unhinged" during meeting with journalists).

Chapter 3

THE OFFICE OF CORONER

TERRITORIAL JURISDICTION

District Coroners

3–23 Since the Local Government (Wales) Act 1994, Sched. 16, para. 82, came into force, a coroner for a Welsh district is to be treated as if he were a coroner for the whole of Wales: section 4A(8) of the Coroners Act 1988.

3–23 *Footnote 6*: For "*supra*", read "*infra*".

PRIVILEGES AND IMMUNITIES

Judicial immunity

3–54 *Footnote 98*: See also *R. v. Bowden* [1995] 4 All E.R. 505; *Three Rivers District Council v. Bank of England (No. 3)* [1996] 3 All E.R. 558, Clarke J.

THE CORONER'S OFFICER

Remuneration and employment

3–59 It is also possible for the coroner's officer to be employed as a "civilian" by the police authority (see para. 3–62, n.22), and this too will avoid the problems arising from the coroner being the employer.

Chapter 4

DEPUTY AND ASSISTANT DEPUTY CORONERS

Power to Act

Exclusions from continuing or completing inquests

Where a coroner opens an inquest but then disqualifies himself from continuing, the deputy or assistant deputy must start again from the beginning. But he is not bound by any decision made by the coroner on the first occasion: *R. v. South London Coroner, ex p. Driscoll* (1993) 159 J.P. 45, D.C. **4–10**

Chapter 5

ASSUMPTION OF JURISDICTION

Basis of Coronial Jurisdiction

5–01 The need for a body to be lying in the coroner's district was overlooked in *R. v. South London Coroner, ex p. Weeks*, unreported, 1996, Scott Baker J., where the death had been registered and the body disposed of some nine months before the matter was referred to the coroner. But the application (for judicial review of the coroner's refusal to hold an inquest) was refused on other grounds in any event.

What Amounts to a Body

5–02 In line 10, for "partially, destroyed", read "partially destroyed".

Deciding whether a body is dead

5–11 *Footnote 27*: *Airedale NHS Trust* is now reported at [1993] A.C. 789. See also *Re Baby A* (1992) 3 Med. L.R. 303, Fam. D., noted 61 *Medico-Legal Journal* 47 (brainstem-dead baby on ventilator held dead for all legal and medical purposes, and accordingly it would not be unlawful to disconnect from ventilator).

Jurisdiction without a Body

Conditions for power to arise

5–13 *Footnote 30*: In *R. v. Home Secretary, ex p. Weatherhead* (1995) 32 B.M.L.R. 72; [1996] C.O.D. 271, May J. held that, for the Home Secretary's discretion to arise, it was not necessary that the coroner believe *for certain* that the person concerned had died; nor was it impermissible to seek to invoke that discretion in order to establish that the death *had* occurred.

Footnote 32: See also *R. v. South London Coroner, ex p. Driscoll* (1993) 159 J.P. 45, D.C. (coroner must be allowed to give an ordinary meaning to ordinary English words). 5–13

See also *R. v. Home Secretary, ex p. Weatherhead* (1995) 32 B.M.L.R. 72; [1996] C.O.D. 271, May J. 5–14

CERTIFICATE OF CAUSE OF DEATH

Certification by a registered medical practitioner

For a study on the ability of clinicians to recognise reportable deaths, see Start *et al.* (1993) 306 B.M.J. 1038; see also (1993) 306 B.M.J. 1018, 1539–1540. 5–18

DEATHS ASSOCIATED WITH OPERATIONS OR ANAESTHESIA

Report by the Registrar of Deaths

It should be made clear that the reference to death within 24 hours of an operation is really a customary means of measuring full recovery from the anaesthetic and does not itself appear in the text of the rule. 5–27

Cause of death

For a study of clinicians' ability to recognise reportable deaths, see Start *et al.* (1993) 306 B.M.J. 1038; see also (1993) 306 B.M.J. 1018, 1539–1540. 5–33

CORONER'S ENQUIRIES

In *R. v. South London Coroner, ex p. Weeks*, unreported, 1996, Scott Baker J. said: 5–48

> "when a coroner is informed of a death within his jurisdiction, he must consider all the relevant material before him and ask whether he has reasonable cause to suspect that the deceased died a violent or unnatural or a sudden death the cause of which is unknown. If he does have cause to suspect, he must hold an inquest. The test is one of objective fact. The matters that fall to be considered are not limited to admissible evidence. See *Hussein v. Chung Fook Kam* [1970] A.C. 942 at 949B."

Order for post-mortem examination

It should be made clear that it is only where a post-mortem examination is made under section 19 of the Act (see para. 6–25 below) and shows that the 5–51 death is natural that the coroner may dispense with an inquest. If the post-mortem examination is made under section 20 or section 21 (see paras. 6–26 and 6–24 below respectively) then there must be an inquest even if the death is established as due to natural causes. What is not clear is whether, if the section 19 examination shows that the death is natural, the coroner has any discretion left as to holding the inquest. Some take the view that he has none. The editors' view is that he has. The coroner is required by section 19(4) to send a certificate of the cause of death ("Pink Form B") to the registrar of deaths, *if* he "is satisfied as a result of [the examination] that an inquest is unnecessary". Assuming that the requirement to send Pink Form B to the registrar implies an *obligation* to discontinue the inquest (which is not clear), the problem is that section 19(4) does not depend on the coroner being satisfied that the death was natural, only that the inquest is "unnecessary". In other words, a coroner might continue to hold an inquest into a case of natural death if there is otherwise reason to do so. In effect, he has a discretion to continue or not, which must be exercised on judicial principles, and will be subject to review in an appropriate case. This interpretation of section 19 is supported by section 19(5), which refers to "*authorising* the coroner to dispense with an inquest", not *requiring* him to do so.

VIOLENT OR UNNATURAL DEATHS

Basic distinctions

5–55 *Footnotes 25, 27*: See also *R. v. East Sussex Coroner, ex p. Homberg* (1994) 158 J.P. 357 D.C. ("*ex p. Thomas* must be confined to the s.8(1)(a) context in which it arose; essentially it decides no more than that a broad common sense view must be taken when deciding the bald question whether a death is unnatural so as to determine whether to hold an inquest": *per* Simon Brown L.J. at 370G).

SUDDEN DEATH OF WHICH THE CAUSE IS UNKNOWN

5–57 *Footnote 30*: See noter-up to para. 5–51 above.

DEATH IN PRISON

5–58 *Footnote 38*: See also *R. v. North Humberside Coroner, ex p. Jamieson* [1995] Q.B. 1, C.A., especially at para. 14 of the Conclusions: "[The coroner] is bound to recognise the acute public concern rightly aroused where deaths occur in custody. He must ensure that the relevant facts are exposed to public scrutiny, particularly if there is evidence of foul play, abuse or inhumanity. . . " (at 26C).

Non-prisoners

5–61 *Footnote 47*: See also the passage from *ex p. Jamieson*, cited in para. 5–58, *supra*, in this Supplement.

REFUSAL TO HOLD AN INQUEST

Application to High Court

See, *e.g. R. v. South Glamorgan Coroner, ex p. Basoodeo Sujeeum* [1993] C.O.D. 366, D.C. **5–90**

See, *e.g. Ex p. Basoodeo Sujeeum*, above. **5–91**

Chapter 6

CORONER'S POWERS BEFORE (OR IN LIEU OF) INQUEST

Exhumation

6–01 *Footnote 3*: Where the Secretary of State for Defence has under the Protection of Military Remains Act 1986 designated (a) a vessel which sank or was stranded while in military service or (b) an area containing such a vessel or an aircraft which crashed on military service, it is an offence (under section 2) to interfere with the military remains concerned, whether by an excavation, exploration, salvage or otherwise, without the Defence Secretary's licence under section 4. This will obviously cover exhumation of human remains inside or near such a vessel or aircraft. The provisions of the Act are *in addition* to other relevant statutory provisions, and not in substitution for them, *pace* the views of the Ministry of Defence and one coroner, who each considered that they alone had exclusive power to exhume: see *The Times*, December 6, 1994. In a case reported in *The Times*, August 31, 1995, the remains of two wartime airmen were found by aviation archaeologists who had been licensed by the Ministry of Defence to dig at an aircraft crash site. The coroner was informed, but a Ministry spokesman did not "anticipate an inquest".

6–01 *Footnote 4*: See also *Re Knight*, *The Times*, January 27, 1994, Const. Ct. (exhumation should be ordered only for "special reasons", and not as matter of course), *Re St Mary's Churchyard, Alderley* [1994] 1 W.L.R. 1478, Const. Ct. (exhumation and reinterment of remains refused where incumbent had exercised his discretion as to place of interment within churchyard), and *Re John Stokes*, *The Times,* September 9, 1995 (exhumation of *cremated* remains for scattering refused). *Cf. Re Horner,* unreported, see *The Times*, July 18, 1995 (body of murder victim to be exhumed and reburied secretly elsewhere to prevent killer visiting grave).

Reference to Coroner

Post-mortem to obviate need for inquest

6–13 In lines 7 and 10 the word "court" should read "cause".

Post-mortem Examinations

Rights of interested persons in relation to post-mortem

6–21 In *Dobson v. North Tyneside Health Authority* [1996] 4 All E.R. 474, the Court of Appeal held that a hospital owed no duty to the administrator of the estate or next of kin of a deceased to retain tissue removed during a post-mortem examination against the possibility that it might be material evidence in civil litigation commenced at some future time. In fact this was the case of a coroner's post-mortem, and so the position of the coroner must be *a fortiori* so far as *civil* litigation is concerned.

Coroner's use of powers

In *Green v. Johnstone* [1995] 2 V.R. 176, Beach J. in the Supreme Court of Victoria, after considering evidence that carrying out an autopsy would be contrary to Aboriginal cultural and religious law, made an order under a specific statutory provision (Coroners Act 1985, s.29(4)) having no equivalent in England and Wales, prohibiting the carrying out of a coroner's autopsy on the body of an Aboriginal child, where the other available evidence suggested that the death was due to sudden infant death syndrome. *Cf. R. v. Greater Manchester Coroner, ex p. Worch* [1988] Q.B. 513, C.A. **6–22**

Selection of a medical practitioner

Where related criminal charges are possible

Another organisation to contact is the British Association of Forensic Medicine, whose membership is restricted to practising pathologists, and of whom approximately one-third are on the "Home Office" list. The Secretary is Dr J. C. Clark of the Department of Forensic Pathology, University of Sheffield, The Medico-Legal Centre, Watery Street, Sheffield, S3 7ES (telephone 0114 273 8721). **6–29**

Where death occurs in hospital

In *R. v. South Glamorgan Coroner, ex p. Basoodeo Sujeeum* [1993] C.O.D. 366, D.C., two post-mortem examinations were made, and it was argued that r. 6(c) had been breached. The court held that, on the evidence, this was not so. **6–31**

Entitlement to representation

In *R. v. South Glamorgan Coroner, ex p. Basoodeo Sujeeum* [1993] C.O.D. 366, D.C., it was argued that a failure to permit the applicant to be represented at the post-mortem examination (in any event an allegation denied by the coroner) could not in the circumstances be a ground for ordering an inquest to be held. **6–41**

SPECIAL EXAMINATION

Purpose of special examinations

A special examination under section 20 can only be ordered by the coroner *once he has decided to open an inquest.* Accordingly it is only in such circumstances that he will be able to pay for it and recover the cost from the relevant council. **6–45**

Chapter 7

DISPOSAL OF HUMAN REMAINS

POSSESSION OF THE BODY

7–01 Since section 14 of the Law of Property (Miscellaneous Provisions) Act 1994 came into force, the property of an intestate has vested on death in the Public Trustee, instead of in the President of the Family Division.

7–02 In *Dobson v. North Tyneside Health Authority* [1996] 4 All E.R. 474, the Court of Appeal held that neither the administrator of the estate nor the next of kin of a deceased had any right to possession of the brain of the deceased, removed for the purposes of a coroner's autopsy, sufficient to maintain an action for damages in conversion, some two years after the death, against the hospital which had since disposed of the brain, the rest of the body having been buried in the meantime.

7–03 *Footnote 16*: See also *Dobson v. North Tyneside Health Authority* [1996] 4 All E.R. 474, C.A., where the deceased had died intestate (so no executor) and no administrator had been appointed by the time the body was buried. The court held that there was no authority that there was a duty to dispose imposed upon the next of kin as such, and that without such a duty there could be no right to possession of the body.

Disputes over disposal

7–04 *Footnotes 17–19*: See *Dobson v. North Tyneside Health Authority* [1996] 4 All E.R. 474 where the Court of Appeal confirmed this to be the position.

Funeral arrangements

7–05 *Footnote 33*: As between estranged parents, see the Australian case of *Calma v. Sesar* (1992) 2 N.T.L.R. 37, noted 67 A.L.J. 149 (burial where the body already was). In *Brown v. Tulloch*, October 18, 1992, and *Burnes v. Richards*, October 6, 1993 (both noted 68 A.L.J. 67) the Supreme Court of New South Wales resolved the dispute between members of the intestate deceased's family by preferring the claim of the person with the higher right to apply for letters of administration to the estate. In *Warner v. Levitt*, unreported, August 23, 1994, the same court preferred blood parents to foster parents, on the basis that the former had the legal duty to bury a deceased child. In *R. v. Inner South London Coroner, ex p. Brinson*, unreported, see *The Times*, July 18, 1995, the wife and the mistress of the deceased both sought possession of the body from the coroner. He refused to release it to either without a court order. He made an affidavit but did not attend the hearing, leaving it to the other parties to fight it out. Owen J. persuaded them ultimately to agree that the body should be released to a named funeral director jointly instructed by the two women, all the funeral arrangements having been agreed between them.

DISPOSAL OF A BODY

Cremation

On cremation generally see White (1993) 33 Med. Sci. Law 151. 7–17

Removal of bodies out of England and Wales

Burial at sea

Footnote 19: The reference should be to the Food and Environment Protection Act 1985, s.5. 7–33

Chapter 8

DEATH

Definition and Diagnosis

Legally accepted test for death

8–02 *Footnote 1*: *Airedale NHS Trust* is at [1993] A.C. 789. See also *Re Baby A* (1992) 3 Med. L.R. 303, Fam. D., noted 61 *Medico-Legal Journal* 47.

Brain-stem Death

8–08 In *Re Baby A* (1992) 3 Med. L.R. 303, Johnson J. in the Family Division held that a baby that was brain-stem dead was dead for all legal purpose, and that doctors who disconnected the ventilation machine would not thereby be legally responsible in any way for the death.

Chapter 9

FORENSIC MEDICINE

Sudden Death from Natural Causes

Pulmonary embolism due to deep venous thrombosis. This must be distinguished from a much rarer cause of sudden death occurring in women during or shortly after labour, namely, amniotic fluid embolism. Definite proof that it is the latter will require extensive pathological investigation. **9–39**

Cardiomyopathy. In individuals with cardiomyopathies vigorous exercise can place a load on the heart which results in death. Hypertrophic cardiomyopathy (idiopathic hypertrophic subaortic stenosis) is a genetically determined disease which may cause no symptoms. In some cases, vigorous exercise precipitates obstruction of blood flow through the heart and consequent sudden death. **9–43**

Disease of the respiratory tract

Pneumonia. A variety of viral infections of the respiratory tract can lead to pneumonia which may cause sudden death. The very young and the old tend to be more susceptible. **9–47**

Poisoning

Some more common poisons

Tranquilizers, sedatives and sleeping tablets. In the last line of this paragraph, for "carbamazapine" read "temazepam". **9–75**

Chapter 10

PRELIMINARIES

Place of Inquest

Council provision of accommodation

10–03 Once the Local Government (Wales) Act 1994, Sched. 16, para. 82, comes into force, section 31 of the 1988 Act will also apply to the council of a Welsh principal area.

Notice of Inquest

Persons to receive notice

10–08 The equivalent rule in New Zealand to rule 19 requires the coroner to notify (*inter alios*) the "immediate relatives" of the deceased. In *Re Sutherland* [1994] 2 N.Z.L.R. 242 the High Court of New Zealand held that where the deceased's daughters were minor children in the care of a guardian, the coroner should notify the guardian.

10–8 *Footnote 26: Re McKerr's Application* is now reported at [1993] N.I. 249.

Witnesses

Power to call witnesses

10–11 See also generally *Re Bradley's Application*, unreported, August 29, 1996, H. Ct. of N.I., where Kerr J. held that a coroner's decision on a resumed inquest not to call witnesses whom he had previously decided to call could not be attacked. Kerr J. said:

> "It is the Coroner's exclusive duty to decide which witnesses are necessary. He should not be swayed or influenced by the views of others except insofar as they affect his own conviction."

Footnotes 37, 40: *Ex p. Clements* is now reported at (1993) 158 J.P. 17. 10–11
Footnote 40: See also *R. v. South Yorkshire Coroner, ex p. Stringer* (1993) 158 J.P. 453, D.C., and *R. v. East Sussex Coroner, ex p. Homberg* (1994) 158 J.P. 357, D.C. (coroner under no duty to call alleged ultimate beneficial owner of house in which persons died through arson of third party, as there was no useful evidence that he could give, even if he had admitted ownership), and *Hay v. Devon Coroner*, unreported, February 10, 1997, C.A. (coroner under no duty to call for investigating officer's report commissioned by Police Complaints Authority after deceased shot by police).

Challenge to coroner's decision on witness

Footnote 46: See also *R. v. East Sussex Coroner, ex p. Homberg*, unreported, June 14, 1993, D.C. and *Re Bradley's Application for Judicial Review*, unreported, August 29, 1996, H.Ct. N.I. 10–13

Subpoena for witness from outside administrative area

Footnote 65: *cf. Morris v. Murjani* [1996] 2 All E.R 384, C.A. 10–18

JURY

Circumstances where jury required

Footnote 77: When *R. v. Poplar Coroner, ex p. Chaudhry* came to a judicial review hearing (December 15, 1993), the application was withdrawn on terms that the coroner would seek the transfer of the matter to another coroner, who would be able to consider the matter afresh. But in a number of exchanges Russell L.J. and Blofeld J. doubted that this case justified a jury. See also *R. v. A.-G., ex p. Ferrante, The Independent*, April 13, 1995, C.A. (death of marine parachutist after accident on training jump did not appear to the coroner to be a case of systematic default, *i.e.* where "the system was so much at fault that, if nothing was done, there would be other deaths," but – at worst – as a case where the deceased should have been differently diagnosed and treated; hence there was no realistic prospect of saying the coroner was wrong not to have sat with a jury), and *R. v. Surrey Coroner, ex p. Wright* [1997] 2 W.L.R. 16, Tucker J. (death of dental patient following surgery under general anaesthetic; coroner's decision not to summon jury not "wrong in a public law sense": the "question of who was in charge on this occasion was entitled to be regarded as an individual rather than a systemic failing"). On the other hand, in *Re Neal, The Times*, December 9, 1995; [1996] C.O.D. 190 the Divisional Court rejected the coroner's argument that section 8(3)(d) did not apply to deaths abroad, and held that it might well have applied to the case of a British holidaymaker who died in Spain of carbon monoxide poisoning as a result of a faulty water heater. (In the event, the court held that the interests of justice did not require another inquest to be held, and so did not decide the point definitively.) 10–22
Footnote 78: The requirement for a jury in a treasure trove inquest is abolished by the Treasure Act 1996, s.7(4). 10–22

It is sometimes suggested that the existence of the coroner's power to report the matter to a person or authority having power to take action to prevent further fatalities, under rule 43 of the Coroners Rules 1984 (see para. 13–42) is relevant to the question whether a jury should be summoned. On principle, this seems wrong. The power is "ancillary to the inquest procedure and not its mainspring", as Pill L.J. observed in *Re Kelly* (1996) 161 J.P. 417, D.C. (see further para. 12–102 in this Supplement). 10–23

Footnote 84: *Ex p. Wigley* is noted at [1993] C.O.D. 364. 10–23

Procedure for summoning of jurors

10–30 *Footnote 4*: *Ex p. Carr* is now reported at [1994] 1 W.L.R. 578.

LEGAL AID

Representation at proceedings

10–36 The references to "legal aid by way of representation" should be simply to "civil legal aid".

Footnote 27: Grants may also be made by the Lord Chancellor under section 4(2)(b) of the Legal Aid Act 1988 to enable there to be representation at proceedings including inquests. In March 1995 the Lord Chancellor made such a grant of up to £200,000 "to enable any of the families involved [in the Marchioness disaster] who wish to be represented to have representation for the whole of the inquest".

PREPARATION FOR THE HEARING

10–37 *Footnote 36*: And see *Re O'Reilly* (1996) 160 J.P. 749, D.C. (inquisition quashed under Coroners Act 1988, s.13, for insufficient inquiry, particularly because coroner relied on oral evidence and did not seek to obtain relevant documents).
Footnote 37: See *Hay v. Devon Coroner*, unreported, February 10, 1997, C.A. (coroner under no duty to obtain investigating officer's report commissioned by Police Complaints Authority after deceased shot by police).

10–38 *Footnote 42*: The Prison Service has recently decided that it will generally be prepared to disclose to a "properly interested person" in advance of the inquest copies of documents which are provided to the coroner for the purposes of the inquest, where the coroner consents to this. Requests from properly interested persons will be handled by the Treasury Solicitor's Department, in consultation with the Prison Service and the coroner.

10–39 In *Re Jordan's Application for Judicial Review*, unreported, December 11, 1995, H. Ct. N.I., Carswell L.J. held that draft depositions of evidence, prepared by the coroner, were;

> "documents in the possession of the Coroner and over which he has control, and I think that it follows that he can deal with them as he sees fit as part of his jurisdiction to control the proceedings of his court. In my view the issue is whether he has come to an unreasonable decision in deciding not to release copies until each witness comes to give evidence . . . In considering this issue it is necessary again to have regard to the inquisitorial nature of the proceedings in an inquest. It does not follow that because a person against whom an accusation is made in a criminal court or who is liable to suffer judgment in a civil court requires the protection of rules and practices designed to ensure that he is not deprived of a fair opportunity to put forward his case, the same must necessarily obtain in an inquest . . . The fact that the next of kin may be less effectively armed than other persons represented at

the inquest is not the immediate issue, as it is a less directly material consideration than in adversarial proceedings."

The Court of Appeal of Northern Ireland, affirming his decision on June 28, 1996, said:

"In these circumstances there is no substance to [the] argument that the coroner is obliged to make such depositions available before the hearing. It is entirely a matter for him to decide when, if ever, as a matter of grace rather than obligation, he will make copies available to those appearing at the inquest . . . ."

The fact that an "interested person" is not entitled to see witness statements **10–39**
serves to emphasise the coroner's responsibility (since he *has* seen them) properly to deal with inconsistencies between the written statement of a witness and what he actually says at the hearing: *cf. Re Cohen* (1993) 158 J.P. 644, D.C., and see also para. 12–93 in this Supplement.

Footnote 46: *Re Mailey* was followed by the High Court of Northern Ireland in *Re Arthurs' Application for Judicial Review*, unreported, July 25, 1996, where the court held that the coroner's refusals (i) to allow the applicant to see witness statements before the relevant witnesses commenced their evidence, (ii) to allow additional time to consider expert and controversial evidence, and (iii) to adjourn to allow an application to be made for judicial review of (i) and (ii) were unimpeachable.
Footnote 49: *Re McKerr's Application* is now reported at [1993] N.I. 249.

Add new paragraph: **10–40**

The relatives of a deceased person may also have rights to obtain documents and information which may be relevant to the inquest's purposes, but entirely outside the inquest procedure. They may, for example, be entitled to see medical and other records relating to the deceased pursuant to the Data Protection Act 1984, the Access to Medical Reports Act 1988 or the Access to Health Records Act 1990. Or they may seek pre-action discovery against a potential defendant, under the Supreme Court Act 1981, or the County Court Act 1984, section 52. It is no objection to seeking such discovery that the inquest has not yet been held: *Stobart v. Nottingham Health Authority* [1992] 3 Med. L.R. 284.

Chapter 11

GENERAL MATTERS AT THE INQUEST

"Interested Persons" and Representation

Coroner's decision as to reasonable interest

11–05 In *R. v. South London Coroner, ex p. Driscoll* (1993) 159 J.P. 45, D.C., the court held that the words "properly interested person" were not technical, but ordinary English words, and it should be left to the coroner to give them an ordinary meaning. The word "properly" imports not only that the interest is reasonable and substantial, but that the coroner may need to be satisfied that the concern of the person involved is genuinely directed to the scope of the inquest under the rules. In that case the court overturned the coroner's ruling that two sisters were not "properly interested persons" in relation to an inquest on their deceased brother, on the basis that he had taken irrelevant matters into account in so ruling.

Publicity

Reporting Restrictions

11–11 In *R. v. Inner West London Coroner, ex p. Dallaglio and Lockwood Croft* [1994] 4 All E.R. 139, the Court of Appeal emphasised how unwise it was for the coroner to discuss any aspect of current legal proceedings with the media. There the coroner's decision not to resume an inquest was quashed for apparent bias after he had referred to the deceased's mother as "unhinged" at a meeting with journalists.

11–12 A problem arises if the child concerned is not a witness. In July 1995 the High Court and the Court of Appeal had to consider the case of a seven-year-old child who lit a fire at home which ultimately caused the death of family members. There was expert evidence of the likelihood of harm to the child if he grew up being known as responsible for the fire and the deaths. But the inquest was about to be held. Although the child would not be called to give evidence, the local authority was concerned that the child should be protected from being identified at the inquest. It therefore sought an injunction against media disclosure of the child's identity. At first instance the judge accepted the local authority's argument that, as the child was neither the subject of proceedings before the coroner, nor to be called as a witness in those proceedings, section 39 of the 1933 Act did not apply. The judge also concluded on the authorities that there was no warrant for exercising the inherent jurisdiction of the court under section 100 of the Children Act 1989 where (as here) there were no other proceedings underway for the protection of the welfare of the child. On appeal, the Court of Appeal, without considering the correctness of the judge's conclusions, invited the local authority instead to issue an originating summons and apply for the child to be warded, so that the court undoubtedly would have jurisdiction. The Court of Appeal thereupon granted an injunction restraining the media from publishing details of the child calculated to lead to his identification as being involved in the events leading to the deaths.

Footnote 36: The coroner considering making an order under section 39 has a complete discretion to allow persons considered to have a legitimate interest in the making of (or opposing) orders under the section (*e.g.* the press, local authorities) to make representations to him before the order is made; the coroner must in deciding whether to exercise the power under section 39 weigh the interest in the full reporting of the events concerned against the need to protect the children involved from further harm: *R. v. Central Criminal Court, ex p. Godwin and Crook* [1995] 1 W.L.R. 139, C.A. **11–12**

Footnote 37: In *Re Jordan's Application for Judicial Review,* unreported, June 28, 1996, C.A. of N.I., MacDermott L.J. said: **11–13**

> "in the exercise of its inherent powers a court . . . may grant anonymity to a witness or screen the witness in whatever manner is appropriate if it is necessary in the interest of justice to take such a course . . . . In considering an application for anonymity any court must engage in a 'balancing exercise'. This Coroner did that . . . .
>
> We would add one additional point: when a witness is to give evidence anonymously he should before commencing his evidence hand to the Judge (or Coroner) a slip of paper bearing his full name and address."

Footnote 38: See also *Birmingham Post and Mail Ltd v. Birmingham City Council, The Times*, November 25, 1993, D.C. **11–13**

Footnote 41–44: See now the Defamation Act 1996, s.14. **11–14**

Footnote 54: See also *R. v. Fellows, The Times*, October 3, 1996, C.A. **11–17**

CONTEMPT OF COURT

Contumacious refusal by a juror to reach any verdict, with the intention of impeding or creating a real risk of prejudicing the administration of justice may amount to contempt of court: *R. v. Schot and Barclay* (1997) 161 J.P. 473, C.A. **11–21**

Footnote 72: See also *A.G. v. Independent Television News Ltd, The Times*, May 22, 1994, D.C. **11–22**

In *Keeber v. Keeber, The Times*, July 14, 1995, the Court of Appeal emphasised the importance, in a non-molestation injunction case, of dealing with contempt proceedings swiftly and not adjourning them to await the conclusion of **11–24** criminal proceedings arising out of the same facts when no real risk of serious prejudice had been made out. It also appears that coroners have no power to detain alleged contemnors to be dealt with later, *e.g.* at the end of the day's sitting; see *Delaney v. Delaney* [1996] 1 All E.R. 367, C.A. Hence coroners must either deal straightaway with contempt in the face of the court, or hope that the contemnor remains to the end of the hearing. (If he is a juror or witness attending pursuant to a summons or *subpoena* the position will of course be different.)

The requirement of fairness

11–25 *Footnote 78*: See also *R. v. Bromell, The Times*, February 9, 1995, C.A. (judge in criminal case should have given appellant opportunity to be represented before making finding of contempt of court), and *R. v. Schot and Barclay* (1997) 161 J.P. 473, C.A. (inadequate legal representation arranged).

11–26 *Footnote 80*: See also *A.G. v. Independent Television News Ltd* [1995] 2 All E.R. 370, D.C. (single broadcast or limited circulation of article in long interval between publication and trial: *held*, no contempt of court).

11–26 *Footnote 81*: See also *R. v. Schot and Barclay* (1997) 161 J.P. 473, C.A. (30 days' imprisonment inappropriate in circumstances).

PERVERTING THE COURSE OF JUSTICE

11–32 The offence of doing acts tending and intended to pervert the course of justice can be committed in relation to an inquest. Thus, in *R. v. Sinha, The Times*, July 13, 1994, a medical practitioner, whose patient's death was the subject of a coroner's inquiry and might also lead to civil or criminal proceedings, falsified the computerised records relating to the patient, so as to make it appear that he was not at fault in connection with the death. The Court of Appeal approved the direction of the trial judge that:

> "An act has such a tendency [*i.e.* to pervert the course of public justice] if it gives rise to the possibility that it will mislead a tribunal concerned with public justice and might cause a miscarriage of justice. Public justice is any judicial proceedings which might arise from the death of [the patient], including an inquest, civil or criminal proceedings."

Chapter 12

PROCEDURE AT THE INQUEST

In the "mini-contents list" the reference to "interested parties" should be to "interested persons".

The Jury

No power to discharge individual juror

12–13 As to discharging jurors who are unwilling to give any verdict, see *R. v. Schot and Barclay* (1997) 161 J.P. 473, C.A.

Footnote 33: *Ex p. Carr* is now reported at [1994] 1 W.L.R. 578.

Composition of the Bench

Invitation to expert to act as assessor

12–17 The coroner will be reluctant to appoint an assessor unless he can be clear that the costs involved will be met by the relevant council (see paras. 18–46—18–48). In order to avoid difficulty later, the coroner would be well advised to secure the council's agreement to the incurring of these costs before doing so.

In *R. v. Surrey Coroner, ex p. Wright* [1997] 2 W.L.R. 16, Tucker J. rejected a challenge to the practice of sitting with an assessor in non-railway cases:

> " . . . it is entirely permissible for a coroner to call for the assistance of an assessor to sit with him if he considers it necessary having regard to the technical nature of the evidence which may have to be considered" (at 23).

Nor was it wrong for such an assessor himself to ask relevant questions

> "of a witness giving technical evidence provided this is done under the coroner's control, and is restricted to matters within the assessor's special experience" (at 24).

However, the judge further held that

> "the role of an assessor should not extend to his giving expert evidence. There is a danger that it might appear (whether justifiably or not) that the evidence of such a witness might attract the special confidence of the coroner, and might carry greater weight than would otherwise be the case" (at 24).

12–18 *Footnote 38*: It appears that in *R. v. Carter* the court did not in fact *order* the coroner to sit with an assessor, but that public funds were provided to enable him to do so.

ADJOURNMENT

Exercise of power

12–29 In *R. v. East Sussex Coroner, ex p. Homberg* (1994) 158 J.P. 357, D.C., the refusal of the coroner to adjourn a hearing so as to enable a challenge to his ruling to be made by way of an application for judicial review was upheld by the Divisional Court.

Compulsory adjournment

Pending criminal proceedings

12–39 *Footnote 90*: *Ex p. Perks* is now reported, *sub nom. R. v. Inner West London Coroner, ex p. Lockwood Croft*, at (1993) 157 J.P. 985. The decision of the Divisional Court was, however, reversed by the Court of Appeal, *sub nom. ex p. Dallaglio and Lockwood Croft* [1994] 4 All E.R. 139. In *Re Downes' Application* [1988] 4 N.I.J.B. 91, H. Ct. of N.I., Carswell J. held that in deciding whether it was necessary to resume an adjourned inquest:

> "the coroner must direct his attention to the question whether it has been sufficiently established who the deceased was, and how, when and where he came by his death. If the coroner, after looking at the facts of the case, considers that these matters have already been sufficiently established in public proceedings, he is quite justified in taking the view that an inquest is not necessary. The fact that the next-of-kin of a deceased person may thus not obtain the opportunity to cross-examine witnesses or tender more evidence does not itself make it necessary for him to hold an inquest. What is material is whether the relevant matters have been established in a manner in which the public interest has been adequately served."

12–39–12–40 Curiously enough, section 16 of the 1988 Act requires an adjournment only when criminal proceedings of the prescribed description are pending or likely *in England and Wales*. Thus if, for example, a person is prosecuted under the Road Traffic Act 1988, s.1, *in Scotland* in relation to a death caused there, and the body is released for disposal in England, not only must the English coroner open an inquest, he cannot adjourn it under section 16, and (what is worse) he is specifically prohibited, by rule 32 of the Coroners Rules 1984, from adjourning the inquest solely because of the pending criminal proceedings. This appears to be a clear *casus omissus*.

Footnote 93: As happened in *ex p. Perks*, n.90 above. **12–40**

The function of examining justices was intended to be abolished by the Criminal Justice and Public Order Act 1994, s.44, and replaced by a procedure for the transfer of trial proceedings. The 1994 Act, by Sched. 4 Part II, paras. 70–71, was to have amended ss. 16 and 17 of the Coroners Act 1988 in consequence, though the changes would not have affected the coroner's procedures in any material way. However, before the 1994 Act came into force, the government changed its mind, and, by s.44 of the Criminal Procedure and Investigations Act 1996, the examining justices' committal procedure was retained, albeit in a modified form. **12–40, 12–43, 12–45**

In the last line, "consistent" should read "inconsistent". **12–53**

Footnote 36: See also *R. v. Home Secretary, ex p. Weatherhead* (1995) 32 B.M.L.R. 72; [1996] C.O.D. 271, May J. (where X was acquitted of murdering Y, and there was no admissible evidence of Y's death, an inquest without a body would be seen as directed at showing that X was the killer, and the Home Secretary's decision to refuse an inquest would be upheld). **12–53**

APPLICATION BY INTERESTED PERSONS

The coroner should generally give reasons for his decisions: *R. v. Lambeth London Borough Council, ex p. Walters, The Times*, October 6, 1993 (not a coroner's case). But it should be noted that in *R. v. Attorney General, ex p. Ferrante* [1995] C.O.D. 18, Popplewell J. reached no conclusion on the question whether the Attorney General should give reasons for refusing his *fiat* under section 13 of the Coroners Act 1988. **12–60**

WITNESSES

Child as witness

Footnote 73: In *R. v. D, The Times,* November 15, 1995, the Court of Appeal held that the test of the competence of a child witness in a criminal trial was now whether the child was able to understand the questions put to him or her, to communicate, and to give a coherent and comprehensible account of the matters in relation to which he or she was giving evidence. Built into that concept was an ability to distinguish between truth and fiction or between fact and fantasy. However, it must be remembered that, since section 33A was added to the Criminal Justice Act 1988 by section 52(1) of the Criminal Justice Act 1991, children's evidence in criminal proceedings is given unsworn. Since all oral evidence at an inquest must be given "on oath" (Coroners Act 1988, s.11(2)), the proposition in the text, representing the common law position, must still apply. **12–70**
Footnote 74: Section 38(1) was in fact repealed by the Criminal Justice Act 1991, s.52(2).

Exceptions to compellability

Footnote 87: The exception applies to *all* judges, whether of superior courts or otherwise: see *Warren v. Warren* [1996] 3 W.L.R. 1129, C.A. **12–76**
Footnote 90: Nor should a coroner give evidence, even formal (such as identification) to himself: *Re Sutherland* [1994] 2 N.Z.L.R. 242.

Oral evidence to be given on oath

12–84 *Footnote 7*: The reference to the Coroners Act 1887, s.4(1), should be to the Coroners Act 1988, s.11(2).

Witnesses not sufficiently fluent to take oath in English

12–87 *Footnote 21*: A good case can be made for treating interpreters as expert witnesses, and hence entitled to be compensated pursuant to para. (3) of the Schedule of Fees and Allowances, *i.e.* in the coroner's discretion. Essentially an interpreter does not say what he or she heard or saw, but using expert skill interprets the primary facts so that the court can understand them. The Lord Chancellor's Department currently sets rates for interpreters in *magistrates' courts* of £70 per half day and £140 per full day.

12–87 *Footnote 22*: The Welsh Language Act 1967, s.1(1), has now been replaced by the Welsh Language Act 1993, s.22(1), in similar terms. The 1993 Act by section 23 enables the Lord Chancellor to make rules prescribing translations into Welsh of any forms of oath or affirmation administered in court, and section 24 empowers him to make rules for the provision of interpreters of the Welsh and English languages.

Order of witnesses

12–88 In *R. v. Maidstone Coroner's Court, ex p. Johnstone* (1994) 158 J.P. 1115, the Divisional Court quashed an inquisition where the pathologist, giving his evidence at the end of the hearing, after having been present during the evidence of witnesses of fact, revised his view of the medical cause of death from that which he had previously intimated to the coroner in the post-mortem examination report. The court stressed that the pathologist had not, "as often happens", given evidence first. This might suggest that a pathologist could only give evidence concerning his findings on examination and any opinion as to cause of death could only be based on such findings: thus the pathologist could not take into account any of the earlier factual evidence. This does not seem consistent with section 20(2), which states that he can be asked to give evidence

> "as to his opinion upon any matter arising out of the examination, *and* as to how, in his opinion the deceased came by his death" (emphasis supplied).

The statute does not limit the pathologist's opinion as to cause of death to the findings of the examination, nor to any written report (as it is, for example, under section 19(1)).

Procedure for examination

12–93 **Examination by Coroner**. If there is an inconsistency between the written statement of a witness and his oral evidence, and the interested persons are not aware of the inconsistency, the coroner must explore and deal with it himself: *Re Cohen* (1993) 158 J.P. 644, D.C. As to putting inconsistent previous statements to witnesses, see the inaptly named Criminal Procedure Act 1865, ss. 3–5, applying also to inquests: section 1. See also para 10.39 in this Supplement.

Footnote 32: In *Re Ministry of Defence's Application*, unreported, June 17, 1994 the Northern Ireland Court of Appeal considered a case where the coroner had refused an application by the Secretary of State for Defence for soldiers giving evidence at an inquest to be screened from the public (though not from coroner, interested persons and their lawyers). The Court of Appeal did not disturb the judge's ruling that the matter be remitted to the coroner for him to reconsider, in the light of the court's ruling on public interest immunity (see para. 12–148), his decision on screening. But Sir Brian Hutton C.J. stated that the court had *itself* caused inquiries to be made as to the practice of screening witnesses in criminal cases in England, and the information supplied by the Lord Chancellor's Department was that the use of screens to protect the identity of witnesses was "now a common occurrence at the Old Bailey", although the majority of such cases were "criminal trials where the victims/witnesses [were] children". Information was given that screening also occurred outside London. But it should be noted that, in *R. v. Schaub and Cooper, The Times*, December 3, 1993 (not referred to in *Re Ministry of Defence's Application)* the Court of Appeal held that it was only in the "most exceptional cases" that screens should be held to prevent eye contact between a defendant and a witness. See also *Re Jordan's Application for Judicial Review*, unreported, June 28, 1996, C.A. of N.I., where the Court refused on the facts to quash the coroner's decision to permit a number of witnesses to be identified merely by letters: see the extract quoted in the noter-up to para. 11–13, n. 37. 12–94

Footnote 33: But the coroner should not consult with witnesses in private: *Matthews v. Hunter* [1993] 2 N.Z.L.R. 683 (H. Ct. of N.Z.).

Examination by interested person. An inability on the part of an interested person to examine witnesses is not a ground for complaint if it arises because he and his legal representative have withdrawn in protest at an allegedly wrong decision by the coroner: *R. v. East Sussex Coroner, ex p. Homberg*, unreported, June 14, 1993, D.C., and subsequently (1994) 158 J.P. 357. See also *Re Arthurs' Application for Judicial Review*, unreported, May 24, 1996, H. Ct. of N.I. 12–95

Examination by legal representative

Footnote 39: *Re McKerr's Application* is now reported at [1993] N.I. 249. 12–100

Direction and relevance of proceedings

In *R. v. East Sussex Coroner, ex p. Homberg* (1994) 158 J.P. 357, the Divisional Court held that the coroner's overriding duty was to inquire "how" the deceased came by his death. But this was confined to matters *directly* causative of death, and did not extend to inquiring into the underlying responsibility for every circumstance which might have contributed to the death. Simon Brown L.J., at p 369F, quoted the final sentence of paragraph 12–101 of the main text ("The question of how . . . ") with apparent approval. In *R. v. North Humberside Coroner, ex p. Jamieson* [1995] Q.B. 1, the Court of Appeal pointed out (at 24A) that: 12–101

> "the task is not to ascertain how the deceased died, which might raise general and far-reaching issues, but 'how . . . the deceased came by his death', a

more limited question directed to the means by which the deceased came by his death."

This was followed by the Northern Ireland Court of Appeal in *Re Ministry of Defence's Application*, unreported, June 17, 1994, and by the Northern Ireland High Court (Nicholson J.) in *Re Inquests into the deaths of Toman, McKerr and others*, unreported, July 11, 1994. See also the extract from *R. v. North Humberside Coroner, ex p. Jamieson* in para. 1–07 to this Supplement, above, and *Re Bradley's Application*, unreported, August 29, 1996, H. Ct. of N.I. (Kerr J.).

Special considerations may apply where a jury has been summoned. In *R. v. East Sussex Coroner, ex p. Homberg* (1994) 158 J.P. 357, Morland J. said (at 381C) that:

> "Rule 36 should not be so interpreted as to defeat the purpose of s.8(3)(d) [death in circumstances prejudicial to public health or safety] . . . [I]f 'the proceedings and evidence' are narrowly confined, the answers to the "how" question will not serve the purpose of this section, the prevention or reduction of the risk of future injuries in similar circumstances."

This was approved by Simon Brown L.J. (the other judge in *ex p. Homberg*) in *R. v. Inner West London Coroner, ex p. Dallaglio and Lockwood Croft* [1994] 4 All E.R. 139. After quoting the passage from *ex p. Jamieson* set out in the noter-up to para. 1–08 above, Simon Brown L.J. said (at 155b-c):

> "[*Ex p. Jamieson*] of course, was a s.8(3)(a) [death in prison] case, but its adaptability to a s.8(3)(d) context is obvious. It is, in short, for the individual coroner to recognise and resolve the tension existing between s.8(3) and (s.11(5)(b) and) Rule 36. The enquiry is almost bound to stretch wider than strictly required for the purposes of a verdict. How much wider is pre-eminently a matter for the coroner whose rulings upon the question will only exceptionally be susceptible to judicial review."

But in *Re Neal*, *The Times*, December 9, 1995; [1996] C.O.D. 190, the Divisional Court (Staughton L.J. and Rougier J.) having considered *Homberg* and *Jamieson* held that the requirement to summon a jury in the cases covered in section 8 could not enlarge the area or scope of the inquiry under section 11(5) or rule 36. All that section 8 did was to identify the cases where a jury was required.

A further question is whether the scope of the inquest can be affected by the power given to the coroner by rule 43 of the Coroners Rules 1984 to report the matter to a person or authority having power to take action to prevent further fatalities (see generally para. 13–42). On principle the answer would seem to be No. In *Re Kelly* (1996) 161 J.P. 417, D.C., Pill L.J., in the context of an application under section 13 of the Coroners Act 1988 for an order quashing the inquisition and ordering a fresh inquest, said:

"A Coroner's power under Rule 43 is a valuable one in the public interest. It is however ancillary to the inquest procedure and not its mainspring. In circumstances such as the present, I cannot regard the fact that the recommendations might be different or fuller if more evidence is given as in itself a main ground, or even a significant supporting ground, for holding another inquest".

Footnote 41: In *Hay v. Devon Coroner*, unreported, February 10, 1997, the Court of Appeal emphasised that it was not "the purpose of inquest proceedings to establish criminal or civil liability". **12–101**

The propriety of questions in examination

It is proper for the coroner or an interested person to ask questions of a witness going to credit in accordance with the inaptly named Criminal Procedure Act 1865, ss. 3–5, as that Act, by s.1, applies to "all courts of judicature . . . and to all persons having, by law or by consent of parties, authority to hear, receive, and examine evidence." **12–103**

EVIDENCE

Common law restrictions

The Civil Evidence Act 1995 has now effectively abolished the rule against the admission of hearsay in civil proceedings. The Law Commission has issued a Consultation Paper (No. 138) on hearsay in criminal proceedings, suggesting various options for reform. **12–106**

Outline of rules of evidence

In *Re Sutherland* [1994] 2 N.Z.L.R. 342 the New Zealand High Court criticised the use of an unsigned police report of an interview with a medical witness to give medical evidence at an inquest. The judge said that although this "double hearsay" was "technically admissible", it was "a particularly unsatisfactory way of conveying evidence of this nature" (at 347). **12–111**

Footnote 56: The reference to *Re Maker's Application* should be to *Re McKerr's Application*, now reported at [1993] N.I. 249. **12–111**

PRIVILEGE

Public interest immunity

The decision of the House of Lords in *R. v. Chief Constable of West Midlands Police, ex p. Wiley* [1995] 1 A.C. 274, in reversing the decision of the Court of **12–143**

Appeal ([1994] 1 W.L.R. 114) has restricted the scope of public interest immunity, and overruled *Neilson v. Laugharne* [1981] Q.B. 736 and the cases that followed it. The particular decision was to the effect that there was no general public interest immunity in respect of documents coming into existence during an investigation into a complaint against the police under Part IX of the Police and Criminal Evidence Act 1984.

12–143 *Footnote 48*: *Makanjuola* was overruled by the House of Lords in *R. v. Chief Constable of West Midlands Police, ex p. Wiley* [1995] 1 A.C. 274.

12–144 *Footnote 50*: But an investigating officer's report commissioned by the Police Complaints Authority following the shooting of the deceased by police was held covered by immunity in *Hay v. Devon Coroner*, unreported, February 10, 1997, C.A.

12–148 *Footnotes 59, 61*: The decision in *Re Ministry of Defence's Application* was affirmed by the Court of Appeal of Northern Ireland on June 17, 1994. See also *Re Inquests into the deaths of Toman, McKerr and others*, unreported, July 11, 1994, Nicholson J. (H. Ct. of N.I.).

DOCUMENTARY EVIDENCE

No power for coroner to order production of documents

12–150 *Footnote 66*: *Re McKerr's Application* is now reported at [1993] N.I. 249.

Other rules on admissibility

12–153 In *R. v. Ceredigion Coroner, ex p. Wiley* [1993] C.O.D. 364, D.C., the court said that material on which the coroner intends to rely at the inquest must be made available to interested persons; it is improper for the court to use material which is not shown and made available at the hearing.

OTHER PROCEDURAL MATTERS

The taking of notes, or tape-recording of evidence by the coroner

12–156 It is desirable that the coroner's notes should identify who asked particular questions of witnesses: *Re Cohen* (1993) 158 J.P. 644, D.C. In *R. v. Ceredigion Coroner, ex p. Wigley* [1993] C.O.D. 364, D.C., the coroner's notes were criticised for not fully and adequately representing all that was said. The court suggested that a shorthand note should have been made, but tape recording is cheaper and easier to arrange, and the relevant council may not be prepared to pay for a shorthand note.

Facts in evidence and matters of law

12–157 *Footnote 88*: See also *R. v. East Sussex Coroner, ex p. Homberg* (1994) 158 JP 357, *per* Morland J.

Summing-up

The coroner must direct the jury with care, and in particular on causation (if lack of care/neglect is available) and on the standard of proof: *R. v. Southwark Coroner's Court, ex p. Epsom Health Care NHS Trust* (1994) 158 J.P. 973 D.C. In *R. v. Reading Coroner, ex p. West Berkshire Housing*, unreported, July 11, 1995, Popplewell J. criticised the coroner's summing up to the jury for not having related the evidence in the case to the directions on the law which he had just given to them. He dealt with both separately, but did not relate the one to the other. The judge expressly asked whether there was any law relating to the coroner's summing up, but was not referred to rule 41 of the Coroners Rules 1984. It is therefore unclear whether the judge's views would have been the same or different if he had known of the rule. **12–158**

Footnote 2: See *Hay v. Devon Coroner*, unreported, February 10, 1997, C.A. **12–161**

Footnote 4: See also *Daley v. R.* [1994] 1 A.C. 117, P.C., and *R. v. Inner North London Coroner, ex p. Keogh*, unreported, July 31, 1995, C.A. **12–162**

Chapter 13

VERDICT AND INQUISITION

Verdict

13–01 *Footnote 4*: See also *R. v. East Sussex Coroner, ex p. Homberg* (1994) 158 J.P. 357, D.C., *R. v. North Humberside Coroner, ex p. Jamieson* [1995] Q.B. 1, C.A., and *Re Ministry of Defence's Application*, unreported, June 17, 1994, C.A. of N.I.

Jury Cases

Consideration of verdict in private

13–04 Once a jury has retired they should not be given any additional evidence, matter or material to assist them: *R. v. Davis* (1975) 62 Cr. App. R. 194; *R. v. Oliver* [1996] 2 Cr. App. R. 514, C.A.

May a coroner's jury separate once it has begun an inquest hearing? This question has never been decided. It has arisen in the context of a criminal trial on indictment. At common law a jury could not separate once the trial had begun (Co. Litt. 227b). This was to prevent interference, and to encourage them to reach a verdict. The Detention of Juries Act 1897, s.1, empowered the court to permit a jury to separate if it had not yet been directed to consider a verdict. But unless it was trivial (*e.g. R. v. Alexander* [1974] 1 W.L.R. 422) any separation after that point was a material irregularity which justified the court in discharging the whole jury and ordering a retrial (*R. v. Goodson* [1975] 1 W.L.R. 549). The Criminal Justice and Public Order Act 1994, s.43, has now extended the court's power to permit a jury to separate to the period *afer* being directed to consider its verdict.

But these statutory changes do not apply to a coroner's inquest jury, which is still governed by the common law on this point. Is the rule the same as it was at common law for trial on indictment, *i.e.* no separation permitted? In favour of the rule being the same is the fact that a jury's conclusion of unlawful killing (say) is a serious matter, requiring the jury to be satisfied beyond reasonable doubt, just like a trial. On the other hand, such a conclusion must not name any person responsible, and since 1977 cannot operate to charge a person with any offence. Even before 1977, a person who *might* be named in an inquisition was not to be treated during the inquest as if he were already on trial. And, unlike on trial on indictment, a coroner had powers, at common law, both to discharge a juror (so long as the minimum remained) and to take a majority verdict. Here the coroner's jury was the functional equivalent of the Grand Jury, who considered whether a case should go to trial, rather than of the petty jury, which actually tried cases.

These important differences suggest that there is no need to apply the common law rule for petty juries to coroners' juries, provided that appropriate steps are taken to minimise any possible interference with the jury. In *R. v. Oliver* [1996] 2 Cr. App. R. 514 the Court of Appeal laid down directions to be given to a jury permitted to separate after retirement. With any necessary modifications, these could be used also in the case of a coroner's jury permitted to separate. In substance, these were that:

(1) the jury must decide the case on the evidence seen and heard in court, and not on anything they might have seen or heard or might see or hear outside court;
(2) the evidence having been completed (as in that case it had) it would be wrong for any juror to seek or receive further evidence or information about the case;
(3) the jury must not talk to anyone about the case, or allow anyone else to talk to them about the case, except other members of the jury, and then only when deliberating in the juryroom;
(4) when they left court they should try to put the case on one side until they returned to court and retired to their jury room to continue the process of deliberating about their verdict.

Such directions should be given in full on the first dispersal by the jury, and then a brief reminder at each subsequent dispersal.

No communication with jury whilst out of court

Footnote 12: For the purposes of section 8, "disclose" means "disclose generally", and hence a newspaper committed contempt of court by publishing an article revealing statements, opinions and arguments, during their deliberations, of some of the jurors in a fraud trial: *A.G. v. Associated Newspapers Ltd* [1994] 2 A.C. 238, H.L. 13–05

Reasonable period for deliberation of jury

Footnote 19: *Ex p. Clements* is now reported at (1993) 158 J.P. 17. See also *Re Bradley's Application for Judicial Review*, unreported, April 7, 1995, H. Ct. of N.I. (final day's sitting 10:30–1:00, 2:00–4:30, 5:45–8:20, jury's verdict finally returned at 10:45p.m.: inquisition quashed, despite facts that jury had wished to sit late to conclude inquest that day, and that no interested person had objected). See also *R. v. Northampton Coroner, ex p. Tompkinson* (1995) 160 J.P. 69, D.C. 13–07

Unanimous and majority verdicts

As to the case where a minority of jurors are unwilling to give any verdict at all, see *R. v. Schot and Barclay* (1997) 161 J.P. 473, C.A. 13–08

13–08 *Footnote 24*: *Ex p. Carr* is now reported at [1994] 1 W.L.R. 578, and *ex p. Clements* at (1993) 158 J.P. 17.

INQUISITION

13–10 *Footnote 30*: *Ex p. Clements* is now reported at (1993) 158 J.P. 17.

(2) Facts Found

13–14 In *R. v. West Yorkshire Coroner, ex p. Stringer* (1993) 158 J.P. 453, the Divisional Court held that a "narrative verdict" should be given under paragraph (3) rather than paragraph (4).

13–15 On "narrative verdicts", see *R. v. West Yorkshire Coroner, ex p. Stringer* (1993) 158 J.P. 453, D.C., *R. v. East Sussex Coroner, ex p. Homberg* (1994) 158 J.P. 357, D.C., and *R. v. North Humberside Coroner, ex p. Jamieson* [1995] Q.B. 1, C.A. In *ex p. Homberg* Simon Brown L.J. said that there was no requirement that the coroner should explicitly invite a jury to reach a "narrative" verdict. Moreover, it was wrong:

> "to incorporate within the verdict itself whatever in the way of contributory causes could ultimately found a successful civil liability claim. That would in my judgment broaden and complicate the approach to inquest verdicts beyond any possible compensating advantage" (at 371E).

In *ex p. Jamieson* the Court of Appeal said (at 24F-G) that:

> "there can be no objection to a verdict which incorporates a brief, neutral, factual statement . . . . But such verdict must be factual, expressing no judgment or opinion, and it is not the jury's function to prepare detailed factual statements."

See also *Re Bradley's Application for Judicial Review*, unreported, April 7, 1995, H. Ct. of N.I.

(c) *"Dependence on drugs/non-dependent abuse of drugs"*

13–20 See also *R. v. Northampton Coroner, ex p. Tompkinson* (1995) 160 J.P. 69, D.C.

(d) *"Suicide"*

13–21 For the difficult interplay between suicide and neglect, see para. 13–37.

13–21 *Footnote 54*: The so-called "year and a day" rule has now been abolished by the Law Reform (Year and a Day Rule) Act 1996, so if the facts of the *De Luca* case recurred, it would be suicide.

13–22 *Footnote 55*: See also *R. v. Birmingham and Solihull Coroner, ex p. Nutt* [1993] C.O.D. 449, D.C. ("the standard of proof remains the same as in a criminal prosecution"). But in *Anderson v. Blashki* [1993]

2 V.R. 89, and in *The Secretary to the Department of Health and Community Services v. Gurrick* [1995] 2 V.R. 69, the Supreme Court of Victoria held that the civil standard of proof applied to *all* findings of coroners, though the graver the allegation, the more cogent must be the evidence, and in *Re Sutherland* [1994] 2 N.Z.L.R. 242, the New Zealand High Court took a similar view: see a note in (1994) 13 C.J.Q. 309.

(g) "*Accident/misadventure*"

This paragraph was cited with approval by Kay J. in *R. v. Birmingham and Solihull Coroner, ex p. Benton*, unreported, July 31, 1997. The judge contrasted two situations when death occurred in the course of medical treatment: 13–24

> "The first is where a person is suffering from a potentially fatal condition and medical intervention does no more than fail to prevent death. In such circumstances the underlying cause of death is the condition that proved fatal and in such a case, the correct verdict would be death from natural causes. This would be the case even if the medical treatment that had been given was viewed generally by the medical profession as the wrong treatment. All the more so is this the case where such a person is not treated at all, even if the failure to give the treatment was negligent . . .
>
> On the other hand, where a person is suffering from a condition which does not in any way threaten his life and such person undergoes treatment which for whatever reason causes death, then assuming that there is no question of unlawful killing the verdict should be death by accident/misadventure. Just as the recording of death by natural causes does not absolve the doctors of fault so the recording of death by accident/misadventure does not imply fault."

(h) *"Unlawful killing"*

As to the elements of the homicide offences concerned, see paras 14–26 – 14–37, 14–46. 13–27

Footnote 84: *Hay v. Devon Coroner*, unreported, February 10, 1997, C.A. 13–30

Footnote 86: See also *Re Oakes*, unreported, see *The Times*, July 7, 1995. 13–30

Footnote 91: See also *Anderson v. Blashki* [1993] 2 V.R. 89, and *The Secretary to the Department of Health and Community Services v. Gurrick* [1995] 2 V.R. 69, Sup. Ct. of Victoria (civil standard of proof applies to *all* findings of coroners, though the graver the allegation, the more cogent must be the evidence). 13–31

(j) *"Self-neglect or lack of care"*

In *R. v. North Humberside Coroner, ex p. Jamieson* [1995] Q.B. 1 at 25B, the Court of Appeal suggested that, in future, it would be preferable to refer to "neglect" rather than to "lack of care", as this is "the obverse of self-neglect". The Court went on to say (at 25E) that: 13–33

"As in the case of self-neglect, neglect [*i.e.*, lack of care] can rarely, if ever, be an appropriate verdict on its own. It is difficult to think of facts on which there would not be a primary verdict other than neglect."

Some of the potential difficulties caused by this decision are referred to in a note in (1994) 110 L.Q.R. 536. The interplay between gross negligence manslaughter and neglect as a free-standing conclusion was discussed in *R. v. Inner South London Coroner, ex p. Douglas-Williams*, unreported, July 31, 1997, Laws J. He said:

"One has to postulate circumstances in which a reasonable jury were not satisfied that unlawful killing (on any basis, but in particular on the footing of gross negligence) was made out, yet could have been satisfied that there was a 'gross failure' to look after the deceased in the condition he was in. I cannot see that on the facts of the case there was any perceptible space for such a scenario. Even if by the ingenuity of counsel such a space could in theory be found, at the very least it was reasonable for the coroner not to leave such a separate verdict. I think that it would only have confused the jury."

Of course, there is one very significant difference between an unlawful killing conclusion and one of neglect. The former requires the criminal standard of proof, the latter only the civil. But the judge did not mention this.

In *R. v. Birmingham Coroner, ex p. Cotton* (1995) 160 J.P. 123, the Divisional Court held that, in the light of the extensive review of earlier case-law on the question of neglect/lack of care in *ex p. Jamieson*, it was that decision that should henceforward be considered, and there was no need to look at the earlier cases. See also *R. v. Surrey Coroner, ex p. Wright* [1997] 2 W.L.R. 16, Tucker J.

13–34 See also *R. v. South Yorkshire Coroner, ex p. Stringer* (1993) 158 J.P. 453, D.C., and *R. v. East Sussex Coroner, ex p. Homberg* (1994) 158 J.P. 357 D.C., where Simon Brown L.J. said that the conclusion of lack of care:

"can arise only in circumstances where the deceased was in a dependent relationship to the putative carer and where the lack of necessary physical care contributed to or aggravated whatever it was about the physical or mental condition of the deceased that required care" (at 370D).

13–34 *Footnote 3*: *Ex p. Jamieson* is now reported at (1993) 158 J.P. 1. The decision was affirmed by the Court of Appeal, though on slightly different grounds: see [1995] Q.B. 1.

13–35 *Footnote 8*: Add *R. v. North Humberside Coroner, ex p. Jamieson* [1995] Q.B. 1, C.A. and *R. v. Southwark Coroner's Court, ex p. Epsom Health Care NHS Trust* (1994) 158 J.P. 973, D.C.

13–36 In *R. v. North Humberside Coroner, ex p. Jamieson* [1995] Q.B. 1, at 25B-D, the Court of Appeal said that

"Neglect [*i.e.* lack of care] in this context means a gross failure to provide adequate nourishment or liquid, or provide or procure basic medical

> attention or shelter or warmth for someone in a dependent position (because of youth, age, illness or incarceration) who cannot provide it for himself. Failure to provide medical attention for a dependent person whose physical condition is such as to show that he obviously needs it may amount to neglect. So it may be if it is the dependent person's mental condition which obviously calls for medical attention . . . . In both cases the crucial consideration will be what the dependent person's condition, whether physical or mental, appeared to be."

This was applied in *R. v. Southwark Coroner's Court, ex p. Epsom Health Care NHS Trust* (1994) 158 J.P. 973, D.C., in *R. v. Birmingham Coroner, ex p. Cotton* (1995) 160 J.P. 123, D.C., in *R. v. South Yorkshire Coroner, ex p. Tremble* (1995) 159 J.P. 761, Owen J., and in *R. v. Surrey Coroner, ex p. Wright* [1997] 2 W.L.R. 16, Tucker J., and in *Re Clegg* (1996) 161 J.P. 521, D.C.

In the *Cotton* case the court held that the words "gross failure" applied just as much to the provision of basic medical attention as to the other matters mentioned. Thus, where a patient dies after clinical judgment had been exercised in relation to her treatment, the fact (if it were the fact) that the judgment had been wrong and had caused death would not justify a neglect/lack of care conclusion. The question whether it was wrong and had caused the death were for civil litigation.

In the *Tremble* case, the deceased was an immature young offender, given to making false threats to commit suicide. A prison officer (knowing of this propensity) saw him with a sheet round his neck and told him to "stop messing about". He was later found hanged, apparently by accident, as the jury negatived suicide. Owen J. said that, although the deceased was a person in a dependent position, there was no evidence of any condition on his part calling for medical attention. Conclusion (11) from *Jamieson* did not assist: this was not a genuine attempt at suicide.

In the *Wright* case, the deceased was a patient under general anaesthetic, recovering from minor dental surgery, who was left alone in the recovery room and suffered brain damage. The judge held (at 25) that

> "the 'neglect' referred to by the Master of the Rolls in *Jamieson* means continuous or at least non-transient neglect. It is not an appropriate description of the negligent lack of care which is alleged to have led to the death in the present case."

In *Re Clegg* the Divisional Court seemed to go back on *Cotton*, holding that:

> "Failure to provide appropriate medical attention to a dependent patient in hospital is capable of constituting 'neglect' ",

and applying that to a case where it appeared that:

"the care which [the deceased] received during [a 12–hour] period suffered from a continuous sequence of shortcomings".

In other words, where care *is* provided but it is the wrong or inadequate treatment, as a result of bad clinical judgment, this is capable of amounting to "neglect". This is directly contrary to *Cotton* which, although cited by the Divisional Court, does not appear to have been made available to the court in transcript or report form.

13–36 *Footnotes 11, 12*: *Ex p. Jamieson* is now reported at (1993) 158 J.P. 1, and *ex p. Clements* at (1993) 158 J.P. 17. The former decision was affirmed by the Court of Appeal, though on slightly different grounds: see [1995] Q.B. 1.

13–36 *Footnote 13*: Add *R. v. North Humberside Coroner, ex p. Jamieson* [1995] Q.B. 1, C.A.

13–37 When *ex p. Jamieson* (from which the extract comes) reached the Court of Appeal ([1995] Q.B. 1), that court held (at 25G-H)) that:

"Where it is established that the deceased took his own life, that must be the verdict. On such facts . . . there is no room for a verdict of neglect [*i.e.* "lack of care"] . . . . It is also inappropriate in such a case . . . to describe that cause of death as aggravated by neglect . . . . On certain facts it could possibly be correct to hold that neglect contributed to that cause of death, but this finding would not be justified simply on the ground that the deceased was afforded an opportunity to take his own life even if it was careless (as that expression is used in common speech or in the law of negligence) to afford the deceased that opportunity. Such a finding would only be appropriate in a case where gross neglect was directly connected with the deceased's suicide . . . "

In *Re Clegg* (1996) 161 J.P. 521, D.C., the deceased took an aspirin overdose, but was taken to hospital before she died. The treatment she received in hospital was inadequate to save her life. The court distinguished *Jamieson* as a case where the alleged "neglect" *preceded* the suicide; in the present case (as also in *ex p. Wright* [1997] 2 W.L.R. 16) the "neglect" followed it. The court said:

"In such circumstances it is much easier to conceive of neglect having a direct causal connection to the death."

13–37 *Footnote 17*: *Ex p. Jamieson* is now reported at (1993) 158 J.P. 1, and *ex p. Clements* at (1993) 158 J.P. 17. The former decision was affirmed by the Court of Appeal, though on slightly different grounds: see [1995] Q.B. 1.

13–39 In *R. v. Sunderland Coroner, ex p. Sunderland City Council*, unreported, October 19, 1994, a case where the deceased died in a home run by the applicant, Beldam L.J., without referring to the authorities cited in this paragraph, referred to Rule 42 of the Coroners Rules, and said:

"The jury . . . returned a verdict that there had been lack of care. It is the contention of the applicants that that verdict infringes the Rules. In my view it does. A verdict expressed in those terms is not a lawful verdict; it is contrary to the Rules."

When, after judgment had been given, counsel referred to *ex p. Hicks* and pointed out that all parties were agreed that the question was not whether the verdict was possible in legal theory, but whether there was any evidence of it to go to the jury, Beldam L.J. commented:

"It seems to me to be a very dangerous course to leave 'lack of care' to the jury in circumstances like this, if the verdict is not to be framed in such a way as to determine any question of civil liability. Lack of care on who else's part?"

Footnote 22: *Ex p. Jamieson* is now reported at (1993) 158 J.P. 1. The decision was affirmed by the Court of Appeal, though on slightly different grounds: see [1995] Q.B. 1. See also *R. v. East Sussex Coroner, ex p. Homberg* (1994) 158 J.P. 357, D.C. **13–40**

Riders and recommendations

In *Re Kelly* (1996) 161 J.P. 417, Pill L.J. said, in the context of an application under section 13 of the Coroners Act 1988 for an order questioning an inquisition and ordering a fresh inquest, **13–43**

"A Coroner's power under Rule 43 is a valuable one in the public interest. It is however ancillary to the inquest procedure and not its mainspring. In circumstances such as the present, I cannot regard the fact that the recommendations might be different or fuller if more evidence is given as in itself a main ground, or even a significant supporting ground, for holding another inquest"(at 427).

See also *Re Clegg* (1996) 161 J.P. 521, D.C.

As to so-called "narrative verdicts", see para. 13–15 *supra*, in this Supplement. **13–43**

Chapter 14

HOMICIDE

PROCEDURE FOLLOWING POST-MORTEM EXAMINATION

Release of the body

14–15 *Footnote 12*: See also *Dobson v. North Tyneside Health Authority* [1996] 4 All E.R. 474, C.A., discussed at para. 6–21 above.

HOLDING THE INQUEST

Suspect untraced or dead

14–18 See also *R. v. Home Secretary, ex p. Weatherhead* (1995) 32 B.M.L.R. 72; [1996] C.O.D. 271, May J.

Where inquest to be adjourned

14–20 *Footnote 19*: The reference given should be to para. 12–49.

THE LAW OF HOMICIDE IN OUTLINE

Substantive offences

(1) *Murder*

14–27 *Footnote 25*: The House of Lords has now held that a person who injures a pregnant woman, wounding the foetus, which is born prematurely as a result but dies because of prematurity can be charged with manslaughter: see *Attorney-General's Reference (No. 3 of 1994)* [1997] 3 All E.R. 936.

(2) *Manslaughter*

14–31 *Footnote 34*: Add *R. v. Marshall* [1993] 4 All E.R. 888, C.A., *R. v. Richens* [1993] 4 All E.R. 877, C.A., *R. v. Rossiter* [1994] 2 All E.R. 752, *R. v. Cambridge* [1994] 2 All E.R. 760, *R. v. Dryden* [1995] 4 All E.R. 987, *R. v. Stewart* [1995] 4 All E.R. 999, *R. v. Humphreys* [1995] 4 All E.R. 1008.

As to the importance of properly distinguishing the two forms of involuntary manslaughter in directing the jury, see *R. v. Inner South London Coroner, ex p. Douglas-Williams*, unreported, July 31, 1997, Laws J. 14–32

It is possible to take into account successive acts by the *same* person, but where *different* persons are concerned the law requires either that the acts of *each individual* amount to the offence or that the rules of joint enterprise are satisfied: *R. v. Inner South London Coroner*, above. 14–33

Footnote 46: *R. v. Scarlett* is now reported, at [1993] 4 All E.R. 629. 14–34

Footnote 49: In *R. v. Adomako* [1995] 1 A.C. 171, the House of Lords held that *Seymour* was no longer good law, as the underlying statutory provisions on which it rested were repealed in 1991. 14–36

The words "more inadvertence" in line 12 of this paragraph should read "mere inadvertence". As to the last sentence of this paragraph, in *R. v. Inner South London Coroner, ex p. Douglas-Williams*, unreported, July 31, 1997, Laws J. said: 14–37

> "I doubt whether a joint enterprise to commit negligence is a concept known to the law . . . I find it difficult to see that there can be any meaningful place for the notion of an intention, formed in advance or nurtured at the time, to participate in acts or omissions which on later examination are condemned for their carelessness, whether gross or otherwise."

Footnotes 50, 51: *R. v. Sulman* is now reported, *sub nom. R. v. Prentice*, at [1994] Q.B. 302. The decision of the Court of Appeal was affirmed by the House of Lords, [1995] 1 A.C. 171, *sub nom. R. v. Adomako*. See also *R. v. Inner North London Coroner, ex p. Keogh*, unreported, July 31, 1995, C.A., and *R. v. Reading Coroner, ex p. West Berkshire Housing*, unreported, July 11, 1995, Popplewell J., and *R. v. Inner South London Coroner, ex p. Douglas-Williams*, unreported, July 31, 1997, Laws J. 14–37

(3) *Road Traffic Offences*

Footnote 52: The Criminal Justice Act 1993, s.67, has increased the maximum penalty for this offence to 10 years imprisonment. 14–39

(6) *Abortion*

The word "second" at the end of the first line should read "section". 14–51

Causation

In unlawful killing cases, the question of *contributory* causes may arise. It is sufficient, for murder or manslaughter, that a person's act was only a contributory cause of death, provided that the contribution was not merely trivial: *R. v. Inner South London Coroner, ex p. Douglas-Williams*, unreported, July 31, 1997, Laws J. 14–55

Causa causans

14–57 In *Hay v. Devon Coroner*, unreported, February 10, 1997, C.A., Kennedy L.J. said:

> "The 'but for' test is useful, but it is necessary to narrow down further the many factual causes which will satisfy that test to the cause or causes which are considered sufficiently major to be adjudged the legal cause or causes . . ."

Footnote 86: This rule has now been abolished by the Law Reform (Year and a Day) Rule Act 1996.

The chain of causation

14–59 In criminal cases, it is sufficient for the prosecution to prove that the injuries inflicted were a significant, if not the only, cause of death; there is no need to prove that a supervening event was *not* a significant cause, or that there was no negligence in the medical treatment of the deceased: *R. v. Mellor* [1996] 2 Cr. App. R. 245, C.A.

Take the victim as you find him

14–60 *Footnote 91*: *Airedale NHS Trust* is now also at [1993] A.C. 789.

Defences

(a) *Infancy*

14–67 In *Curry v. D.P.P.* [1996] 1 A.C. 1, the Divisional Court had swept away the rebuttable presumption that a child between 10 and 14 was incapable of committing a crime in English law, and the so-called "twilight zone" was effectively abolished. However, on appeal by the Crown, the House of Lords ([1996] 1 A.C. 1) put it back again, holding that the rebuttable presumption was a rule of the common law that could only be abrogated by statute.

(c) *Automatism*

14–73 The condition known as "driving without awareness" cannot support a defence of automatism: *Att.-Gen.'s Reference (No. 2 of 1992)* [1994] Q.B. 91, C.A.

(d) *Mistake*

14–76 *Footnote 23*: *R. v. Scarlett* is now reported at [1993] 4 All E.R. 629.

(e) *Intoxication*

In a landmark decision, the House of Lords in *R. v. Kingston* [1994] 3 All E.R. 353 reversed the decision of the Court of Appeal, [1994] Q.B. 81, and held that involuntary intoxication did not provide a defence to a defendant who was proved to have had the necessary criminal intent when he committed the offence. **14–78**

(f) *Necessity*

In *R. v. Pommell* [1995] 2 Cr. App. R.607 the Court of Appeal held that the limited defence of "duress of circumstance", developed in relation to road traffic offences, was closely related to "duress by threats", and applied to all crimes except murder, attempted murder, and some forms of treason. But the feature causative of the defendent committing the offence must be extraneous to the defendent: *R. v. Rodger, The Times*, July 30, 1997, C.A. **14–79**

(g) *Duress*

In relation to the defence of duress, a low I.Q., short of mental impairment or mental defectiveness, is not a relevant characteristic: *R. v. Bowen* [1996] 2 Cr. App. R. 157, C.A. **14–80**

On the scope and elements of the defence of coercion, see *R. v. Shortland* [1996] 1 Cr. App. R. 116, C.A. **14–81**

(i) *Superior Orders*

In *R. v. Yip Chiu-cheung* [1995] 1 A.C. 111, D was convicted in Hong Kong of conspiring with N to traffic in heroin. In fact N was an undercover agent permitted by the relevant authorities to carry the drugs concerned in order to break a drugs ring. D appealed on the basis that N could not have been convicted of conspiracy (having been authorised to carry out the relevant acts) and hence there could be no conspiracy. Lord Griffiths, for the Privy Council, said (at 118C-E): **14–86**

> "Neither the police, nor customs, nor any other member of the executive have any power to alter the terms of the [Hong Kong] Ordinance forbidding the export of heroin, and the fact that they may turn a blind eye when the heroin is exported does not prevent it from being a criminal offence.
>
> The High Court of Australia in *A v. Hayden (No. 2)* (1984) 156 C.L.R. 532 declared emphatically that there was no place for a general defence of superior orders or of Crown or Executive fiat in Australian criminal law. Gibbs C.J. said (at 540):
>
> > 'It is fundamental to our legal system that the executive has no power to authorise a breach of the law and that it is no excuse for an offender to say that he acted under the orders of a superior officer.'

This statement of the law applies with the same force in England and Hong Kong as it does in Australia."

Accordingly D's appeal was dismissed.

PARTICIPATION IN CRIME

14–89 *Footnote 60*: See also *R. v. Rook* [1993] 2 All E.R. 955 at 960–961.

14–91 *Footnote 71*: And see *R. v. Rook* [1993] 2 All E.R. 955, C.A., which also deals with the question of withdrawal from participation.

14–92 *Footnote 72*: See also *R. v. Powell* [1996] 1 Cr. App.R.14, C.A.

Chapter 15

NOTIFIABLE ACCIDENTS AND PRESCRIBED DISEASES

NOTIFIABLE ACCIDENTS AND OCCURRENCES

The 1985 Regulations have been replaced as from April 1, 1996, by the Reporting of Injuries, Diseases and Dangerous Occurrences Regulations 1995 (S.I. 1995 No. 3163), the relevant parts of which are printed in Appendix 2. The new Regulations are substantially the same as, but by no means indentical to, the old. **15–04**

Footnote 11: In reg. 3(1)(b) "person" is not confined to employees, self-employed persons and trainees, but extends to visitors, customers and other invitees on the premises: *Woking Borough Council v. B.H.S. plc* (1994) 159 J.P. 427, D.C. **15–04**

Regulations requiring special notification

Footnote 26: Railway accidents are now notifiable pursuant to reg. 3(1)(e) of RIDDOR 1995, and the 1986 Order has been repealed by *ibid.*, reg. 14(1). **15–09**
Footnote 29: Section 13(2) of the 1900 Act has been repealed by reg. 14(1) of RIDDOR 1995.

Effect on coroner's responsibility of duty to notify enforcing authority

In the third line from the bottom of the paragraph, for "probable" read "probably". **15–10**

NOTIFIABLE DISEASES

In line 8, for "health or any" read "health of any". **15–19**

Chapter 16

TREASURE TROVE

DEFINITION

Ownership where object not treasure trove

16–08 *Footnote 22*: See also *Waverley Borough Council v. Fletcher* [1996] Q.B. 334, C.A. (local authority held entitled to medieval brooch dug up by member of public with metal detector in a park owned by it but to which the public had free access for recreation).

THE TREASURE ACT 1996

16–37 This is the first significant statutory reform in the history of the law relating to treasure trove. The drafting is unnecessarily complex and user-friendly, but broadly speaking, the Act (according to its long title) purports to abolish the medieval law of treasure trove and to replace it with a broader, more modern concept of "treasure". The coroner's inquest still plays a significant role in relation to treasure, although the procedure has been modified in a number of ways.

Section 11 of the Act (dealing with the Code of Practice) came into force on March 13, 1997: see the Treasure Act 1996 (Commencement No. 1) Order 1997 (S.I. 1997 No. 760). The remaining provisions came into force on September 24, 1997: see the Treasure Act 1996 (Commencement No. 2) Order 1997 (S.I. 1997 No. 1977). From the commencement date any "treasure" (as defined) subsequently found cannot be treasure trove under the old law, but can only be claimed by the Crown or a franchisee as treasure under this Act. The coroner continues to have jurisdiction to hold a treasure trove inquest under the old law in relation to anything found before the commencement of section 4 (section 7(2)), but, in relation to anything found after that commencement, coroners have jurisdiction under section 30 of the Coroners Act 1988 to hold a treasure inquest under the new law (section 7(1)).

16–38 The right to treasure trove under the old law is abolished for the future (section 4(3)), and is replaced by the new right to "treasure", which when found vests in the franchisee if there is one, but otherwise in the Crown (section 4(1)).

There is a complex definition of "treasure" in section 1 of the Act, supplemented by section 3. There are now four categories of treasure, one of which (despite the Act's long title) actually *preserves* the old law of treasure trove, because it comprises "any object which would have been treasure trove if found before the commencement of section 4". This is likely to be significant only in relation to objects less than 300 years old, or less than 200 years old and not designated by the Secretary of State under section 2(1), because objects at least 300 years old, or 200 years old and so designated, will usually fall within other (new) categories of "treasure". (The main exception is a single gold or silver coin.)

The most important new such category comprises objects at least 300 years old, which, not being coins, have metallic content of at least 10 per cent by weight of gold or silver, or which, being coins, are at least two in number with the same percentage of gold or silver or at least ten in number altogether. Thus, a hoard of at least ten non gold or silver coins at least 300 years old would be treasure, although it could not have been treasure trove. The third category of treasure is an object at least 200 years old when found, belonging to a class designated by the Secretary of State under section 2(1) which he considers to be of outstanding historical, archaeological, or cultural importance. There is a fourth category of treasure, which covers objects found as part of the same find as something else which falls within the categories of treasure.

There are certain exclusions from the definition of treasure. In particular, it **16–39** does not include objects which are unworked natural objects or minerals extracted from a natural deposit, or wreck within the meaning of Part IX of the Merchant Shipping Act 1995. In addition, the Secretary of State has power to designate a class of objects which are thereupon excluded from the definition. But for something to vest in the Crown or a franchisee as treasure, it is generally no longer necessary to show any intention on the part of the last possessor to retrieve the object subsequently (section 4(4)). (Of course this will still be necessary in relation to an object which is within the scope of "treasure" only because it would have been treasure trove under the old law.)

There is now a statutory duty on a person finding an object which he has grounds for believing to be treasure to notify the coroner for the district in which it was found before the end of a 14-day notice period (section 8(1), (2)). Failure to notify is a criminal offence (section 8(3)). A coroner proposing to conduct a treasure inquest must notify the British Museum, if his district is in England, or the National Museum of Wales, if it is in Wales (section 9(2)). He must also take reasonable steps to notify the apparent finder of the treasure and the occupier of the land where it was found, and this is an obligation which continues during the inquest if not successfully achieved before it (section 9(3), (4)). It also gives rise to an obligation to take reasonable steps to obtain from any person so notified the names and addresses of other interested persons and to notify them of the inquest (section 9(5)). The coroner must then take reasonable steps to give any interested person (as defined by section 9(7)) so notified of the inquest the opportunity to examine witnesses at the inquest (see section 9(6)).

Any inquest held under this Act is to be held without a jury, unless the coroner otherwise decides (section 7(4)).

But no change has been made to the rule that the decision of an inquest is not binding on anyone, and so anyone unhappy with the result can litigate the question of title to the object(s) concerned in the ordinary courts without regard to that decision (and it is not even admissible evidence in the subsequent litigation).

16–40 The Act also contains various other provisions dealing with rewards (section 10), codes of practice (section 11), and an obligation on the Secretary of State to report to Parliament on the operation of the Act (section 12), though these are likely to be of less concern to coroners. The Code of Practice was approved by the House of Commons on March 18, 1997, and by the House of Lords on March 20, 1997. It does not have the force of law. Relevant sections of the Code of Practice can be found at Appendix 6.

It is to be regretted that the opportunity was not taken to make a more root and branch modernisation and simplification of the law in this area, and to draft in a clearer fashion (particularly given that it is an area in which non-lawyers are usually involved), but, most of all, to exclude the coroner system—unsuited as it is to dealing with the preservation of archaeological and historical artefacts—entirely from the law of treasure.

Chapter 17

MAJOR DISASTERS

In October 1994 a National Working Party published a report on dealing with fatalities during disasters, which addresses many of the matters covered in this chapter.

Chapter 18

MATTERS AFTER THE INQUIRY

Functus Officio

Prior inquest pursuant to the Coroners Act 1988

18–02 *Footnote 5*: In Hong Kong, for example, English case law is heavily relied on: *Re Dr Steven Lee* [1991] 1 H.K.L.R. 122; *China Light & Power Co. Ltd v. Banks* [1994] H.K. Digest, 829. For a survey of the differing systems in the United States, see Hansen, "Body of Evidence", (June 1995) *ABA Journal. Coronial Law in South Wales* should read *Coronial Law in New South Wales*.

18–04 It should also be borne in mind that the body may be released in Scotland or Northern Ireland for disposal in England and Wales *before* the fatal accident inquiry or inquest is concluded in the country of origin. In such a case the Home Office argument does not even get off the ground: the coroner in England or Wales will (assuming the relevant criteria to be satisfied) have to open an inquest, as indeed happened in relation to the soldiers and civil servants killed in Scotland when their Chinook helicopter crashed on the Mull of Kintyre on June 2, 1994. But for the criteria to be satisfied, the coroner must be informed. It is to be noted that, where a certificate for disposal is issued in Scotland or Northern Ireland for use in England or Wales, it is unlikely that the English or Welsh coroner will be informed of the presence of the body, as no statutory regulation requires this to be done in such a case.

Post-inquiry Duties

Certificate after inquest

18–12 Before 1993, the Registrar-General's Form 99 REV did not explicitly ask the coroner to notify the conclusion as to death. It now does so (calling it "verdict"), though as part of the box headed "cause of death". If the coroner supplies this information, it will be recorded on the register and will appear on every copy death certificate thereafter produced. But the coroner's obligation is that under section 11(7) of the 1988 Act, which refers simply to the "cause of death". It is submitted that this expression does not extend to the conclusion as to death. The former is a purely factual statement, whereas the latter is a value judgment on a question of classification, referring to the circumstances in which the cause of death arose or occurred. In the prescribed form of inquisition (1984 Rules, App. 4, Form 2), they are treated as entirely distinct matters, appearing in Boxes 2 and 4 respectively. Accordingly, coroners are under no duty to provide this information under section 11(7).

Stillbirths

Footnote 30: Form 99A has recently been redesigned following changes made to the forms prescribed for the registration of stillbirths under the Registration of Births and Deaths (Amendment) Regulations 1995: see HOC 19/1995. **18–14**

Entry in register of deaths

Footnote 47: This "certificate" may simply be a letter, signed by the coroner, informing the registrar that he has received evidence on oath or by statutory declaration satisfying him of the existence of the error in the certificate after inquest and of the true state of affairs. The coroner has no power to issue a fresh certificate after inquest since he has *ex hypothesi* already issued one, and section 29(4) by the word "certify" is referring to a document stating very limited facts, *not* repeating all the information on the certificate after inquest. In some cases it may be possible to correct the certificate after inquest, but if the coroner does this he must re-date it as at the date of correction, otherwise the certificate will be telling a lie about itself, *i.e.* forgery, and then the five-day time limit in section 11(7) may cause difficulties. **18–17**

OTHER RETURNS

Notification to government departments

Footnote 62: Coroner's Newsletter No. 17 (April 19, 1995) reminded coroners of the "yellow card scheme" for reporting adverse drug reactions to the Committee on Safety of Medicines and Medicines Control Agency, at Market Towers, 1 Nine Elms Lane, London SW8 5BR (Tel: 0171 273 0189). It also reminded coroners of the role of the Medical Devices Agency of the Department of Health in relation to the reporting of all adverse incidents involving medical equipment and devices to the MDA Adverse Incident Centre; contact the Agency at 14 Russell Square, London WC1B 5EP (Tel: 0171 972 8140). **18–23**

Footnote 63: The Drugs Branch of the Home Office ceased to collect statistics from coroners as from March 31, 1997. **18–23**

ACCESS TO DOCUMENTS

On the question of supply of post-mortem and special examination reports before the inquest, it may be argued that, since there are three sections of the Act (sections 19–21) under which a post-mortem examination may be made, but only in one (section 19) is there a reference to making a written report to the coroner (the others refer simply to giving evidence at the inquest), therefore the reference in rule 57 to a "report" of a post-mortem examination must be only to one under section 19. But the words of rule 57 are inconsistent with this argument: first, because the rule qualifies the word "report" by adding the words "including one made under" section 19—thus showing that it covers reports under other provisions; and second, because "report" also covers the **18–32** report of a "special examination" which can only take place under section 20. Obviously if in a given case there is no written report before the inquest there is nothing on which rule 57 can bite. But if there is such a report in the coroner's hands, then prima facie rule 57 extends to it. See also *R. v. Cleveland County Council* [1995] 2 All E.R. 236 at 243–244. It is doubtful that rule 57 can be avoided merely by labelling the written report as "provisional" or "subject to confirmation", as it is nonetheless a report to the coroner pursuant to the statutory provision.

18–35 Home Office Circular 62/1994 in principle endorses the recommendation of the Clothier Report (Beverly Allitt Inquiry) that:

> "coroners should send copies of post-mortem reports to any consultant who has been involved in the patient's care prior to death, whether or not demanded under Rule 57 of the Coroners Rules 1984" (see para 4.2.9 of the Report).

But the Home Secretary does not propose to amend the rules so as to *require* the coroner to supply such copies to consultants without prior request.

In *Cleveland County Council v. F* [1995] 2 All E.R. 236, Hale J. directed that the coroner inquiring into the death of a sibling of children in care proceedings be asked to release a post-mortem examination report to the parties in the proceedings as soon as possible.

GENERAL ADMINISTRATIVE MATTERS

Reimbursement of fees and expenses

18–46 Since the Local Government (Wales) Act 1994, Sched. 16, para. 82, came into force, the provision for apportionment of expenses applies also where the district lies in two or more Welsh principal areas.

18–48 *Footnote 48*: But see *Re Clegg* (1996) 161 J.P. 521, discussed in this Supplement at para. 19–15.

Chapter 19

REVIEWING INQUISITIONS AND CORONIAL DECISIONS

Statutory Power

Prerequisites for the quashing of an inquisition

It is not at all clear whose is the responsibility, and what is the mechanism, for obtaining a different coroner to hold a further inquest, if the court so orders. The court does not normally name the new coroner, but simply orders that the matter be remitted, *e.g.* "to be heard by a different coroner". See also para. 19–49. **19–06**

Circumstances held to have satisfied pre-requisites

Footnote 30: Add *Re O'Reilly* (1996) 160 J.P. 749, D.C. (apparently drunk man who had suffered a fall arrested and detained in police cell; condition deteriorated, taken to hospital and died; coroner relied on oral evidence at inquest and did not obtain custody record, police surgeon's notes and hospital consultant's report). **19–07**

Footnote 33: Add *R. v. Maidstone Coroner's Court, ex p. Johnstone* (1994) 158 J.P. 1115, D.C. (pathologist heard factual evidence earlier in hearing and changed his mind about cause of death in light of that). **19–08**

Critical test of whether "necessary or desirable in the interests of justice"

Footnote 37: See also *Herron v. A.G. for New South Wales* (1987) 8 N.S.W.L.R. 601, C.A. of N.S.W., *Re Neal The Times*, December 9, 1995; [1996] C.O.D. 190, D.C. and *Re Kelly* (1996) 61 J.P. 417, D.C. **19–10**

Likelihood of different verdict

Footnote 38: *Cf. Re O'Reilly* (1996) 160 J.P. 749, D.C. (because of insufficient inquiry by coroner, impossible to say whether fresh inquest would come to different conclusion: held, not determinative factor); *Re Clegg* (1996) 161 J.P. 521 (possibility of different verdict if fresh evidence admitted at new inquest points towards desirability of fresh inquest, but not conclusive; must bear in mind purposes of request and extent to which order for new inquest will further those purposes). **19–11**

19–12 But in *Re Taylor* (1990) 154 J.P. 933, D.C., it was said that it was not necessary that the new inquest would be likely to come to a different conclusion in the light of the new evidence.

19–12 *Footnote 42*: See also *Re Kelly* (1996) 161 J.P. 417, D.C. *Ex p. Wigley* is noted at [1993] C.O.D. 364.

19–12 *Footnote 43*: See also *Re Sutherland* [1994] 2 N.Z.L.R. 242, H. Ct. of N.Z.: "a fresh inquest can be ordered, if only to allay the disquiet of relatives".

Application by any person with sufficient interest

19–13 *Footnote 49*: In *R. v. A.G., ex p. Ferrante* [1995] C.O.D. 18, Popplewell J. followed *Gouriet*, and held that the court had no power to review the Attorney General's refusal to give his fiat for an application under section 13. On appeal, the Court of Appeal did not deal with this point, but held that the Attorney General in any event did not err in law in applying as a test for giving his *fiat* whether there was a reasonable prospect of satisfying the court that it was necessary or desirable in the interests of justice that another inquest should be held, for any of the reasons stated in section 13(1)(b). See also *R. v. Solicitor General, ex p. Taylor, The Times*, August 14, 1995, D.C.

Costs

19–15 The costs position is reviewed in more detail in an article (by Paul Matthews) in the Winter issue for 1995 of *Public Law*, at pp. 526–538. But this has been partly overtaken by the Divisional Court's decision on costs in *Re Clegg* (1996) 161 J.P. 521. In that case an application under section 13 of the 1988 Act was met by opposition from the coroner, on grounds which the court ultimately held bad. However, the applicant failed on the question of discretion (see (1996) 161 J.P. 521). The coroner had filed an affidavit, but was neither present nor represented, his local authority having expressly refused to indemnify him or to provide representation. The court awarded the *unsuccessful* applicant his costs against the coroner personally, though expressing the view that the local authority (not party to the proceedings) was obliged to indemnify him.

There are three main points. First, the court expressly considered and preferred *Ex p. Johnstone* (see noter-up to para. 19–16, n. 70) to the earlier cases, adding:

> "Nor do we see any reason why a finding of 'strong disapproval' should be made before costs can be awarded against a coroner who is not represented but opposes the application, for example, in an affidavit . . . "

Secondly, the court considered that the fact that the application had *failed* did not prevent a costs order being made against the coroner. This was so even though section 13(2)(b) (which gives the court power to order the coroner to pay costs) in part of section 13, and section 13(1) states that:

> "This section applies where . . . the High Court is satisfied . . . that . . . it is necessary or desirable in the interests of justice that another inquest should be held."

In the instant case, of course, the Court was *not* so satisfied. Hence the condition for the application of the section was not fulfilled.

Lastly, the court considered:

> "that costs ordered against a coroner under s.13(2)(b) of the Act are 'disbursements in accordance with the provisions of this Act', for which, under s.27 of the Act, the local authority has an obligation to reimburse a coroner".

This cannot be right. The normal meaning of "disbursement" is payment for services or goods rendered or supplied to oneself, *not* the *reimbursement* of what another has paid for such goods or services for himself. And in the context of the Act itself, section 27(1) in fact refers to "*fees, allowances or disbursements* in accordance with the provisions of this Act". This phrase is a clear reference to "fees, allowances and disbursements" in sections 24(2)(a), 24(3)(b) and 26(1). But none of these provisions contemplates payment even of the *coroner's* own legal costs on a judicial review, let alone those of any other party. And it is notable that none of the words "fees, allowances or disbursements" appears in section 13, which refers simply to "costs".

Footnote 62: See also *R. v. Inner North London Coroner, ex p. Keogh* (1995) 159 J.P. 739, D.C., and *R. v. Birmingham Coroner, ex p. Cotton* (1995) 160 J.P. 123 D.C., where the unsuccessful applicant for judicial review argued that the coroner should not have an order for costs, as the applicant if successful could not have obtained one against him. The court nonetheless made the order in favour of the coroner. In cases where more than one public authority is involved on the same side, the losing applicant should not normally pay more than one set of costs: *Bolton Metropolitan District Council v. Secretary of State for the Environment (No. 2)* [1995] 1 W.L.R. 1176, H.L. **19–15**

Footnote 64: *Ex p. Clements* is now reported at (1993) 158 J.P. 17. Such an order was also made in *R. v. Birmingham Coroner, ex p. Cotton* (1995) 160 J.P. 123, D.C. **19–15**

The text deals with the case where the coroner is the *respondent* to a successful application. In *Re Kelly* (1996) 161 J.P. 417 the coroner himself applied, unsuccessfully under section 13 of the Coroners Act 1988, for an order quashing the inquisition and holding a fresh inquest. Two "interested persons" from the inquest appeared at the hearing to argue (successfully) that the coroner's application should fail, though they were not technically respondents. Both sought their costs from the coroner. The coroner cited the article in *Public Law* referred to at 19–15 above, and the cases referred to. The court held that: **19–16**

(i) no regard should be had to the fact that the interested persons were not legally aided (see section 31 of the Legal Aid Act 1988);

(ii) some regard had to be had to the position of the coroner, and that in cases where he was respondent he had not been required to pay the costs;

(iii) the court must look at the particular facts, *i.e.* that the coroner's application had failed but that one of the interested persons had been at fault in not disclosing a relevant statement to the coroner.

Ultimately the court held that the coroner should pay the costs of the interested person who had not been criticised for non-disclosure, but not those of the person who had.

19–16 *Footnote 65*: Add: *R. v. Huntingdon Magistrates' Court, ex p. Percy, The Times*, March 4, 1994. *Footnote 66*: Add: *R. v. Southwark Coroner, ex p. Epsom Hospital NHS Trust* (1994) 158 J.P. 973, D.C.

19–16 *Footnote 69*: Add: *R. v. South London Coroner, ex p. Driscoll* (1993) 159 J.P. 45, D.C. In *R. v. Inner West London Coroner, ex p. Dallaglio and Lockwood Croft* [1994] 4 All E.R. 139, the Court of Appeal ordered the respondent coroner (who had won below) to pay the successful appellant's costs there and below, in a case where his decision not to resume an inquest had been quashed for apparent bias. But no cases (and particularly not those cited in n.70 below) were cited to the court, which appears to have been unaware of the practice on costs established by the caselaw. Whilst it may be different for a coroner who loses at first instance and then unsuccessfully appeals, it is submitted that a coroner who wins at first instance and then loses the appeal to which he is taken should not be treated differently from the coroner who loses at first instance, and that the practice in the cases cited in n.70 should prevail.

Footnote 70: Add: *Re Cohen* (1993) 158 J.P. 644, D.C., and *R. v. Reading Coroner, ex p. West Berkshire Housing*, unreported, July 11, 1995, Popplewell J. *Ex p. Carr* is now reported at [1993] 4 All E.R. 65. But in *R. v. Maidstone Coroner's Court, ex p. Johnstone* [1995] 6 Med. L.R. 116, 123–127, *The Times*, October 19, 1994, the Divisional Court held that the coroner who had gone wrong in law but of whom they made no criticism, should nevertheless pay the applicant's costs (the report at 158 J.P. 1115 does not deal with costs). This is out of line with earlier (and later) authority. But it has been expressly followed, in preference to the other (earlier) authorities, by the Divisional Court in *Re Clegg* (1996) 161 J.P. 521. *Cf. Re Kelly* (1996) 161 J.P. 467, D.C., where the *coroner's* application failed and he was ordered to pay the costs of an interested person who had opposed it.

Footnote 71: The reference to *ex p. Linnane* should be (1989) *Casebook on Coroners*, p. 279. *Ex p. Diesa Koto* is now reported at (1993) 157 J.P. 857.

19–16 At the end, add new footnote 72a:

Footnote 72a: In *Re Cohen* (1993) 158 J.P. 644, D.C., the (legally-aided) successful applicants sought such a costs order, but after hearing argument the Court declined to make any order as to costs.

19–16 Add a new paragraph:

An appeal may be brought to the Court of Appeal against the decision of the High Court under section 13. Unlike the position in judicial review (see para. 19–46), there is no requirement for leave, as the Rules of the Supreme Court (Amendment) 1993 (S.I. 1993 No. 2133), r. 6, introducing a new rule Order 59 rule 1B, does not refer to applications under section 13. Given that judicial review *is* included, and leave to appeal now required in such cases, this may have been an oversight on the part of the Rules Committee.

JUDICIAL REVIEW

To what extent is the coroner susceptible to review?

19–18 The word "fact" at the end of line 4 should read "face".

What kind of decisions in coroner's court are susceptible to review?

19–21 *Footnote 91*: *cf. R. v. East Sussex Coroner, ex p. Homberg* (1994) 158 J.P. 357 (coroner's refusal to call witness who could give no useful evidence upheld).

Footnote 99: Add: *R. v. Birmingham and Solihull Coroner, ex p. Nutt* [1993] C.O.D. 499, D.C. (failure to direct jury on standard of proof in a suicide case). 19–21

Footnote 18: *Ex p. Perks* is now reported, *sub nom. ex p. Lockwood Croft* (1993) 157 J.P. 985. The decision of the Divisional Court was, however, reversed by the Court of Appeal, *sub nom. Ex p. Dallaglio and Lockwood Croft:* [1994] 4 All E.R. 139. 19–22

As to a refusal by the coroner to adjourn, see *R. v. East Sussex Coroner, ex p. Homberg* (1994) 158 J.P. 357, D.C. 19–22

Distinction between review and appeal

In *R. v. Poplar Coroner, ex p. Chaudhry*, unreported, December 15, 1993, D.C. (application withdrawn on basis that coroner would seek to persuade another coroner to take matter over) Russell L.J. made clear that the Court was reviewing the coroner's decision not to summon a jury on the basis of the information then before him, and not on the basis of the evidence now available. 19–23

Judicial review is a discretionary remedy

Footnote 27: See also *R. v. Inner South London Coroner, ex p. Douglas-Williams*, unreported, July 31, 1997, Laws J. 19–25

Locus standi

On the other hand, in *R. v. North Cambridgeshire Coroner, ex p. Chaney*, unreported, May 19, 1995, the Court of Appeal held that the applicant, who was not a relative of, and had never met, the deceased (a convicted prisoner who died in prison), but had corresponded with him after his conviction, had no *locus standi* to bring judicial review proceedings in respect of the inquest into his death. 19–30

Procedure for application for leave

An application for judicial review should not ordinarily be embarked upon before the decision-maker has received a complaint and has been given an opportunity to say whether or not he accepts it and, if not, to give his reasons: *R. v. Horsham District Council, ex p. Wenman* [1995] 1 W.L.R. 680 (not a coroner's case). 19–31

Footnote 44: See *Hay v. Devon Coroner*, unreported, February 10, 1997, C.A., for a case where delay was fatal, and *R. v. South London Coroner, ex p. Weeks*, unreported, 1996, Scott Baker J., for one where it was significant in refusing the application.

Various procedural matters relating to Crown Office business, including the lodging of skeleton arguments and paginated bundles, and the amendment of grounds of relief and further affidavits, are dealt with in a Practice Direction given on October 25, 1994: [1994] 1 W.L.R. 1551. 19–35

Recently, the Crown Office has taken to listing coroners' judicial reviews before a single judge, instead of a Divisional Court, as formerly. This is in contrast with applications under section 13 of the 1988 Act, which must go to a Divisional Court: see para. 19–13, n. 53.

Procedure for application for judicial review

Orders prior to hearing

19–39 Once an application for judicial review of a coroner's interlocutory decision has been launched, the court is unlikely to accede to any attempt by the applicant to adjourn the application generally or until the inquest concerned has taken place. Thus, in *R. v. Inner North London Coroner, ex p. Keogh*, unreported, February 1, 1994, Potts J. refused an application, by the applicant for judicial review of the coroner's refusal to call a named person as witness, to adjourn the hearing of the application for judicial review pending the hearing of the inquest, when it would be known if the coroner in fact did or did not call the named person. The judge said:

> "I am quite satisfied that leave having been granted, and the hearing [ordered to be] expedited, it is in the interests of justice that the matter be determined as quickly as possible. It should not go into limbo until the conclusion of the inquest, or until such time as the applicant chooses to re-activate the application."

On the other hand, in *R. v. Birmingham Coroner, ex p. Najada* (1995) 160 J.P. 210, the Court of Appeal upheld Popplewell J.'s decision (on the application of the coroner) to stay a judicial review of an inquest until the termination of pending criminal proceedings against the applicant arising out of the same facts.

Agreement on disposal prior to hearing

19–41 *Footnote 67*: See now Practice Direction (Crown Office List: Consent Orders) [1997] 2 All E.R. 799.

The finding of the court

19–42 In *R. v. Inner West London Coroner, ex p. Dallaglio and Lockwood Croft* [1994] 4 All E.R. 139, the Court of Appeal, having concluded that the coroner's decision not to resume inquests under section 16(3) of the 1988 Act was vitiated by apparent bias, considered at some length whether in the exercise of their discretion they should remit the matter to be reconsidered by another coroner. Ultimately they decided that they should, notwithstanding the lapse of some five years since the deaths in question. It appears the most important factor weighing with the court was the absence, during that time, of any other form of inquiry into the circumstances surrounding the deaths.

Footnote 69: See also *R. v. South Yorkshire Coroner, ex p. Stringer* (1993) 158 J.P. 453, D.C. **19–42**

Footnote 76: See also *R. v. South Yorkshire Coroner, ex p. Stringer* (1993) 158 J.P. 453 D.C., and *R. v. East Sussex Coroner, ex p. Homberg*, unreported, June 14, 1993, D.C., and (on a further hearing) (1994) 158 J.P. 357, D.C. In *R. v. South London Coroner, ex p. Weeks*, unreported, 1996, an application for an inquest failed because it was "doubtful if anything new would be learned". **19–43**

Remedies

In *R. v. Sunderland Coroner, ex p. Sunderland City Council*, unreported, October 19, 1994, the Divisional Court quashed paragraph 4 for misdirection of the jury but deferred consideration as to whether to order a fresh inquest or to leave the inquisition as it was, until the deceased's brother had had an opportunity to put to the court new evidence which, he said, justified a new inquest. In Northern Ireland, see *Re Bradley's Application for Judicial Review*, unreported, April 7, 1995, H. Ct. of N.I. See also *R. v. Northampton Coroner, ex p. Tompkinson* (1995) 160 J.P. 69, D.C. **19–44**

Footnote 82: In *R. v. Birmingham and Solihull Coroner, ex p. Nutt* [1993] C.O.D. 449 the Divisional Court refused to do this in a jury case, as the same jury would not be available. **19–44**

Footnote 83: In *ex p. Nutt*, above, the Divisional Court insisted on remitting the matter to the coroner's court for a fresh inquest, following *ex p. Jones*. In *R. v. Southwark Coroner, ex p. Epsom Hospital N.H.S. Trust* (1994) 158 J.P. 973, the Divisional Court deleted *part* of a conclusion ("aggravated by lack of care") without remitting the inquisition to the coroner's court. In *R. v. Reading Coroner, ex p. West Berkshire Housing*, unreported, August 7, 1995, Popplewell J. (having concluded on July 11, 1995 that the conclusion of unlawful killing at the previous inquest should be quashed) declined to make any order for a fresh inquest to be held. In *R. v. Birmingham and Solihull Coroner, ex p. Benton*, unreported, July 31, 1997, Kay J. quashed the conclusion (of natural causes) without substituting any other conclusion, and expanded the "narrative verdict" in box 3, without remitting the matter to the coroner or ordering a new inquest. **19–44**

Renewal of application following refusal of leave

Footnote 88: See *e.g. R. v. North Cambridgeshire Coroner, ex p. Chaney*, unreported, May 19, 1995, C.A. (appeal dismissed); *R. v. Inner North London Coroner, ex p. Keogh*, unreported, July 31, 1995, C.A. (appeal dismissed); *Hay v. Devon Coroner*, unreported, February 10, 1997, C.A. (appeal 19 weeks out of time: dismissed for delay). **19–46**

Footnote 91: But since October 1, 1993 leave to appeal has been required, by virtue of R.S.C. Ord. 59 r. 1B(1)(c), inserted by R.S.C. (Amendment) 1993 (S.I. 1993 No. 2133), rule 6. Curiously, this does not apply to cases under the Coroners Act 1988, s.13. **19–46**

LEGAL AID

The reference to "legal aid by way of representation" should be to "civil legal aid". **19–48**

CONSEQUENCES

19–49 For the logistical problems that arise when the court orders a different coroner to hold a fresh inquest, see noter-up to para. 19–06. In *R. v. Inner West London Coroner, ex p. Dallaglio and Lockwood Croft* [1994] 4 All E.R. 139, the Court of Appeal quashed a coroner's decision under section 16(3) of the Coroners Act 1988 not to resume an inquest, and ordered that the matter be remitted to a coroner for a different district to consider and to decide again whether the inquest should be resumed or not.

Unlike section 13 of the 1988 Act, which explicitly empowers the court to order that a different coroner hold a new inquest, there is no statutory power for the court to order a coroner for a different district to retake an interlocutory decision such as this was. The Home Secretary has power under section 14(3) to direct a particular coroner to hold an inquest, where it appears to another coroner *that an inquest ought to be held.* But this does not cover the case where the coroner is directed to take the decision *whether* to resume an inquest.

Two questions arise. One is how a coroner who *volunteers* to take on the matter can thereby acquire jurisdiction to do so. The other is what the court will do if in such a case no coroner volunteers: does it just pick one? Prima facie, if the original coroner is unable to act, the deputy coroner should. (In this case the deputy coroner had sat with the coroner in making the quashed decision, so it should devolve on the assistant deputy.) It is true that section 5(3) provides that "a coroner may act as coroner for another coroner in the same administrative area" (here, Greater London) in certain circumstances, but that is permissive, rather than compulsory.

At a further hearing in *ex p. Dallaglio and Lockwood-Croft,* on July 20, 1994, the Court of Appeal, after hearing of the difficulties experienced in finding a coroner to take on the matter, and one of the other Greater London coroners being willing to take on the matter *if ordered by the court to do so,* the Court made an order that he be appointed the coroner to take the decision ordered by the Court on the earlier hearing, *i.e.* whether or not the inquest should be resumed.

Appendix 1

STATUTES AND STATUTORY EXTRACTS

Coroners Act 1988

The Coroners Act has been further amended by the Local Government (Wales) Act 1994, and the Criminal Justice and Public Order Act 1994, and S.I. 1995 No. 655, though the amendments by the Criminal Justice and Public Order Act 1994 were effectively reversed by the Criminal Procedure and Investigation Act 1996, section 44. **A1–80– A1–126**

Coroners Act 1988

CORONERS

Appointment of coroners

1.—[(1) Coroners shall be appointed— **A1–80**

(a) for each coroner's district in a metropolitan county, Greater London or Wales;
(b) for each coroner's district constituted by an order under section 17 of the Local Government Act 1992 which lies partly in each of two or more non-metropolitan counties;
(c) for each non-metropolitan county in England none of which is included in such a coroner's district as is mentioned in paragraph (b) above;
(d) in the case of a non-metropolitan county in England part of which is included in such a coroner's district as is mentioned in paragraph (b) above, for so much of that county as is not so included; and
(e) for the City.

(1A) Coroners shall be appointed by the relevant council, that is to say—

(a) in the case of a coroner's district consisting of or included in a metropolitan district or London borough, the council of that district or borough;
(b) in the case of a coroner's district consisting of two or more metropolitan districts or London boroughs, such one of the councils of those districts of boroughs as may be designated by an order made by the Secretary of State by statutory instrument;
(c) in the case of a coroner's district consisting of or included in a Welsh principal area, the council of that area;
(d) in the case of a coroner's district lying partly in each or two or more Welsh principal areas, such one of the councils of those areas as may be designated by an order made by the Secretary of State by statutory instrument;
(e) in a case falling within subsection (1)(b) above, such one of the councils of the non-metropolitan counties in question as may be designated by an order under section 17 of the Local Government Act 1992;
(f) in a case falling within subsection (1)(c) or (d) above, the council of the non-metropolitan county in question; and
(g) in the case of the City, the Common Council.][91a]

[91a] Words substituted by S.I. 1996 No. 655.

(2) A relevant council falling within paragraphs (a) or (b) of subsection [(1A)][91b] above shall not appoint a coroner except with the approval of the Secretary of State; and a relevant council falling within paragraph (b) [(d) or (e)][91c] of that subsection shall not appoint a coroner except after consultation with the other council or councils in question.

(3) Subject to subsection (2) above, where a vacancy occurs in the office of coroner, the relevant council shall—

(a) immediately give notice of the vacancy to the Secretary of State;
(b) within three months of the vacancy occurring or within such further period as the Secretary of State may allow, appoint a person to that office; and
(c) immediately after making the appointment, give notice of the appointment to the Secretary of State.

Qualifications for appointments as coroner

A1–81 **2.**—(1) No person shall be qualified to be appointed as coroner [unless

(a) he has a five year general qualification, within the meaning of section 71 of the Courts and Legal Services Act 1990; or
(b) he is a][92] legally qualified medical practitioner of not less than five years' standing [. . .][93]

[(2) A person shall, so long as he is a councillor of a metropolitan district or London borough, and for six months after he ceases to be one, be disqualified for being a coroner for a coroner's district which consists of, includes or is included in that metropolitan district or London borough.

[(2A) A person shall, so long as he is a councillor of a Welsh principal area, and for six months after he ceases to be one, be disqualified for being a coroner for a coroner's district which, or any part of which, falls within that area.][93a]

(3) A person shall, so long as he is an alderman or a councillor of a non-metropolitan county [in England],[93b] and for six months after he ceases to be one, be disqualified

[(a) in the case of a county none of which is included in such a coroner's district as is mentioned in section 1(1)(b) above, for being a coroner for that county;
(b) in the case of a county the whole or part of which is included in such a coroner's district as is mentioned in section 1(1)(b) above, for being a coroner for that coroner's district and for so much of that county (if any) as is not so included.][93bb]

(4) A person shall, so long as he is an alderman of the City or a common councillor, and for six months after he ceases to be one, be disqualified for being a coroner for the City.

Terms on which coroners hold office

A1–82 **3.**—(1) The provisions of Schedule 1 to this Act have effect with respect to the payment of salaries and the grant of pensions to coroners.

(2) Except as authorised by this or any other Act, a coroner shall not take any fee or remuneration in respect of anything done by him in the execution of his office.

[91b] *ibid.*
[91c] *ibid.*
[92] Words substituted by the Courts and Legal Services Act 1990, s.71(2), Sched. 10, para. 70.
[93] Words repealed by *ibid.*, s.125(7), Sched. 20.
[93a] Words inserted by the Local Government (Wales) Act 1994, s.66, Sched. 16, para. 82.
[93b] *ibid.*
[93bb] Words inserted by S.I. 1996 No. 655.

(3) A coroner may resign his office by giving notice in writing to the relevant council, but the resignation shall not take effect unless and until it is accepted by the council.

(4) The Lord Chancellor may, if he thinks fit, remove any coroner from office for inability or misbehaviour in the discharge of his duty.

(5) A coroner who is guilty of corruption, wilful neglect of his duty or misbehaviour in the discharge of his duty shall be guilty of an offence and liable on conviction on indictment to imprisonment for a term not exceeding two years or to a fine or to both.

(6) Where a coroner is convicted of an offence under subsection (5) above, the court may, unless his office as coroner is annexed to any other office, order that he be removed from office and be disqualified for acting as coroner.

Coroner's districts

4.—(1) The Secretary of State may by order divide, amalgamate or otherwise alter the coroners' districts for the time being existing in a metropolitan county or Greater London; and before making any such order, the Secretary of State shall consult the councils and coroners appearing to him to be affected by the order and such other persons as he thinks appropriate. **A1–83**

(2) The council of a non-metropolitan county [in England][93c] may, and shall if directed to do so by the Secretary of State, after complying with such requirements as to notice and consideration of objections as may be prescribed, submit to the Secretary of State a draft order providing—

(a) for such alteration of any existing division of the county into coroners' districts as appears to them suitable; or

(b) where there is no such division, for the division of the county into such coroners' districts as they think expedient;

and the Secretary of State, after taking into consideration any objections to the draft made in the prescribed manner and within the prescribed time, may make the order, either in the terms of the draft submitted to him or with such modifications as he thinks fit.

(3) If by reason of any order under subsection (2) above it is in the opinion of the Secretary of State necessary that the number of coroners for a non-metropolitan county should be increased,

(a) the council shall appoint such number of additional coroners for that county as the Secretary of State may direct; and

(b) section 1(3) above shall apply with respect to any such appointment as if a vacancy had occurred in the office of coroner for that county.

(4) Where a non-metropolitan county [in England][93d] is divided into coroners' districts, each of the coroners for that county shall be assigned to one of those districts; and where a non-metropolitan county is not so divided, the following provisions of this Act shall have effect as if the whole of that county were a coroner's district.

(5) Except as provided by this Act, a coroner appointed for or assigned to a coroner's district—

(a) shall for all purposes be regarded as a coroner for the whole administrative area [in England][93e] which includes that district; and

(b) shall have the same jurisdiction, rights, powers and authorities throughout that area as if he had been appointed as coroner for that area or, as the case may be, had not been assigned to that district.

[93c] *ibid.*

[93d] *ibid.*

[93e] *ibid.*

[(5A) Subsections (2) to (5) above shall not apply to a non-metropolitan county the whole of which is included in such a coroner's district as is mentioned in section 1(1)(b) above.

(5B) In the application of this section to a non-metropolitan county part of which is included in such a coroner's district as is mentioned in section 1(1)(b) above, any reference in subsections (2)(a) and (b), (3) and (4) to a county shall be construed as a reference to so much of that county as is not so included.][93ee]

(6) The power to make orders under this section shall be exercisable by statutory instrument; and a statutory instrument containing an order under this section shall be laid before each House of Parliament after being made.

(7) An order under subsection (2) above shall be published in the London Gazette and particulars of any order under that subsection shall be published by the council of the non-metropolitan county in such manner as may be prescribed.

(8) In this section "prescribed" means prescribed by the Secretary of State either by general rules made by statutory instrument or by directions given as respects any particular occasion.

[Coroners' districts: Wales

4A.—(1) The Secretary of State may by order divide, amalgamate or otherwise alter—

(a) any coroner's district for the time being existing in Wales; or
(b) any such coroners' districts.

(2) Before making any order under subsection (1) above, the Secretary of State shall consult the councils and coroners appearing to him to be affected by the order and such other persons as he thinks appropriate.

(3) The Secretary of State may, in relation to any area in Wales (the "review area"), direct the council or councils for each Welsh principal area which, or any part of which, falls within the review area to consider any of the following questions—

(a) whether any alteration should be made in a boundary between coroners' districts which falls within the review area;
(b) whether a new coroner's district should be created for the whole or any part of the review area;
(c) whether a coroner's district which falls wholly within the review area should be abolished.

(4) The council or councils to whom such a direction is given shall submit their conclusions to the Secretary of State, together with a statement of their reasons for reaching those conclusions.

(5) In making an order under subsection (1) above in a case where he has given a direction under subsection (3) above, the Secretary of State shall have regard to any proposals made to him under subsection (4) above.

(6) Where the Secretary of State intends to give effect to any such proposals without modification, subsection (2) above shall not require him to consult the council or councils who made those proposals.

(7) An order made under subsection (1) above may make such incidental, consequential, transitional or supplemental provision as appears to the Secretary of State to be appropriate.

(8) Except as provided by this Act, a coroner appointed for any coroner's district in Wales—

(a) shall for all purposes be regarded as a coroner for the whole of Wales; and
(b) shall have the same jurisdiction, rights, powers and authorities throughout Wales as if he had been appointed as coroner for the whole of Wales.

[93ee Words inserted by S.I. 1996 No. 655.

(9) The power to make orders under this section shall be exercisable by statutory instrument.

(10) Any such statutory instrument shall be laid before each House of Parliament after being made.][93f]

Jurisdiction of coroners

5.—(1) Subject to subsection (3) and sections 7 and 13 to 15 below, an inquest into a death shall be held only by the coroner within whose district the body lies. **A1–84**

(2) Subject to subsection (3) and section 13 below, a coroner shall hold inquests only within his district.

(3) A coroner may act as coroner for another district in the same administrative area—

(a) during the illness, incapacity or unavoidable absence of the coroner for that district; or

(b) where there is a vacancy in the office of coroner for that district;

and the inquisition returned in respect of an inquest held under this subsection shall certify the cause of the coroner's holding the inquest and shall be conclusive evidence of any matter stated in it which falls within paragraph (a) or (b) above.

DEPUTY CORONERS

Appointment of deputy coroners

6.—(1) Every coroner— **A1–85**

(a) shall appoint as his deputy a person approved by the chairman of the relevant council; and

(b) may appoint as his assistant deputy a person so approved.

(2) A coroner may at any time revoke an appointment made under subsection (1) above; but a revocation of an appointment made under paragraph (a) of that subsection shall not take effect until the appointment of a successor to the deputy has been approved by the chairman of the relevant council.

(3) The following, namely—

(a) every appointment made under subsection (1) above; and

(b) every revocation of an appointment made under paragraph (b) of that subsection,

shall be in writing under the hand of the coroner; and a copy of every such appointment or revocation shall be sent to the relevant council and be kept with the council's records.

(4) Subsection (1) of section 2 above shall apply in relation to the office of deputy or assistant deputy coroner as it applies in relation to the office of coroner; and subsections (2) to (4) of that section shall apply in relation to, or to persons holding, the office of deputy coroner as they apply in relation to, or to persons holding, the office of coroner.

(5) In this section "chairman", in relation to the Common Council, means the Lord Mayor.

Functions of deputy coroners

7.—(1) A deputy coroner may act for his coroner in the following cases but no other, namely— **A1–86**

(a) during the illness of the coroner;

[93f] *ibid.*

(b) during the coroner's absence for any lawful or reasonable cause; or
(c) at an inquest for the holding of which the coroner is disqualified.

(2) Where a coroner vacates office, his deputy—
(a) shall continue in office until a new deputy is appointed;
(b) shall act as coroner while the office remains vacant; and
(c) shall be entitled to receive in respect of the period of the vacancy the same remuneration as the vacating coroner.

(3) An assistant deputy coroner—
(a) may act as coroner where the deputy coroner would be entitled to act as coroner but is unable so to act owing to illness or absence for any reasonable cause; and
(b) where the coroner vacates office, may act for the deputy coroner in like manner while the office of coroner is vacant.

(4) In relation to an inquest or act which he is authorised to hold or do, a deputy or assistant deputy to a coroner shall—
(a) have the same jurisdiction and powers;
(b) be subject to the same obligations, liabilities and disqualifications; and
(c) generally be subject to the provisions of this Act and the law relating to coroners in the same manner,

as if he were the coroner.

INQUESTS: GENERAL

Duty to hold inquest

A1–87 **8.**—(1) Where a coroner is informed that the body of a person ("the deceased") is lying within his district and there is reasonable cause to suspect that the deceased—
(a) has died a violent or an unnatural death;
(b) has died a sudden death of which the cause is unknown; or
(c) has died in prison or in such a place or in such circumstances as to require an inquest under any other Act,

then, whether the cause of death arose within his district or not, the coroner shall as soon as practicable hold an inquest into the death of the deceased either with or, subject to subsection (3) below, without a jury.

(2) In the case of an inquest with a jury—
(a) the coroner shall summon by warrant not less than seven nor more than eleven persons to appear before him at a specified time and place, there to inquire as jurors into the death of the deceased; and
(b) when not less than seven jurors are assembled, they shall be sworn by or before the coroner diligently to inquire into the death of the deceased and to give a true verdict according to the evidence.

(3) If it appears to a coroner, either before he proceeds to hold an inquest or in the courts of an inquest begun without a jury, that there is reason to suspect—
(a) that the death occurred in prison or in such a place or in such circumstances as to require an inquest under any other Act;
(b) that the death occurred while the deceased was in police custody, or resulted from an injury caused by a police officer in the purported execution of his duty;
(c) that the death was caused by an accident, poisoning or disease notice of which is required to be given under any Act to a government department, to any inspector or other officer of a government department or to an inspector appointed under section 19 of the Health and Safety at Work etc. Act 1974; or

(d) that the death occurred in circumstances the continuance or possible recurrence of which is prejudicial to the health or safety of the public or any section of the public,

he shall proceed to summon a jury in the manner required by subsection (2) above.

(4) If it appears to a coroner, either before he proceeds to hold an inquest or in the course of an inquest begun without a jury, that there is any reason for summoning a jury, he may proceed to summon a jury in the manner required by subsection (2) above.

(5) In the case of an inquest or any part of an inquest held without a jury, anything done by or before the coroner alone shall be as validly done as if it had been done by or before the coroner and a jury.

(6) Where an inquest is held into the death of a prisoner who dies within a prison, neither a prisoner in the prison nor any person engaged in any sort of trade or dealing with the prison shall serve as a juror at the inquest.

Qualifications of jurors

9.—(1) A person shall not be qualified to serve as a juror at an inquest held by a coroner unless he is for the time being qualified to serve as a juror in the Crown Court, the High Court and county courts in accordance with section 1 of the Juries Act 1974. **A1–88**

(2) If a person serves on a jury knowing that he is ineligible for such service under Group A, B or C in Part I of Schedule 1 to that Act, he shall be guilty of an offence and liable on summary conviction to a fine not exceeding level 3 on the standard scale.

(3) If a person serves on a jury knowing that he is disqualified for such service under Part II of that Schedule, he shall be guilty of an offence and liable on summary conviction to a fine not exceeding level 5 on the standard scale.

(4) The appropriate officer may at any time put or cause to be put to any person who is summoned under section 8 above such questions as he thinks fit in order to establish whether or not the person is qualified to serve as a juror at an inquest.

(5) Where a question is put to any person under subsection (4) above, if that person—

(a) refuses without reasonable excuse to answer;

(b) gives an answer which he knows to be false in a material particular; or

(c) recklessly gives an answer which is false in a material particular,

he shall be guilty of an offence and liable on summary conviction to a fine not exceeding level 3 on the standard scale.

(6) If any person—

(a) duly summoned as a juror at an inquest makes, or causes or permits to be made on his behalf, any false representation to the coroner or the appropriate officer with the intention of evading service as such juror; or

(b) makes or causes to be made on behalf of another person who has been so summoned any false representation to the coroner or the appropriate officer with the intention of enabling that other person to evade such service,

he shall be guilty of an offence and liable on summary conviction to a fine not exceeding level 3 on the standard scale.

(7) A coroner may authorise a person to perform the functions conferred on the appropriate officer by subsection (4) above and references in this section to the appropriate officer shall be construed as references to the person so authorised.

Attendance of jurors and witnesses

10.—(1) Where a person duly summoned as a juror at an inquest— **A1–89**

(a) does not, after being openly called three times, appear to the summons; or

(b) appears to the summons but refuses without reasonable excuse to serve as a juror,

the coroner may impose on that person a fine not exceeding [£1000].[94]

(2) Where a person duly summoned to give evidence at an inquest—

(a) does not, after being openly called three times, appear to the summons; or

(b) appears to the summons but refuses without lawful excuse to answer a question put to him,

the coroner may impose on that person a fine not exceeding [£1000].[95]

(3) The powers conferred upon a coroner by this section shall be in addition to and not in derogation of any other power which the coroner may possess—

(a) for compelling any person to appear and give evidence before him in any inquest or other proceeding; or

(b) for punishing any person for contempt of court in not so appearing and giving evidence;

but a person shall not be fined by the coroner under this section and also be punished under any such other power.

(4) Notwithstanding anything in the foregoing provisions of this section, a juror shall not be liable to any penalty for non-attendance on a coroner's jury unless the summons requiring him to attend was duly served on him no later than six days before the day on which he was required to attend.

Proceedings at inquest

A1–90 **11.**—(1) It shall not be obligatory for a coroner holding an inquest into a death to view the body; and the validity of such an inquest shall not be questioned in any court on the ground that the coroner did not view the body.

(2) The coroner shall, at the first sitting of the inquest, examine on oath concerning the death all persons who tender evidence as to the facts on the death and all persons having knowledge of those facts whom he considers it expedient to examine.

(3) In the case of an inquest held with a jury, the jury shall, after hearing the evidence—

(a) give their verdict and certify it by an inquisition; and

(b) inquire of and find the particulars for the time being required by the Births and Deaths Registration Act 1953 (in this Act referred to as "the 1953 Act") to be registered concerning the death.

(4) In the case of an inquest held without a jury, the coroner shall, after hearing the evidence—

(a) give his verdict and certify it by an inquisition; and

(b) inquire of and find the particulars for the time being required by the 1953 Act to be registered concerning the death.

(5) An inquisition—

(a) shall be in writing under the hand of the coroner and, in the case of an inquest held with a jury, under the hands of the jurors who concur in the verdict;

(b) shall set out, so far as such particulars have been proved—

(i) who the deceased was; and

(ii) how, when and where the deceased came by his death; and

(c) shall be in such form as the Lord Chancellor may by rules made by statutory instrument from time to time prescribe.

---

[94] Words substituted by the Criminal Justice Act 1991, s.17(3)(a), Sched. 4, Pt. I.

[95] *ibid.*

(6) At a coroner's inquest into the death of a person who came by his death by murder, manslaughter or infanticide, the purpose of the proceedings shall not include the finding of any person guilty of the murder, manslaughter or infanticide; and accordingly a coroner's inquisition shall in no case charge a person with any of those offences.

(7) Where an inquest into a death is held, the coroner shall, within five days after the finding of the inquest is given, send to the registrar of deaths a certificate under his hand—

(a) giving information concerning the death;

(b) specifying the finding with respect to the particulars which under the 1953 Act are required to be registered concerning the death and with respect to the cause of death; and

(c) specifying the time and place at which the inquest was held.

(8) In the case of an inquest into the death of a person who is proved—

(a) to have been killed on a railway; or

(b) to have died in consequence of injuries received on a railway,

the coroner shall within seven days after holding the inquest, make a return of the death, including the cause of death, to the Secretary of State in such form as he may require; and in this subsection "railway" has the same meaning as in the Railway Regulation Act 1842.

Failure of jury to agree

12.—(1) This section applies where, in the case of an inquest held with a jury, the jury fails to agree on a verdict. **A1–91**

(2) If the minority consists of not more than two, the coroner may accept the verdict of the majority, and the majority shall, in that case, certify the verdict under section 11(3) above.

(3) In any other case of disagreement the coroner may discharge the jury and issue a warrant for summoning another jury and, in that case, the inquest shall proceed in all respects as if the proceedings which terminated in the disagreement had not taken place.

Inquests: Special Cases

Order to hold inquest

13.—(1) This section applies where, on an application by or under the authority of the Attorney-General, the High Court is satisfied as respects a coroner ("the coroner concerned") either— **A1–92**

(a) that he refuses or neglects to hold an inquest which ought to be held; or

(b) where an inquest has been held by him that (whether by reason of fraud, rejection of evidence, irregularity of proceedings, insufficiency of inquiry, the discovery of new facts or evidence or otherwise) it is necessary or desirable in the interest of justice that another inquest should be held.

(2) The High Court may—

(a) order an inquest or, as the case may be, another inquest to be held into the death either—

(i) by the coroner concerned; or

(ii) by the coroner for another district in the same administrative area;

(b) order the coroner concerned to pay such costs of and incidental to the application as to the court may appear just; and

(c) where an inquest has been held, quash the inquisition on that inquest.

(3) In relation to an inquest held under subsection (2)(a)(ii) above, the coroner by whom it is held shall be treated for the purposes of this Act as if he were the coroner for the district of the coroner concerned.

Inquest out of jurisdiction

A1–93 **14.**—(1) If it appears to a coroner that, in the case of a body lying within his district, an inquest ought to be held into the death but it is expedient that the inquest should be held by some other coroner, he may request that coroner to assume jurisdiction to hold the inquest; and if that coroner agrees he, and not the coroner within whose district the body is lying, shall have jurisdiction to hold the inquest.

(2) If the coroner who has been requested to assume jurisdiction declines to assume it, the coroner who has made the request may apply to the Secretary of State for a direction designating the coroner who is to hold the inquest.

(3) On the making of an application under subsection (2) above, the Secretary of State—

(a) shall determine by which coroner (whether one of the two mentioned in that subsection or another) the inquest should in all the circumstances be held; and

(b) shall direct him to assume jurisdiction or, as the case may be, to exercise his jurisdiction to hold the inquest;

and where a direction is given under this subsection directing a coroner to assume jurisdiction, he, and not the coroner within whose district the body is lying, shall have jurisdiction to hold the inquest and shall hold it accordingly.

(4) Where jurisdiction to hold an inquest is assumed under this section, it shall not be necessary to remove the body into the district of the coroner who is to hold the inquest.

(5) Any request made or agreement given, any application for a direction and any direction under any of the foregoing provisions of this section shall be made or given in writing.

(6) Notice of the making of an application under subsection (2) above shall be given to the coroner who declined to assume jurisdiction and notice of the direction given pursuant to such an application shall be given—

(a) in a case where the direction is given to the coroner who made the application or the coroner who had notice of it, to the other coroner; and

(b) in a case where the direction is given to some other coroner, to the coroner who made the application and to the coroner who had notice of it.

(7) On the assumption by a coroner of jurisdiction to hold an inquest under this section, the coroner—

(a) shall also assume, in relation to the body and the inquest, all the powers and duties which would belong to him if the body were lying within his district (including the power to order its exhumation under section 23 below); and

(b) may exercise those powers notwithstanding that the body remains outside his district or, having been removed into it, is removed out of it by virtue of any order of his for its examination or burial.

(8) On the assumption of the powers and duties referred to in subsection (7) above by the coroner who assumes jurisdiction to hold the inquest, the coroner within whose district the body is lying shall cease to have any powers or duties in relation to the body or the inquest, notwithstanding that the body remains within his district or comes to be buried there.

(9) It shall be for the coroner who assumes, and not for the coroner who ceases to have, jurisdiction to hold an inquest under this section to pay any fees or other expenses incurred in the course of his duties by the latter coroner before he ceased to have

jurisdiction; and any such fees or other expenses shall be accounted for and repaid accordingly.

Inquest where body destroyed or irrecoverable

15.—(1) Where a coroner has reason to believe— A1–94

(a) that a death has occurred in or near his district in such circumstances that an inquest ought to be held; and

(b) that owing to the destruction of the body by fire or otherwise, or to the fact that the body is lying in a place from which it cannot be recovered, an inquest cannot be held except in pursuance of this section,

he may report the facts to the Secretary of State.

(2) Where a report is made under subsection (1) above, the Secretary of State may, if he considers it desirable to do so, direct a coroner (whether the coroner making the report or another) to hold an inquest into the death.

(3) Where a coroner is directed under this section to hold an inquest, the provisions of this Act and the law relating to coroners and coroners' inquests shall apply with such modifications as may be necessary in consequence of the inquest being one into the death of a person whose body does not lie within the coroner's district.

Adjournment of inquest in certain cases

16.—(1) If on an inquest into a death the coroner before the conclusion of the inquest— A1–95

(a) is informed by the clerk of a magistrates' court under section 17(1) below that some person has been charged before a magistrates' court with—

(i) the murder, manslaughter or infanticide of the deceased;

(ii) an offence under [section 1 or 3A of the Road Traffic Act 1988 (dangerous driving or careless driving when under the influence of drink or drugs)][96] committed by causing the death of the deceased; or

(iii) an offence under section 2(1) of the Suicide Act 1961 consisting of aiding, abetting, counselling or procuring the suicide of the deceased; or

(b) is informed by the Director of Public Prosecutions that some person has been charged before examining justices[96a] with an offence (whether or not involving the death of a person other than the deceased) alleged to have been committed in circumstances connected with the death of the deceased, not being an offence within paragraph (a) above, and is requested by the Director to adjourn the inquest,

then subject to subsection (2) below, the coroner shall, in the absence of reason to the contrary, adjourn the inquest until after the conclusion of the relevant criminal proceedings and, if a jury has been summoned, may, if he thinks fit, discharge them.

(2) The coroner—

(a) need not adjourn the inquest in a case within subsection (1)(a) above if, before he has done so, the Director of Public Prosecutions notifies him that adjournment is unnecessary; and

(b) may in any case resume the adjourned inquest before the conclusion of the relevant criminal proceedings if notified by the Director that it is open to him to do so.

---

[96] Words substituted by the Road Traffic Act 1991, s.48, Sched. 4, para. 40.

[96a] The words substituted or added by the Criminal Justice and Public Order Act 1994, s.44, Sched. 4, para. 70 have been repealed by the Criminal Procedure and Investigations Act 1996, s.44, Sched. 5.

(3) After the conclusion of the relevant criminal proceedings, or on being notified under paragraph (b) of subsection (2) above before their conclusion, the coroner may, subject to the following provisions of this section, resume the adjourned inquest if in his opinion there is sufficient cause to do so.

(4) Where a coroner adjourns an inquest in compliance with subsection (1) above, he shall send to the registrar of deaths a certificate under his hand stating, so far as they have been ascertained at the date of the certificate, the particulars which under the 1953 Act are required to be registered concerning the death.

(5) Where a coroner does not resume an inquest which he has adjourned in compliance with subsection (1) above, he shall (without prejudice to subsection (4) above) send to the registrar of deaths a certificate under his hand stating the result of the relevant criminal proceedings.

(6) Where a coroner resumes an inquest which has been adjourned in compliance with subsection (1) above and for that purpose summons a jury (but not where he resumes without a jury, or with the same jury as before the adjournment)—

(a) he shall proceed in all respects as if the inquest had not previously begun; and
(b) subject to subsection (7) below, the provisions of this Act shall accordingly as if the resumed inquest were a fresh inquest.

(7) Where a coroner resumes an inquest which has been adjourned in compliance with subsection (1) above—

(a) the finding of the inquest as to the cause of death must not be inconsistent with the outcome of the relevant criminal proceedings;
(b) the coroner shall supply to the registrar of deaths after the termination of the inquest a certificate under his hand stating the result of the relevant criminal proceedings; and
(c) the provisions of section 11(7) above shall not apply in relation to that inquest.

(8) In this section "the relevant criminal proceedings" means the proceedings before examining justices[96b] and before any court to which the person charged is committed[96c] for trial.

Provisions supplementary to section 16

A1–96 **17.**—(1) Where a person is charged before a magistrates' court with—

(a) murder, manslaughter or infanticide;
(b) an offence under [section 1 or 3A of the Road Traffic Act 1988 (dangerous driving or careless driving when under the influence of drink or drugs)][97]; or
(c) an offence under section 2(1) of the Suicide Act 1961 consisting of aiding, abetting, counselling or procuring the suicide of another,

the clerk of the court shall inform the coroner who is responsible for holding an inquest into the death of the making of the charge and of the result of the proceedings before that court.

(2) Where[97a] a person charged with—

(a) murder, manslaughter or infanticide;
(b) an offence under [section 1 or 3A of the Road Traffic Act 1988 (dangerous driving or careless driving when under the influence of drink or drugs)][98]; or

---

[96b] *ibid.*

[96c] *ibid.*

[97] Words substituted by the Road Traffic Act 1991, s.48, Sched. 4, para. 40.

[97a] The words substituted or added by the Criminal Justice and Public Order Act 1994, s.44, Sched. 4, para. 71 have been repealed by the Criminal Procedure and Investigations Act 1996, s.44, Sched. 5.

[98] Words substituted by the Road Traffic Act 1991, s.48, Sched. 4, para. 40.

(c) an offence under section 2(1) of the Suicide Act 1961 consisting of aiding, abetting, counselling or procuring the suicide of another,

is committed[98a] for trial to the Crown Court, the appropriate officer of the Crown Court at the place where the person charged is tried shall inform the coroner of the result of the proceedings before that court.

(3) Where the Director of Public Prosecutions has under section 16(1)(b) above requested a coroner to adjourn an inquest, then whether or not the inquest is adjourned as a result, the Director shall—

(a) inform the coroner of the result of the proceedings before the magistrates' court in the case of the person charged as mentioned in that paragraph; and

(b) if that person is committed[98b] for trial to the Crown Court, inform the coroner of the result of the proceedings before that court.

Inquests into road deaths in London

18.—(1) Where an accident occurs within Greater London or the City resulting in the death of a person, and it is alleged that the accident was due to— **A1–97**

(a) the nature or character of a road or road surface; or

(b) a defect in the design or construction of a vehicle or in the materials used in the construction of a road or vehicle;

the coroner holding the inquest into the death shall send to the Secretary of State, or to such officer of his as the Secretary of State may direct, notice in writing of the time and place of holding the inquest, and of any adjourned inquest.

(2) An officer appointed by the Secretary of State for the purpose shall be at liberty at any such inquest to examine any witness, subject nevertheless to the power of the coroner to disallow any question which in his opinion is not relevant or is otherwise not a proper question.

(3) In this section "road" has the same meaning as in [section 182 of the Road Traffic Act 1988].[99]

Post-mortem examination without inquest

19.—(1) Where a coroner is informed that the body of a person is lying within his district and there is reasonable cause to suspect that the person has died a sudden death of which the cause is unknown, the coroner may, if he is of opinion that a post-mortem examination may prove an inquest to be unnecessary— **A1–98**

(a) direct any legally qualified medical practitioner whom, if an inquest were held, he would be entitled to summon as a medical witness under section 21 below; or

(b) request any other legally qualified medical practitioner,

to make a post-mortem examination of the body and to report the result of the examination to the coroner in writing.

(2) For the purposes of a post-mortem examination under this section, the coroner and any person directed or requested by him to make the examination shall have the like powers, authorities and immunities as if the examination were a post-mortem examination directed by the coroner at an inquest into the death of the deceased.

[98a] The words substituted or added by the Criminal Justice and Public Order Act 1994, s.44, Sched. 4, para. 71, have been repealed by the Criminal Procedures and Investigations Act 1996, s.44, Sched. 5.

[98b] *ibid.*

[99] Words substituted by the Road Traffic (Consequential Provisions) Act 1988, s.4, Sched. 3, para. 37(3).

(3) Where a post-mortem examination is made under this section and the coroner is satisfied as a result of it that an inquest is unnecessary, he shall send to the registrar of deaths a certificate under his hand stating the cause of death as disclosed by the report of the person making the examination.

(4) Nothing in this section shall be construed as authorising the coroner to dispense with an inquest in any case where there is reasonable cause to suspect that the deceased—

(a) has died a violent or an unnatural death; or

(b) has died in prison or in such a place or in such circumstances as to require an inquest under any other Act.

Request to specially qualified person to make post-mortem and special examinations

A1–99 **20.**—(1) Without prejudice to the power of a coroner holding an inquest to direct a medical witness whom he may summon under section 21 below to make a post-mortem examination of the body of the deceased, the coroner may, at any time after he has decided to hold an inquest—

(a) request any legally qualified medical practitioner to make a post-mortem examination of the body or a special examination of the body or both such examinations; or

(b) request any person whom he considers to possess special qualifications for conducting a special examination of the body to make such an examination.

(2) If any person who has made a post-mortem or special examination in pursuance of such a request is summoned by the coroner as a witness, he may be asked to give evidence as to his opinion upon any matter arising out of the examination, and as to how, in his opinion, the deceased came by his death.

(3) Where a person states upon oath before the coroner that in his belief the death of the deceased was caused partly or entirely by the improper or negligent treatment of a medical practitioner or other person, that medical practitioner or other person—

(a) shall not be allowed to perform or assist at any post-mortem or special examination made for the purposes of the inquest into the death; but

(b) shall have the right, if he so desires, to be represented at any such post-mortem examination.

(4) In this section "special examination", in relation to a body, means a special examination by way of analysis, test or otherwise of such parts or contents of the body or such other substances or things as ought in the opinion of the coroner to be submitted to analyses, tests or other examination with a view to ascertaining how the deceased came by his death.

Summoning of medical witnesses and direction of post-mortem examinations

A1–100 **21.**—(1) In the case of an inquest into a death, the coroner may summon as a witness—

(a) any legally qualified medical practitioner appearing to him to have attended at the death of the deceased or during the last illness of the deceased; or

(b) where it appears to him that no such practitioner so attended the deceased, any legally qualified medical practitioner in actual practice in or near the place where the death occurred;

and any medical witness summoned under this section may be asked to give evidence as to how, in his opinion, the deceased came by his death.

(2) Subject to subsection (3) below, the coroner may, either in his summons for the attendance of a medical witness or at any time between the issuing of that summons and

the end of the inquest, direct the medical witness to make a post-mortem examination of the body of the deceased.

(3) Where a person states upon oath before the coroner that in his belief the death of the deceased was caused partly or entirely by the improper or negligent treatment of a medical practitioner or other person, that medical practitioner or other person shall not be allowed to perform or assist at the post-mortem examination of the deceased.

(4) If, in the case of an inquest with a jury, a majority of the jury are of opinion that the cause of death has not been satisfactorily explained by the evidence of the medical practitioner or of other witnesses brought before them, they may in writing require the coroner—

(a) to summon as a witness some other legally qualified medical practitioner named by them; and

(b) to direct a post-mortem examination of the deceased to be made by a practitioner summoned under this subsection, whether or not such an examination has been previously made;

and if the coroner fails to comply with such a requisition, he shall be liable on conviction on indictment to a term of imprisonment not exceeding two years or to a fine or to both.

(5) Where a medical practitioner fails to obey a summons of a coroner issued in pursuance of this section, he shall, unless he shows a good and sufficient cause for not having obeyed the summons, be liable on summary conviction, on the prosecution of the coroner or of any two of the jury, to a fine not exceeding [£1000].[1]

Removal of body for post-mortem examination

22.—(1) Subject to subsection (2) below, where by the direction or at the request of a coroner, a post-mortem examination of a body is to be made, the coroner may order the removal of the body to any place which may be provided for the purpose either within his district or within an adjoining district of another coroner. **A1–101**

(2) A coroner shall not order the removal of a body upon which a post-mortem examination is to be made to any place other than a place within his district provided by a local authority except with the consent of the person or authority by whom the place is provided.

(3) The removal of a body in pursuance of an order made by a coroner under this section to any place outside his district shall not affect his powers and duties in relation to the body or the inquest into the death nor shall it confer or impose any rights, powers or duties upon any other coroner.

(4) Where a coroner—

(a) orders under this section the removal of a body to any place outside his district; and

(b) does not authorise the disposal of the body after examination,

he shall order the removal of the body after examination to a place within his district.

(5) The expenses of any removal ordered by a coroner under this section shall be defrayed as part of the expenses incurred by him in the course of his duties.

(6) In this section—

"disposal" has the same meaning as in the 1953 Act;

"local authority" means the council of a [district, London borough or Welsh principal area][1a] or the Common Council.

---

[1] Words substituted by the Criminal Justice Act 1991, s.17(3)(a), Sched. 4, Pt. I.

[1a] Words substituted by the Local Government (Wales) Act 1994, s.66, Sched. 16, para. 82.

Exhumation of body for examination

A1–102 **23.**—(1) A coroner may order the exhumation of the body of a person buried within his district where it appears to him that it is necessary for the body to be examined—

(a) for the purpose of his holding an inquest into that person's death or discharging any other function of his in relation to the body or the death; or

(b) for the purposes of any criminal proceedings which have been instituted or are contemplated in respect of the death of that person or of some other person who came by his death in circumstances connected with the death of the person whose body is needed for examination.

(2) The power of a coroner under this section shall be exercisable by warrant under his hand.

(3) No body shall be ordered by a coroner to be exhumed except under this section.

EXPENSES AND RETURNS OF INQUEST

Fees and allowances payable on holding inquest

A1–103 **24.**—(1) The fees and allowances which may be lawfully paid by coroners—

(a) to witnesses and persons summoned to attend as witnesses; and

(b) to medical practitioners making post-mortem examinations by the coroner's direction or at the coroner's request.

shall be such as may be determined by the Secretary of State with the consent of the Treasury; but nothing in this subsection shall apply in relation to the fees payable in respect of a special examination under section 20 above.

(2) A relevant council—

(a) may from time to time make a schedule of the fees, allowances and disbursements which may be lawfully paid or made by a coroner in the course of his duties, other than fees and allowances to which subsection (1) above applies;

(b) may at any time vary a schedule so made; and

(c) shall cause a copy of every schedule so made or so varied to be sent to every coroner concerned.

(3) The Secretary of State may by rules made by statutory instrument prescribe—

(a) the fees payable to corners or other persons for furnishing copies of inquisitions, depositions or other documents in their custody relating to an inquest; and

(b) where in the opinion of the Secretary of State adequate provision is not made for them by a schedule under subsection (2) above, the fees, allowances and disbursements which may be lawfully paid or made by a coroner in the course of his duties, other than fees and allowances to which subsection (1) above applies.

Payments to jurors

A1–104 **25.**—(1) A person who serves as a juror in a coroner's court shall be entitled, in respect of his attendance at court for the purpose of performing jury service, to receive payments, at the rates determined by the Secretary of State with the consent of the Treasury and subject to any prescribed conditions, by way of allowance—

(a) for travelling and subsistence; and

(b) for financial loss where in consequence of his attendance for that purpose—

(i) he has incurred any expenditure (otherwise than on travelling and subsistence) to which he would not otherwise be subject; or

(ii) he has suffered any loss of earnings which he would otherwise have made or any loss of benefit under the enactments relating to national insurance and social security which he would otherwise have received.

(2) The amount due to any person in respect of such service shall be ascertained and paid over to him by the coroner.

(3) For the purposes of this section a person who, in obedience to a summons to serve on a jury, attends for service as a juror shall be deemed to serve as a juror notwithstanding that he is not subsequently sworn.

(4) In this section "prescribed" means prescribed by regulations made by statutory instrument by the Secretary of State with the consent of the Treasury.

Payment of expenses by coroner

26.—(1) A coroner holding an inquest shall, immediately after the termination of the proceedings, pay— **A1–105**

(a) the fees of every medical witness;

(b) the allowance of every juror; and

(c) all expenses reasonably incurred in and about the holding of the inquest,

not exceeding the fees, allowances and disbursements which may be lawfully paid or made under this Act.

(2) Any fees, allowances or disbursements so paid or made shall be repaid to the coroner in manner provided by this Act.

Accounts to be laid before relevant council

27.—(1) Every coroner shall within four months after paying or making any fees, allowances or disbursements in accordance with the provisions of this Act, cause a full and true account of all fees, allowances and disbursements so paid or made by him under this Act to be laid before the relevant council. **A1–106**

(2) Every account under this section shall be accompanied by such vouchers as under the circumstances may to the relevant council seem reasonable; and the relevant council may, if they think fit, examine the coroner on oath as to any such account.

(3) On being satisfied of the correctness of any such account, the relevant council shall order their treasurer to pay to the coroner the sum due; and the treasurer shall without any abatement or deduction pay that sum—

(a) in the case of a metropolitan district or London borough council, out of the general [. . .][2] fund;

[(aa) in the case of a non-metropolitan district council, out of the general fund][2a]

(b) in the case of a non-metropolitan county council [in England],[2aa] out of the county fund;

[(bb) in the case of the council of a Welsh principal area, out of the council fund.][2b]

(c) in the case of the Common Council, out of the [City fund].[3]

and shall be allowed that sum on passing his accounts.

(4) In the case of a coroner for a coroner's [district—

(a) consisting of two or more metropolitan districts or London boroughs, or

(b) which lies partly in each of two or more Welsh principal areas, [or

(c) which lies partly in each of two or more non-metropolitan counties in England,][3a]

---

[2] Words repealed by S.I. 1990 No. 1285.

[2a] Words inserted by S.I. 1995 No. 655.

[[2aa] Words inserted by the Local Government (Wales) Act 1994, s.66, Sched. 16, para. 82.

[2b] *ibid.*

[3] Words substituted by S.I. 1990 No. 1285.

[3a] Words inserted by S.I. 1995 No. 655.

the expenses of the councils of those districts, boroughs [areas or counties][[3aa in respect of the coroner's service shall be apportioned between those councils in such manner as they may agree or, in default of agreement, as may be determined by the Secretary of State.

Annual returns to be made to Secretary of State

A1–107 **28.**—(1) Every coroner shall on or before 1st February in every year furnish to the Secretary of State a return in writing, in such form and containing such particulars as the Secretary of State may direct, of all cases in which an inquest has been held by him, or by some other person acting for him, during the year ending on the immediately preceding 31st December.

(2) Every coroner shall also, as and when required by the Secretary of State, furnish to the Secretary of State returns in relation to inquests held and deaths inquired into by him in such form and containing such particulars as the Secretary of State may direct.

MISCELLANEOUS

Coroner of the Queen's household

A1–108 **29.**—(1) The coroner of the Queen's household shall continue to be appointed by the Lord Steward for the time being of the Queen's household.

(2) The coroner of the Queen's household shall have exclusive jurisdiction in respect of inquests into the deaths of persons whose bodies are lying—

(a) within the limits of any of the Queen's palaces; or

(b) within the limits of any other house where Her Majesty is then residing.

(3) The limits of any such palace or house shall be deemed to extend to any courts, gardens or other places within the curtilage of the palace or house but not further; and where a body is lying in any place beyond those limits, the coroner within whose district the body is lying, and not the coroner for the Queen's household, shall have jurisdiction to hold an inquest into the death.

(4) The jurors on an inquest held by the coroner of the Queen's household shall consist of officers of that household, to be returned by such officer of the Queen's household as may be directed to summon the jurors by the warrant of the coroner.

(5) All inquisitions, depositions and recognizances shall be delivered to the Lord Steward of the Queen's household to be filed among the records of his office.

(6) The coroner of the Queen's household—

(a) shall make his declaration of office before the Lord Steward of the Queen's household; and

(b) shall reside in one of the Queen's palaces or in such other convenient place as may from time to time be allowed by the Lord Steward of the Queen's household.

(7) The provisions of Schedule 2 to this Act shall have effect with respect to the application of this Act and the law relating to coroners to the coroner of the Queen's household.

Treasure trove

A1–109 **30.** A coroner shall continue to have jurisdiction—

(a) to inquire into any treasure which is found in his district; and

(b) to inquire who were, or are suspected of being, the finders;

and the provisions of this Act shall, so far as applicable, apply to every such inquest.

[3aa *ibid.*

Provision of accommodation

31. [The council (whether or not a relevant council) of any of the following, that is to say— **A1–110**

(a) a metropolitan district,
(b) a London borough,
(c) a Welsh principal area; or
(d) in the case of such a coroner's district as is mentioned in section 1(1)9b) above, a non-metropolitan county the whole or part of which is included in that coroner's district][3b]

may provide and maintain proper accommodation for the holding of inquests in their area.

Power to make rules

32.—(1) The Lord Chancellor may, with the concurrence of the Secretary of State, make rules for regulating the practice and procedure at or in connection with inquests and post-mortem examinations and, in particular (without prejudice to the generality of the foregoing provision), such rules may provide— **A1–111**

(a) as to the procedure at inquests held without a jury;
(b) as to the issue by coroners of orders authorising burials;
(c) for empowering a coroner or his deputy or assistant deputy to alter the date fixed for the holding of any adjourned inquest within the district of the coroner;
(d) as to the procedure to be followed where a coroner decides not to resume an adjourned inquest; and
(e) as to the notices to be given, and as to the variation or discharge of any recognisances entered into by jurors or witnesses, where the date fixed for an adjourned inquest is altered or where a coroner decides not to resume an adjourned inquest.

(2) Without prejudice to the generality of subsection (1) above, rules under this section may make provision for persons to be excused service as jurors at inquests in such circumstances as the rules may specify.

(3) The power of the Lord Chancellor under this section to make rules with respect to any matter shall include power—

(a) to prescribe the forms to be used in connection with that matter;
(b) to revoke or amend, or substitute new forms for, any forms which are directed or authorised by or under any enactment to be used in connection with that matter.

(4) The power to make rules under this section shall be exercisable by statutory instrument.

Savings for ex-officio coroners and judicial powers

33.—(1) Nothing in this Act shall prejudice or affect the jurisdiction of a judge exercising the jurisdiction of a coroner by virtue of his office. **A1–112**

(2) Nothing in this Act shall prejudice or affect—

(a) the jurisdiction of the Lord Chancellor or the High Court in relation to the removal of a coroner otherwise than in the manner provided by this Act; or
(b) the jurisdiction of the High Court in relation to or over a coroner or his duties.

[3b] Words inserted by S.I. 1996 No. 655.

Application of Act to Isles of Scilly

A1–113 **34.**—(1) Subject to subsection (2) below, this Act shall apply in relation to the Isles of Scilly as if those Isles were a non-metropolitan county and the Council of those Isles were the council of that county.

(2) The power conferred on the Secretary of State by section 265 of the Local Government Act 1972 (application of that Act to the Isles of Scilly) shall include power to make an order providing for regulating the application of this Act to those Isles otherwise than as mentioned in subsection (1) above and such an order may amend or repeal that subsection accordingly.

Interpretation

A1–114 **35.**—(1) In this Act, unless the context otherwise requires—

"the 1953 Act" means the Births and Deaths Registration Act 1953;

"administrative area" means [,subject to subsection (1B) below,][3bb [Wales,][3c a metropolitan or non-metropolitan county [in England][3d or Greater London;

"the Common Council" means the Common Council of the City of London and "common councillor" shall be construed accordingly;

"the City" means the City of London (including the Inner Temple and the Middle Temple);

"Greater London" does not include the City;

"relevant council" has the meaning given by section [1(1A)][3dd above.

["Welsh principal area" means Welsh county or county borough.][3e

[(1A) In this Act any reference to a council of a non-metropolitan county includes in relation to an area for which there is a district council but no county council a reference to a district council, and any reference to a councillor of a non-metropolitan county shall be construed accordingly.

(1B) In the application of sections 4(5), 5(3) and 13(2) above to a non-metropolitan county part of which is included in such a coroner's district as is mentioned in section 1(1)(b) above, any reference in those provisions to an administrative area shall be construed as a reference to so much of that county as is not so included.][3f

(2) In this Act references to an inquest held with a jury include, and references to an inquest held without a jury do not include, references to an inquest part of which is held with a jury.

Consequential amendments, repeals, transitional and provisions and savings

A1–115 **36.**—(1) The enactments mentioned in Schedule 3 to this Act shall have effect subject to the amendments there specified, being amendments consequential on the provisions of this Act.

(2) The enactments and instruments mentioned in Schedule 4 to this Act (which include some that are spent) are hereby repealed to the extent specified in the third column of that Schedule.

[3bb Words inserted by S.I. 1996 No. 655.

[3c] Words inserted by the Local Government (Wales) Act 1994, s.66, Sched. 16, para. 82.

[3d] *ibid.*

[3dd] Words inserted by S.I. 1996 No. 655.

[3e] *ibid.*

[3f] Words inserted by S.I. 1996 No. 655.

(3) Where any period of time specified in an enactment repealed by this Act is current at the commencement of this Act, his Act shall have effect as if the corresponding provision of this Act had been in force when that period began to run.

(4) Notwithstanding the repeal by this Act of section 13 of the Local Government Act 1985—

(a) any corner holding office immediately before 1st April 1986 and assigned to a coroner's district in a metropolitan county or in Greater London shall be deemed to have been duly appointed by the relevant council; and

(b) any orders made under section 12 of the Coroners (Amendment) Act 1926 and in force immediately before that date shall, so far as they affect a metropolitan county or Greater London, have effect as if made under section 4(1) above.

(5) Notwithstanding the repeal by this Act of the Coroners Act 1887, anything mentioned in subsection (5) of section 45 of that Act which, immediately before the commencement of this Act, was in force by virtue of that subsection shall, except so far as it is inconsistent with this act, remain in force.

(6) Nothing in this section shall be taken as prejudicing the operation of sections 15 to 17 of the Interpretation Act 1978 (which relate to the effect of repeals).

Short title, commencement and extent

37.—(1) This Act may be cited as the Coroners Act 1988. **A1–116**

(2) This Act shall come into force at the end of the period of two months beginning with the day on which it is passed.

(3) This Act extends to England and Wales only.

SCHEDULES

Section 3(1)

SCHEDULE 1

SALARIES AND PENSIONS

Coroners' salaries

1.—(1) Subject to the provisions of this paragraph, a coroner shall be paid by the relevant council an annual salary at such rate as may be fixed by agreement between the coroner and that council. **A1–117**

(2) If at any time a coroner and the relevant council cannot agree with respect to any proposed alteration of the rate of his salary—

(a) the Secretary of State may, on the application of either party, fix the rate of that salary at such rate as he thinks proper; and

(b) subject to sub-paragraph (4) below, the rate so fixed shall come into force as from such date as he may determine.

(3) In fixing the rate of the salary payable to a coroner under this paragraph, regard shall be had to the nature and extent of his duties and to all the circumstances of the case.

(4) A date determined under sub-paragraph (2) above shall be not less than three years from the date when the rate of the coroner's salary as last fixed came into force, unless in the opinion of the Secretary of State the coroner's district has in the meantime been materially altered.

Coroners' pensions

A1–118 **2.**—(1) On the retirement, after not less than five years' service, of a coroner—
(a) who held office as a coroner immediately before April 6, 1978; and
(b) who did not elect in accordance with article 3(b) of the Social Security (Modification of Coroners (Amendment) Act 1926) Order 1978 that the provisions of the Coroners (Amendment) Act 1926 relating to pensions should not apply to him,

(that is to say, a coroner who is not a pensionable employee for the purposes of the Local Government Superannuation Regulations 1986) the relevant council may, if either of the conditions mentioned in sub-paragraph (2) below is satisfied, grant to him a pension of such amount as may be agreed between him and the council not exceeding the scale contained in paragraph 3 below.

(2) The said conditions are—
(a) that the coroner has attained the age of sixty-five years;
(b) that the relevant council is satisfied by means of a medical certificate that the coroner is incapable of discharging his duties whether on mental or physical grounds and that such incapacity is likely to be permanent.

(3) A coroner to whom this paragraph applies—
(a) shall, at any time after he has completed fifteen years' service and has attained the age of sixty-five years, vacate his office if required to do so by the relevant council; but
(b) shall, in that case and in the absence of any agreement to the contrary, be entitled to receive the maximum pension which the council is empowered to grant him under this paragraph having regard to the length of his service.

(4) A pension payable to a coroner under this paragraph shall be reduced by the amount of any additional component of his retirement pension (within the meaning of section 6(1)(b) of the Social Security Pensions Act 1975) which is payable to him.

(5) In this paragraph "service" means service, whether before or after the commencement of this Act, as a coroner in the same administrative area; and for this purpose "administrative area" includes the City.

(6) Notwithstanding the reproduction of article 3 of the Social Security (Modification of Coroners (Amendment) Act 1926) Order 1978 as paragraphs (a) and (b) of sub-paragraph (1) above and of article 4 of that Order as sub-paragraph (4) above—
(a) those provisions may be amended or repealed; and
(b) any question as to the validity of those provisions may be determined,

as though they were contained in an order made under section 65 of the Social Security Act 1973.

Scale of pensions

A1–119 **3.**—(1) An annual pension not exceeding ten sixtieths of the last annual salary may be granted after the completion of five years' service.

(2) Where the completed service exceeds five years, there may be granted an annual pension not exceeding the aggregate of—
(a) ten-sixtieths of the last annual salary; and
(b) an amount; not exceeding one-fortieth of that salary for each completed year's service after five years.

so however that no such pension shall be of an amount exceeding two-thirds of that salary.

(3) For the purposes of this paragraph the last annual salary of a coroner shall be taken to be the salary paid to him in his last completed year of service as coroner, after deducting so much (if any) of that salary as was paid to him with a view to his providing

at his own expense for any necessary expenditure in connection with his duties as coroner.

(4) If any dispute arises as to the amount to be deducted under sub-paragraph (3) above in computing the last annual salary of a coroner, the dispute shall be referred to the Secretary of State, whose decision shall be final.

Payment of salaries and pensions

4. The salary of a coroner and any pension payable to a person in respect of his service as a coroner shall be deemed to accrue from day to day and, in the absence of agreement to the contrary, shall be payable quarterly. **A1–120**

Section 29(7)

SCHEDULE 2

CORONER OF THE QUEEN'S HOUSEHOLD

Section 29(7)

1. Sections 1 to 5 of this Act (except subsections (4) to (6) of section 3), sections 6 and 7 of this Act so far as relating to the appointment and functions of assistant deputy coroners and Schedule 1 to this Act shall not apply to the coroner of the Queen's household. **A1–121**

2. Sections 6 and 7 of this Act, so far as relating to the appointment and functions of deputy coroners, shall apply with the necessary modifications to the coroner of the Queen's household as they apply to other coroners and, in particular, with the following modifications, namely— **A1–122**

(a) that the appointment of a deputy to the coroner of the Queen's household shall be subject to the approval of the Lord Steward of the Queen's household; and
(b) that copies of such appointments shall be sent to and kept by him.

3. Sections 9 and 32(2) of this Act shall not apply in relation to any inquest held by the coroner of the Queen's household. **A1–123**

4. Section 25 of this Act shall not apply in relation to service on a jury on an inquest held by the coroner of the Queen's household but that shall not affect any entitlement to payment that might otherwise be enjoyed by a juror for service on such a jury. **A1–124**

5. Subject to the provisions of this Schedule and section 29 of this Act, the coroner of the Queen's household shall, within the limits laid down in subsection (3) of that section— **A1–125**

(a) have the same jurisdiction and powers; and
(b) be subject to the same obligations, liabilities and disqualifications; and
(c) generally be subject to the provisions of this Act and the law relating to coroners in the same manner,

as any other coroner.

SCHEDULE 3

CONSEQUENTIAL AMENDMENTS

[*Makes consequential amendments to various Acts.*] **A1–126**

SCHEDULE 4A1–136A

REPEALS

[*Makes certain repeals.*]

Criminal Procedure Act 1865

(28 & 29 VICT C. 18)

1 Section 2 to apply to all trials for felony or misdemeanor; sections 3 to 8 to all courts and persons authorized to hear evidence

A1–136A [. . .] The provisions of section two of this Act shall apply to every trial [. . .]; and [. . .] the provisions of sections from three to eight, inclusive, of this Act shall apply to all courts of judicature, as well criminal as all others, and to all persons having, by law or by consent of parties, authority to hear, receive, and examine evidence.[4]

4 As to proof of contradictory statements of adverse witness

If a witness, upon cross-examination as to a former statement made by him relative to the subject matter of the indictment or proceeding, and inconsistent with his present testimony, does not distinctly admit that he has made such statement, proof may be given that he did in fact make it; but before such proof can be given the circumstances of the supposed statement, sufficient to designate the particular occasion, must be mentioned to the witness, and he must be asked whether or not he has made such statement.

5 Cross-examinations as to previous statements in writing

A witness may be cross-examined as to previous statements made by him in writing, or reduced into writing, relative to the subject matter of the indictment or proceeding, without such writing being shown to him; but if it is intended to contradict such witness by the writing, his attention must, before such contradictory proof can be given, be called to those parts of the writing which are to be used for the purpose of so contradicting him: Provided always, that it shall be competent for the judge, at any time during the trial, to require the production of the writing for his inspection, and he may thereupon make such use of it for the purposes of the trial as he may think fit.

Law Reform (Year and a Day Rule) Act 1996

(1996 C. 19)

A1–164A An Act to abolish the "year and a day rule" and, in consequence of its abolition, to impose a restriction on the institution in certain circumstances of proceedings for a fatal offence. [17th June 1996]

Abolition of "year and a day rule"

1. The rule known as the "year and a day rule" (that is, the rule that, for the purposes of offences involving death and of suicide, an act or omission is conclusively presumed

[4] The words omitted were repealed by the SLR Act 1893, the Criminal Law Act 1967, s.10(2), Sched. 3, Pt. III, and the Criminal Law Act (Northern Ireland) 1967, s.15(2),Sched. 2.

not to have caused a person's death if more than a year and a day elapsed before he died) is abolished for all purposes.

Restriction on institution of proceedings for a fatal offence

2.—(1) Proceedings to which this section applies may only be instituted by or with the consent of the Attorney General.

(2) This section applies to proceedings against a person for a fatal offence if—

(a) the injury alleged to have caused the death was sustained more than three years before the death occurred, or

(b) the person has previously been convicted of an offence committed in circumstances alleged to be connected with the death.

(3) In subsection (2) "fatal offence" means—

(a) murder, manslaughter, infanticide or any other offence of which one of the elements is causing a person's death, or

(b) the offence of aiding, abetting, counselling or procuring a person's suicide.

(4) No provision that proceedings may be instituted only by or with the consent of the Director of Public Prosecutions shall apply to proceedings to which this section applies.

(5) In the application of this section to Northern Ireland—

(a) the reference in subsection (1) to the Attorney General is to the Attorney General for Northern Ireland, and

(b) the reference in subsection (4) to the Director of Public Prosecutions is to the Director of Public Prosecutions for Northern Ireland.

Short title, commencement and extent

3.—(1) This Act may be cited as the Law Reform (Year and a Day Rule) Act 1996. **A1–164B**

(2) Section 1 does not affect the continued application of the rule referred to in that section to a case where the act or omission (or the last of the acts or omissions) which caused the death occurred before the day on which this Act is passed.

(3) Section 2 does not come into force until the end of the period of two months beginning with the day on which this Act is passed; but that section applies to the institution of proceedings after the end of that period in any case where the death occurred during that period (as well as in any case where the death occurred after the end of that period).

(4) This Act extends to England and Wales and Northern Ireland.

Local Government Act 1992

Implementation of recommendations

Implementation of recommendations by order

17.—(1) Where the Local Government Commission submit to the Secretary of State a report on a review together with its recommendations, he may, if he thinks fit, by order give effect to all or any of the recommendations, with or without modifications. **A1–166A**

(2) No order under this section shall be made before the end of the period of six weeks beginning with the submission of the report; and before making such an order, the Secretary of State may by a direction require the Local Government Commission to supply him with such additional information as may be described in the direction.

(3) An order under this section may, in particular, include provision which, for the purpose of giving effect (with or without modifications) to recommendations of the Local Government Commission, makes provision with respect to—

(a) the area of any authority and the name of any such area;
(b) the name of any authority;
(c) the establishment of any new authority for any county or district or the winding up and dissolution of any existing authority;
(d) the total number of councillors of any authority, the apportionment of councillors among electoral areas, the assignment of existing councillors to new or altered electoral areas, and the first election of councillors for any new or altered electoral area;
(e) without prejudice to paragraph (d) above, the holding of a fresh election of councillors for all electoral areas in a local government area where substantial changes have been made to some of those areas, or the order of retirement of councillors for any electoral areas in the local government area in question;
(f) in the case of an order relating to the system of election of district councillors, the ordinary year of election and the order of retirement of parish councillors for any parish situated in the district;
(g) the constitution and election of public bodies in any area affected by the order;
(h) the abolition or establishment, or the restriction or extension, of the jurisdiction of any public body in or over any part of any area affected by the order.

(4) The power to make an order under this section shall include power to make any such provision in relation to the other provisions of that order, or to the provisions of any previous order under this section, as is equivalent to that which may be contained in regulations under section 19 below or in an agreement under section 20 below.

(5) Without prejudice to the preceding provisions of this section, where charter trustees have been constituted under section 246 of the 1972 Act for an area which is altered by an order under this section and subsection (8) of that section (incorporation of whole or part of trustees' area in parish) does not apply, the order may make such provision with respect to the charter trustees as appears to the Secretary of State to be appropriate.

Regulations for supplementing orders

A1–166B **19.**—(1) The Secretary of State may by regulations of general application make such incidental, consequential, transitional or supplementary provision as he thinks necessary or expedient for the purposes or in consequence of any orders under section 17 above, or for giving full effect to orders under that section.

(2) Regulations under this section may, in particular, include provision of general application with respect to—

(a) the transfer of functions, property, rights or liabilities from a local authority for any area to another local authority whose area consists of or includes the whole or any part of that area;
(b) the transfer of property, rights or liabilities, and of related functions, from an authority which ceases to exist to a residuary body established under section 22 below;
(c) the management or custody of transferred property (whether real or personal);
(d) the functions or areas of jurisdiction of any public body or of any of the following persons—
    (i) any justice of the peace, stipendiary magistrate, coroner or keeper of the rolls for a commission area (within the meaning of the Justices of the Peace Act 1979);

(ii) any lord-lieutenant, lieutenant or high sheriff;
(iii) any other officers (including police officers) within the area of any local authority affected by any such order,

and the costs and expenses of such public bodies and persons.

(3) In their application in relation to any order under section 17 above, regulations under this section shall have effect subject to any provision made under that section.

(4) Any regulations under section 67 of the 1972 Act (regulations in connection with implementation of proposals under Part IV of that Act) which are in force at the commencement of this section shall have effect, without prejudice to their operation in relation to any order made under that Part after the commencement of this section (whether by virtue of section 24(3) below or otherwise) and subject to any regulations under this section, as if orders under section 17 above were orders under that Part.

The Regulation of Railways Act 1871 has been amended by the Reporting of Injuries, Diseases and Dangerous Occurrences Regulations 1995, regulation 14(2) (printed in Appendix 2), as from April 1, 1996. Section 6 of that Act was repealed by *ibid.*, regulation 14(1), as from the same date. The obligation to report railway accidents is now contained in the 1995 Regulations themselves, regulation 3(1)(e) and Schedule 2 Part IV. **A1–193**

Treasure Act 1996

(1996 C. 24)

An Act to abolish treasure trove and to make fresh provision in relation to treasure. [4th July 1996] **A1–203A**

Be it enacted by the Queen's most Excellent Majesty, by and with the advice and consent of the Lords Spiritual and Temporal, and Commons, in this present Parliament assembled, and by the authority of the same, as follows–

Meaning of "treasure"

1.—(1) Treasure is—
(a) any object at least 300 years old when found which—
(i) is not a coin but has metallic content of which at least 10 per cent by weight is precious metal;
(ii) when found, is one of at least two coins in the same find which are at least 300 years old at that time and have that percentage of precious metal; or
(iii) when found, is one of at least ten coins in the same find which are at least 300 years old at that time;
(b) any object at least 200 years old when found which belongs to a class designated under section 2(1);
(c) any object which would have been treasure trove if found before the commencement of section 4;
(d) any object which, when found, is part of the same find as—
(i) an object within paragraph (a), (b) or (c) found at the same time or earlier; or
(ii) an object found earlier which would be within paragraph (a) or (b) if it had been found at the same time.

(2) Treasure does not include objects which are—
(a) unworked natural objects, or
(b) minerals as extracted from a natural deposit,
or which belongs to a class designated under section 2(2).

A1–203B 2.—(1) The Secretary of State may by order, for the purposes of section 1(1)(b), designate any class of object which he considers to be of outstanding historical, archaeological or cultural importance.

(2) The Secretary of State may by order, for the purposes of section 1(2), designate any class of object which (apart from the order) would be treasure.

(3) An order under this section shall be made by statutory instrument.

(4) No order is to be made under this section unless a draft of the order has been laid before Parliament and approved by a resolution of each House.

A1–203C 3.—(1) This section supplements section 1.

(2) "Coin" includes any metal token which was, or can reasonably be assumed to have been, used or intended for use as or instead of money.

(3) "Precious metal" means gold or silver.

(4) When an object is found, it is part of the same find as another object if—
(a) they are found together,
(b) the other object was found earlier in the same place where they had been left together,
(c) the other object was found earlier in a different place, but they had been left together and had become separated before being found.

(5) If the circumstances in which objects are found can reasonably be taken to indicate that they were together at some time before being found, the objects are to be presumed to have been left together, unless shown not to have been.

(6) An object which can reasonably be taken to be at least a particular age is to be presumed to be at least that age, unless shown not to be.

(7) An object is not treasure if it is wreck within the meaning of Part IX of the Merchant Shipping Act 1995.

Ownership of treasure

A1–203D 4.—(1) When treasure is found, it vests, subject to prior interests and rights—
(a) in the franchisee, if there is one;
(b) otherwise, in the Crown.

(2) Prior interests and rights are any which, or which derive from any which—
(a) were held when the treasure was left where it was found, or
(b) if the treasure had been moved before being found, were held when it was left where it was before being moved.

(3) If the treasure would have been treasure trove if found before the commencement of this section, neither the Crown nor any franchisee has any interest in it or right over it except in accordance with this Act.

(4) This section applies—
(a) whatever the nature of the place where the treasure was found, and
(b) whatever the circumstances in which it was left (including being lost or being left with no intention of recovery).

A1–203E 5.—(1) The franchisee for any treasure is the person who—
(a) was, immediately before the commencement of section 4, or
(b) apart from this Act, as successor in title, would have been,
the franchisee of the Crown in right of treasure trove for the place where the treasure was found.

(2) It is as franchisee in right of treasure trove that Her Majesty and the Duke of Cornwall are to be treated as having enjoyed the rights to treasure trove which belonged respectively to the Duchy of Lancaster and the Duchy of Cornwall immediately before the commencement of section 4.

6.—(1) Treasure vesting in the Crown under this Act is to be treated as part of the hereditary revenues of the Crown to which section 1 of the Civil List Act 1952 applies (surrender of hereditary revenues to the Exchequer). **A1–203F**

(2) Any such treasure may be transferred, or otherwise disposed of, in accordance with directions given by the Secretary of State.

(3) The Crown's title to any such treasure may be disclaimed at any time by the Secretary of State.

(4) If the Crown's title is disclaimed, the treasure—

(a) is deemed not to have vested in the Crown under this Act, and

(b) without prejudice to the interests or rights of others, may be delivered to any person in accordance with the code published under section 11.

Coroners' jurisdiction

7.—(1) The jurisdiction of coroners which is referred to in section 30 of the Coroners Act 1988 (treasure) is exercisable in relation to anything which is treasure for the purposes of this Act. **A1–203G**

(2) That jurisdiction is not exercisable for the purposes of the law relating to treasure trove in relation to anything found after the commencement of section 4.

(3) The Act of 1988 and anything saved by virtue of section 36(5) of that Act (saving for existing law and practice etc.) has effect subject to this section.

(4) An inquest held by virtue of this section is to be held without a jury, unless the coroner orders otherwise.

8.—(1) A person who finds an object which he believes or has reasonable grounds for believing is treasure must notify the coroner for the district in which the object was found before the end of the notice period. **A1–203H**

(2) The notice period is fourteen days beginning with—

(a) the day after the find; or

(b) if later, the day on which the finder first believes or has reason to believe the object is treasure.

(3) Any person who fails to comply with subsection (1) is guilty of an offence and liable on summary conviction to—

(a) imprisonment for a term not exceeding three months;

(b) a fine of an amount not exceeding level 5 on the standard scale; or

(c) both.

(4) In proceedings for an offence under this section, it is a defence for the defendant to show that he had, and has continued to have, a reasonable excuse for failing to notify the coroner.

(5) If the office of coroner for a district is vacant, the person acting as coroner for that district is the coroner for the purposes of subsection (1).

9.—(1) In this section, "inquest" means an inquest held under section 7. **A1–203I**

(2) A coroner proposing to conduct an inquest must notify—

(a) the British Museum, if his district is in England; or

(b) the National Museum of Wales, if it is in Wales.

(3) Before conducting the inquest, the coroner must take reasonable steps to notify—

(a) any person who it appears to him may have found the treasure; and

(b) any person who, at the time the treasure was found, occupied land which it appears to him may be where it was found.

(4) During the inquest the coroner must take reasonable steps to notify any such person not already notified.

(5) Before or during the inquest, the coroner must take reasonable steps—

(a) to obtain from any person notified under subsection (3) or (4) the names and addresses of interested persons; and

(b) to notify any interested person whose name and address he obtains.

(6) The coroner must take reasonable steps to give any interested person notified under subsection (3), (4) or (5) an opportunity to examine witnesses at the inquest.

(7) In subsections (5) and (6), "interested person" means a person who appears to the coroner to be likely to be concerned with the inquest—

(a) as the finder of the treasure or otherwise involved in the find;

(b) as the occupier, at the time the treasure was found, of the land where it was found, or

(c) as having had an interest in that land at that time or since.

Rewards, codes of practice and report

A1–203J **10.**—(1) This section applies if treasure—

(a) has vested in the Crown under section 4; and

(b) is to be transferred to a museum.

(2) The Secretary of State must determine whether a reward is to be paid by the museum before the transfer.

(3) If the Secretary of State determines that a reward is to be paid, he must also determine, in whatever way he thinks fit—

(a) the treasure's market value;

(b) the amount of the reward;

(c) to whom the reward is to be payable; and

(d) if it is to be payable to more than one person, how much each is to receive.

(4) The total reward must not exceed the treasure's market value.

(5) The reward may be payable to—

(a) the finder or any other person involved in the find;

(b) the occupier of the land at the time of the find;

(c) any person who had an interest in the land at that time, or has had such an interest at any time since then.

(6) Payment of the reward is not enforceable against a museum or the Secretary of State.

(7) In a determination under this section, the Secretary of State must take into account anything relevant in the code of practice issued under section 11.

(8) This section also applies in relation to treasure which has vested in a franchisee under section 4, if the franchisee makes a request to the Secretary of State that it should.

A1–203K **11.**—(1) The Secretary of State must—

(a) prepare a code of practice relating to treasure;

(b) keep the code under review; and

(c) revise it when appropriate.

(2) The code must, in particular, set out the principles and practice to be followed by the Secretary of State—

(a) when considering to whom treasure should be offered;

(b) when making a determination under section 10; and

(c) where the Crown's title to treasure is disclaimed.

(3) The code may include guidance for—

(a) those who search for or find treasure; and
(b) museums and others who exercise functions in relation to treasure.

(4) Before preparing the code or revising it, the Secretary of State must consult such persons appearing to him to be interested as he thinks appropriate.

(5) A copy of the code and of any proposed revision of the code shall be laid before Parliament.

(6) Neither the code nor any revision shall come into force until approved by a resolution of each House of Parliament.

(7) The Secretary of State must publish the code in whatever way he considers appropriate for bringing it to the attention of those interested.

(8) If the Secretary of State considers that different provision should be made for—
(a) England and Wales, and
(b) Northern Ireland,
or that different provision should otherwise be made for treasure found in different areas, he may prepare two or more separate codes.

12. As soon as reasonably practicable after each anniversary of the coming into force of this section, the Secretary of State shall lay before Parliament a report on the operation of this Act in the preceding year. **A1–203L**

Miscellaneous

13. In the application of this Act to Northern Ireland— **A1–203M**
(a) in section 7—
 (i) in subsection (1), for "section 30 of the Coroners Act 1988" substitute "section 33 of the Coroners Act (Northern Ireland) 1959";
 (ii) in subsection (3), for the words from "1988" to "practice etc.)" substitute "1959";
(b) in section 9(2), for the words from "British Museum" to the end substitute "Department of the Environment for Northern Ireland".

14.—(1) In section 33 of the Coroners Act (Northern Ireland) 1959 (inquest on treasure trove), for "treasure trove" substitute "treasure". **A1–203N**

(2) In section 54(3) of the Ancient Monuments and Archaeological Areas Act 1979 (saving for rights in relation to treasure trove) for "in relation to treasure trove" substitute "under the Treasure Act 1996".

(3) In Article 42 of the Historic Monuments and Archaeological Objects (Northern Ireland) Order 1995 (reporting of archaeological objects)—
(a) after paragraph (10) insert—
"(10A) This Article does not apply in relation to an object if the person who found it believes or has reasonable grounds for believing that the object is treasure within the meaning of the Treasure Act 1996.";
(b) in paragraph (11)(a) for "treasure trove" substitute "any treasure within the meaning of the Treasure Act 1996".

(4) Subsections (2) and (3)(b) have effect in relation to any treasure found after the commencement of section 4.

(5) Subsection (3)(a) has effect in relation to any object found after the commencement of section 8.

15.—(1) This Act may be cited as the Treasure Act 1996. **A1–203O**

(2) This Act comes into force on such day as the Secretary of State may by order made by statutory instrument appoint; and different days may be appointed for different purposes.

(3) This Act does not extend to Scotland.

THE WELSH LANGUAGE ACT 1993

A1–215– A1–217 The Welsh Language Act 1967 has been repealed and replaced by the Welsh Language Act 1993, as from December 21, 1993. Section 22(1) of the 1993 Act replaces section 1(1) of the 1967 Act. Section 23 deals with oaths and affirmations, and section 24 with the provision of interpreters.

The Welsh Language Act 1993

PART III

MISCELLANEOUS

Welsh in legal proceedings

Use of Welsh in legal proceedings

22.—(1) In any legal proceedings in Wales the Welsh language may be spoken by any party, witness or other person who desires to use it, subject in the case of proceedings in a court other than a magistrates' court to such prior notice as may be required by rules of court; and any necessary provision for interpretation shall be made accordingly.

(2) Any power to make rules of court include powers to make provision as to the use, in proceedings in or having a connection with Wales, of documents in the Welsh language.

Oaths and affirmations

23. The Lord Chancellor may make rules prescribing a translation in the Welsh language of any form for the time being prescribed by law as the form of any oath or affirmation to be administered and taken or made by any person in any court, and an oath or affirmation administered and taken or made in any court in Wales in the translation prescribed by such rules shall, without interpretation, be of the like effect as if it had been administered and taken or made in the English language.

Provision of interpreters

24.—(1) The Lord Chancellor may make rules as to the provision and employment of interpreters of the Welsh and English languages for the purposes of proceedings before courts in Wales.

(2) The interpreters shall be paid, out of the same fund as the expenses of the court are payable, such remuneration in respect of their services as the Lord Chancellor may determine.

(3) The Lord Chancellor's powers under this section shall be exercised with the consent of the Treasury.

Appendix 2

STATUTORY INSTRUMENTS

Add: The Avon (Coroners) Order 1996, S.I. 1996 No. 656. **A2–04A**

The Avon (Coroners) Order 1996

(1996 No. 656)

1.—(1) This Order may be cited as the Avon (Coroners) Order 1996 and shall come into force on 1st April 1996.

(2) In this Order "the 1988 Act" means the Coroners Act 1988.

2.—(1) There shall be a single coroner's district, called the Avon Coroner's District, for the Counties of Bath and North East Somerset, the City of Bristol, North West Somerset and South Gloucestershire (which counties come into existence on 1st April 1996 by virtue of article 6(1) of the Avon (Structural Change) Order 1995).

(2) The Council of the City of Bristol shall be the relevant council within the meaning of section 1(1A) of the 1988 Act for the coroner's district constituted by paragraph (1) above.

(3) The person who, at 31st March 1996, is the coroner for the Council of Avon shall be deemed on 1st April 1996 to be appointed coroner for the coroner's district constituted by paragraph (1) above.

(4) Any agreement between the person to whom paragraph (3) above applies and Avon County Council (as the relevant council for the purposes of section 1 of the 1988 Act prior to 1st April 1996) as to his salary and pension as a coroner shall be deemed on and after 1st April 1996 to have effect as if originally made between him and the City of Bristol Council.

(5) Any person who, at 31st March 1996, is a deputy or assistant deputy coroner for the County of Avon shall be deemed on 1st April 1996 to be appointed deputy or, as the case may be, assistant deputy coroner for the coroner's district constituted by paragraph (1) above.

3. On 1st April 1996, all rights and liabilities (including those in connection with legal proceedings) of Avon County Council, in its capacity prior to that date as the relevant council for the purposes of the 1988 Act for coroners in the County of Avon shall be transferred to the City of Bristol Council, in its capacity as the relevant council for those purposes for coroners in the coroner's district constituted by article 2(1) above.

4.—(1) On 1st April 1996, any process issued, order made, direction given, inquest begun or other thing done by or to the coroner for the County of Avon shall be deemed to have been issued, made, given, begun or done by or to the coroner for the coroner's district constituted by article 2(1) above.

(2) All documents, exhibits, registers and other things in the custody of the coroner for the County of Avon in connection with inquests or post-mortem investigations shall be transferred to the coroner for the coroner's district constituted by article 2(1) above.

(3) In this article "coroner" includes any deputy coroner or assistant deputy coroner.

A2–04B Add The Bedfordshire (Coroners) Order 1997, S.I. 1997, No. 494.

The Bedfordshire (Coroners) Order 1997

(1997 No. 494)

1. This Order may be cited as the Bedfordshire (Coroners) Order 1997 and shall come into force on 1st April 1997.

2.—(1) There shall be a single coroner's district, called the Bedfordshire and Luton Coroner's District, for the Counties of Bedfordshire and Luton (which county comes into existence on 1st April 1997 by virtue of article 8(2) of the Bedfordshire (Borough of Luton) (Structural Change) Order 1995).

(2) The Council of the County of Bedfordshire shall be the relevant council within the meaning of section 1(1A) of the Coroners Act 1988 for the coroner's district constituted by paragraph (1) above.

(3) The person who, at 31st March 1997, is the coroner for the County of Bedfordshire shall be deemed on 1st April 1997 to be appointed coroner for the coroner's district constituted by paragraph (1) above.

(4) Any person who, at 31st March 1997, is a deputy or assistant deputy coroner for the County of Bedfordshire shall be deemed on 1st April 1997 to be appointed deputy or, as the case may be, assistant deputy coroner for the coroner's district constituted by paragraph (1) above.

3.—(1) On 1st April 1997, any process issued, order made, direction given, inquest begun or other thing done by or to the coroner for the County of Bedfordshire shall be deemed to have been issued, made, given, begun or done by or to the coroner for the coroner's district constituted by article 2(1) above.

(2) All documents, exhibits, registers and other things in the custody of the coroner for the County of Bedfordshire in connection with inquests or post-mortem investigations shall be transferred to the coroner for the coroner's district constituted by article 2(1) above.

(3) In this article "coroner" includes any deputy coroner or assistant deputy coroner.

A2–04C Add: The Buckinghamshire (Coroners) Order 1997, S.I. 1997 No. 495.

The Buckinghamshire (Coroners) Order 1997

(1997 No. 495)

1. This Order may be cited as the Buckinghamshire (Coroners) Order 1997 and shall come into force on 1st April 1997.

2. The North Buckinghamshire Coroner's District and the South Buckinghamshire Coroner's District shall be abolished.

3.—(1) On 1st April 1997, any process issued, order made, direction given, inquest begun or other thing done by or to the coroner for the existing North Buckinghamshire Coroner's District or the coroner for the existing South Buckinghamshire Coroner's District shall be deemed to have been issued, made, given, begun or done by or to the coroner for the County of Buckinghamshire.

(2) All documents, exhibits, registers and other things in the custody of the coroner for the existing North Buckinghamshire Coroner's District or the coroner for the existing South Buckinghamshire Coroner's District in connection with inquests or post-mortem investigations shall be transferred to the coroner for the County of Buckinghamshire.

(3) In this article "coroner" includes any deputy coroner or assistant deputy coroner.

Add: The Cleveland (Coroners) Order 1996, S.I. 1996 No. 657. A2–09A

The Cleveland (Coroners) Order 1996

(1996 No. 657)

1.—(1) This Order may be cited as the Cleveland (Coroners) Order 1996 and shall come into force on 1st April 1996.

(2) In this Order "the 1988 Act" means the Coroners Act 1988.

2.—(1) There shall be a single coroner's district, called the Teesside Coroner's District, for the Counties of Middlesbrough, Redcar and Cleveland and Stockton-on-Tees (which counties come into existence on 1st April 1996 by virtue of article 3 of the Cleveland (Further Provision) Order 1995).

(2) The Council of the City of the Borough of Middlesbrough shall be the relevant council within the meaning of section 1(1A) of the 1988 Act for the coroner's district constituted by paragraph (1) above.

(3) The person who, at 31st March 1996, is the coroner for the existing Central Cleveland Coroner's District of the County of Cleveland by virtue of having been appointed for or assigned to that district shall be deemed on 1st April 1996 to be appointed coroner for the coroner's district constituted by paragraph (1) above.

(4) Any agreement between the person to whom paragraph (3) above applies and Cleveland County Council (as the relevant council for the purposes of section 1 of the 1988 Act prior to 1st April 1996) as to his salary and pension as a coroner shall be deemed on and after 1st April 1996 to have effect as if originally made between him and Middlesbrough Borough Council.

(5) Any person who, at 31st March 1996, is a deputy or assistant deputy coroner for the existing Central Cleveland Coroner's District shall be deemed on 1st April 1996 to be appointed deputy or, as the case may be, assistant deputy coroner for the coroner's district constituted by paragraph (1) above.

3.—(1) The person who, at 31st March 1996, is the coroner for the existing North Cleveland Coroner's District of the County of Cleveland by virtue of having been appointed for or assigned to that district shall be deemed on 1st April 1996 to be appointed coroner for the County of Hartlepool (which county comes into existence on 1st April 1996 by virtue of article 3 of the Cleveland (Further Provision) Order 1996).

(2) Any agreement between the person to whom paragraph (1) above applies and Cleveland County Council (as the relevant council for the purposes of section 1 of the 1988 Act prior to 1st April 1996) as to his salary and pension as a coroner shall be

deemed on and after 1st April 1996 to have effect as if originally made between him and Hartlepool Borough Council.

(3) Any person who, at 31st March 1996, is a deputy or assistant deputy coroner for the existing North Cleveland Coroner's District shall be deemed on 1st April 1996 to be appointed deputy or, as the case may be, assistant deputy coroner for the coroner's district constituted by paragraph (1) above.

4. On 1st April 1996, all rights and liabilities (including those in connection with legal proceedings) of Cleveland County Council, in its capacity prior to that date as the relevant council for the purposes of the 1988 Act for coroners—

(a) in the existing Central Cleveland Coroner's District of the County of Cleveland shall be transferred to Middlesbrough Borough Council in its capacity as the relevant council for those purposes for coroners in the coroner's district constituted by article 2(1) above; and

(b) in the existing North Cleveland Coroner's District of the County of Cleveland shall be transferred to Hartlepool Borough Council in its capacity as the relevant council for those purposes for coroners in the County of Hartlepool.

5.—(1) On 1st April 1996, any process issued, order made, direction given, inquest begun or other thing done by or to the coroner for an existing coroner's district shall be deemed to have been issued, given, made, begun or done by or to the coroner for the relevant new coroner's district.

(2) All documents, exhibits, registers and other things in the custody of the coroner for an existing coroner's district in connection with inquests or post-mortem investigations shall be transferred to the coroner for the relevant new coroner's district.

(3) In paragraphs (1) and (2) above—

(a) Teesside Coroner's District is the relevant new coroner's district for the existing Central Cleveland Coroner's District of the County of Cleveland, and

(b) the County of Hartlepool is the relevant new coroner's district for the existing North Cleveland Coroner's District of the County of Cleveland.

(4) In this article "coroner" includes any deputy coroner or assistance deputy coroner.

A2–09B Add: The Cornwall (Coroners' Districts) (Amendment) Order 1996 No. 2403

The Cornwall (Coroners' Districts) (Amendment) Order 1996

(1996 No. 2403)

Citation

A2–09B/1 **1.** This Order may be cited as the Cornwall (Coroners' Districts) (Amendment) Order 1996.

Commencement and application

A2–09B/2 **2.**—(1) This Order shall come into force on 1st October 1996.

(2) This Order shall not have effect in relation to any inquest begun before the day on which it comes into force or to any post-mortem examination which, before that day, a coroner has directed or requested a medical practitioner to make.

Alteration and renaming of coroners' districts

3.—(1) The existing Number One coroner's district and Number Two coroner's district shall be amalgamated to form a new coroner's district to be named the West Cornwall coroner's district. **A2–09B/3**

(2) The existing Number Three coroner's district shall be renamed the East Cornwall coroner's district.

4.—(1) The Cornwall (Coroners' Districts) Order 1974 shall accordingly be amended as follows:

(a) in article 3, for the word "three" there shall be substituted the word "two"; and

(b) for the Schedule. there shall be substituted the Schedule to this Order.

(2) The Cornwall (Coroners' Districts) (Amendment) Order 1991 is hereby revoked.

SCHEDULE

(1) *Name of Coroner's District*	(2) *Area comprised in Coroner's District named in column 1*
East Cornwall coroner's district	The districts of Caradon, North Cornwall and Restormel
West Cornwall coroner's district	The districts of Carrick, Kerrier and Penwith

Add: Coroners Districts (Designation of Relevant Councils) Order 1985, S.I. 1985 No. 1933. **A2–09C**

The Coroners' Districts (Designation of Relevant Councils) Order 1985

(1985 No. 1933)

1. This Order may be cited as the Coroners' Districts (Designation of Relevant Councils) Order 1985 and shall come into operation on 1st April 1986. **A2–09D**

2. The councils listed in the Schedule to this Order are hereby designated for the purposes of section 13 of the Local Government Act 1985 (arrangements for coroners' service in Greater London and metropolitan counties) as the relevant councils for the coroners' districts also listed there.

Coroner's District	Relevant Council
GREATER LONDON	
Inner North London coroner's district	The council of the London Borough of Camden
Inner South London coroner's district	The council of the London Borough of Southwark
Inner West London coroner's district	The council of the City of Westminster
Eastern coroner's district	The council of the London Borough of Waltham Forest
Northern coroner's district	The council of the London Borough of Haringey
Southern coroner's district	The council of the London Borough of Croydon
Western coroner's district	The council of the London Borough of Hammersmith
GREATER MANCHESTER	
North coroner's district	The council of the Metropolitan Borough of Rochdale
South coroner's district	The council of the Metropolitan Borough of Stockport
West coroner's district	The council of the Metropolitan Borough of Bolton
MERSEYSIDE	
Knowsley, St. Helens and Sefton coroner's district	The council of the Metropolitan Borough of Sefton
SOUTH YORKSHIRE	
East coroner's district	The council of the Metropolitan Borough of Doncaster
West coroner's district	The council of the City of Sheffield
TYNE AND WEAR	
Gateshead and South Tyneside coroner's district	The council of the Metropolitan Borough of South Tyneside
WEST MIDLANDS	
Birmingham coroner's district	The council of the City of Birmingham
WEST YORKSHIRE	
Eastern coroner's district	The council of the City of Wakefield
Western coroner's district	The council of the City of Bradford

Add: The Coroners' Districts (Wales) Order 1996, S.I. 1996 No. 661. A2–09E

The Coroners' Districts (Wales) Order 1996

(1996 No. 661)

1. This Order may be cited as the Coroners' Districts (Wales) Order 1996 and shall come into force on 1st April 1996.

2.—(1) Coroners' districts in the Counties of Clwyd, Gwent, Gwynedd, Mid Glamorgan, Powys, South Glamorgan and West Glamorgan, as those counties existed immediately before 1st April 1996, shall be amalgamated and altered so that the areas of those districts are divided into the coroners' districts, for which the alternative names in English and Welsh are given where applicable, set out in column (1) of Schedule 1 to this Order and each such district shall comprise the area specified in respect thereof in column (2) of that Schedule.

(2) The areas described in column (2) of that Schedule are local government areas in Wales as they exist on 1st April 1996 by virtue of the amendments made by section 1 of, and Schedule 1 to, the Local Government (Wales) Act 1994.

3.—(1) On 1st April 1996, any process issued, order made, direction given, inquest begun or other thing done by or to the coroner for an existing coroner's district shall be deemed to have been issued, made, given, begun or done by or to the coroner for the relevant new coroner's district.

(2) All documents, exhibits, registers and other things in the custody of the coroner for an existing coroner's district in connection with inquests or post-mortem investigations shall be transferred to the coroner for the relevant new coroner's district.

(3) In this article, the relevant new coroner's district in relation to an existing coroner's district is the new district, for which the alternative names in English and Welsh are given where applicable, specified in column (2) of Schedule 2 to this Order opposite the name of the existing district (or districts) in column (1) of that Schedule.

(4) In this article "coroner" includes any deputy coroner or assistant deputy coroner.

(5) This article is without prejudice to paragraph 23 of Schedule 17 to the Local Government (Wales) Act 1994 (transitional provisions: coroners).

SCHEDULE 1 **Article 2**

NEW CORONERS' DISTRICTS IN WALES

Column (1)	Column (2)
Coroners' districts	Area comprised therein
Bridgend and Glamorgan Valleys/ Pen-y-bont a Chymoedd Morgannwg	The County Boroughs of Bridgend, Merthyr Tydfil and Rhondda, Cynon, Taff
Cardiff and The Vale of Glamorgan/ Caerdydd a Bro Morgannwg	The County of Cardiff and the County Borough of the Vale of Glamorgan
Central North Wales/Canol Gogledd Cymru	The County of Denbighshire and the County Borough of Aberconwy and Colwyn

Column (1)	Column (2)
Coroners' districts	Area comprised therein
Gwent	The County of Monmouthshire, the County Boroughs of Blaenau Gwent, Caerphilly, Newport and Torfaen
Neath and Port Talbot/Castell-nedd a Phort Talbot	The County Borough of Neath and Port Talbot
North East Wales/Gogledd Dwyrain Cymru	The County of Flintshire and the County Borough of Wrexham
North West Wales/Gogledd Gorllewin Cymru	The Counties of Anglesey and Caernarfonshire and Merionethshire
Powys	The County of Powys
Swansea/Abertawe	The County of Swansea

SCHEDULE 2 **Article 3**

TRANSITIONAL PROVISION: RELEVANT NEW CORONERS' DISTRICTS

Column (1)	Column (2)
Existing coroner's district	Relevant new coroner's district
Mid Glamorgan	Bridgend and Glamorgan Valleys/ Pen-y-bont a Chymoedd Morgannwg
South Glamorgan	Cardiff and The Vale of Glamorgan/ Caerdydd a Bro Morgannwg
Gwynedd Eryri and Clwyd West	Central North Wales/Canol Gogledd Cymru
Gwent	Gwent
West Glamorgan	Neath and Port Talbot/Castell-nedd a Phort Talbot
Clwyd East and Clwyd South	North East Wales/Gogledd Dwyrain Cymru
Gwynedd Llŷn ac Eifionydd, Gwynedd Meirionydd and Gwynedd Ynys Môn	North West Wales/Gogledd Gorllewin Cymru
Powys	Powys
Swansea and Gower	Swansea/Abertawe

Add: The Coroners' Districts (Designation of Relevant Councils) (Wales) Order 1996, S.I. 1996 No. 662. A2–09F

The Coroners' Districts (Designation of Relevant Councils) (Wales) Order 1996

(1996 No. 662)

1. This Order may be cited as the Coroners' Districts (Designation of Relevant Councils) (Wales) Order 1996 and shall come into force on 1st April 1996.

2. For each coroner's district listed in column 1 of the Schedule to this Order, being a coroner's district created by the Coroners' Districts (Wales) Order 1996 lying partly in each of two or more Welsh counties or county boroughs, the council specified opposite thereto in column 2 of that Schedule is hereby designated as the relevant council for the purposes of the Coroners Act 1988.

SCHEDULE **Article 2**

RELEVANT COUNCILS FOR THE PURPOSES OF THE CORONERS ACT 1988

Column (1)	Column (2)
Coroner's district	Relevant council
Bridgend and Glamorgan Valleys/ Pen-y-bont a Chymoedd Morgannwg	Rhondda, Cynon, Taff County Borough Council
Cardiff and The Vale of Glamorgan/ Caerdydd a Bro Morgannwg	The Vale of Glamorgan County Borough Council
Central North Wales/Canol Gogledd Cymru	Denbighshire County Council
Gwent	Newport County Borough Council
North East Wales/Gogledd Dwyrain Cymru	Wrexham County Borough Council
North West Wales/Gogledd Gorllewin Cymru	Caernarfonshire and Merionethshire County Council

Add: The Derbyshire (Coroners) Order 1997, S.I. 1997 No. 496. A2–133A

The Derbyshire (Coroners) Order 1997

(1997 No. 496)

1. This Order may be cited as the Derbyshire (Coroners) Order 1997 and shall come into force on 1st April 1997.

2.—(1) There shall be a single coroner's district, called the Derby and South Derbyshire Coroner's District, for the County of Derby (which county comes into existence on 1st April 1997 by virtue of article 8(2) of the Derbyshire (City of Derby) (Structural Change) Order 1995 and for so much of the County of Derbyshire as is not included in the High Peak or Scarsdale Coroners' Districts.

(2) The Council of the County of Derbyshire shall be the relevant council within the meaning of section 1(1A) of the Coroners Act 1988 for the coroner's district constituted by paragraph (1) above.

(3) The person who, at 31st March 1997, is the coroner for the existing Derby and South Derbyshire Coroner's District shall be deemed on 1st April 1997 to be appointed coroner for the coroner's district constituted by paragraph (1) above.

(4) Any person who, at 31st March 1997, is a deputy or assistant deputy coroner for the existing Derby and South Derbyshire Coroner's District shall be deemed on 1st April 1997 to be appointed deputy or, as the case may be, assistant deputy coroner for the coroner's district constituted by paragraph (1) above.

3.—(1) On 1st April 1997, any process issued, order made, direction given, inquest begun or other thing done by or to the coroner for the existing Derby and South Derbyshire Coroner's District shall be deemed to have been issued, made, given, begun or done by or to the coroner's district constituted by article 2(1) above.

(2) All documents, exhibits, registers and other things in the custody of the coroner for the existing Derby and South Derbyshire Coroner's District in connection with inquests or post-mortem investigations shall be transferred to the coroner for the coroner's district constituted by article 2(1) above.

(3) In this article "coroner" includes any deputy coroner or assistant deputy coroner.

A2–133B Add: The Dorset (Coroners) Order 1997, S.I. 1997 No. 497.

The Dorset (Coroners) Order 1997

(1997 No. 497)

1.—(1) This Order may be cited as the Dorset (Coroners) Order 1997 and shall come into force on 1st April 1997.

(2) In this Order "the 1988 Act" means the Coroners Act 1988.

2.—(1) There shall be a single coroner's district, called the Bournemouth, Poole and Eastern Dorset Coroner's District, for the Counties of Bournemouth and Poole (which counties come into existence on 1st April 1997 by virtue of article 8(2) and (3) of the Dorset (Boroughs of Poole and Bournemouth) (Structural Change) Order 1995) and for so much of the County of Dorset as is not included in the Western Dorset Coroner's District.

(2) The Council of the Borough of Bournemouth shall be the relevant council within the meaning of section 1(1A) of the 1988 Act for the coroner's district constituted by paragraph (1) above.

(3) The person who, at 31st March 1997, is the coroner for the existing Eastern Dorset Coroner's District shall be deemed on 1st April 1997 to be appointed coroner for the coroner's district constituted by paragraph (1) above.

(4) Any agreement between the person to whom paragraph (3) above applies and Dorset County Council (as the relevant council for the purposes of section 1 of the 1988 Act prior to 1st April 1997) as to his salary and pension as a coroner shall be deemed on and after 1st April 1997 to have effect as if originally made between him and Bournemouth Borough Council.

(5) Any person who, at 31st March 1997, is a deputy or assistant deputy coroner for the existing Eastern Dorset Coroner's District shall be deemed on 1st April 1997 to be appointed deputy or, as the case may be, assistant deputy coroner for the coroner's district constituted by paragraph (1) above.

3.—(1) On 1st April 1997, any process issued, order made, direction given, inquest begun or other thing done by or to the coroner for the existing Eastern Dorset Coroner's District shall be deemed to have been issued, made, given, begun or done by or to the coroner for the coroner's district constituted by article 2(1) above.

(2) All documents, exhibits, registers and other things in the custody of the coroner for the existing Eastern Dorset Coroner's District in connection with inquests or post-mortem investigations shall be transferred to the coroner for the coroner's district constituted by article 2(1) above.

(3) In this article "coroner" includes any deputy coroner or assistant deputy coroner.

Add: The Durham (Coroners) Order 1997, S.I. 1997 No. 498. **A2–133C**

The Durham (Coroners) Order 1997

(1997 No. 498)

1. This Order may be cited as the Durham (Coroners) Order 1997 and shall come into force on 1st April 1997.

2.—(1) There shall be a single coroner's district, called the Darlington and South Durham Coroner's District, for the County of Darlington (which county comes into existence on 1st April 1997 by virtue of article 8(2) of the Durham (Borough of Darlington) (Structural Change) Order 1995 and for so much of the County of Durham as is not included in the North Durham Coroner's District.

(2) The Council of the County of Durham shall be the relevant council within the meaning of section 1(1A) of the Coroners Act 1988 for the coroner's district constituted by paragraph (1) above.

(3) The person who, at 31st March 1997, is the coroner for the existing South Durham Coroner's District shall be deemed on 1st April 1997 to be appointed coroner for the coroner's district constituted by paragraph (1) above.

(4) Any person who, at 31st March 1997, is a deputy or assistant deputy coroner for the existing South Durham Coroner's District shall be deemed on 1st April 1997 to be appointed deputy or, as the case may be, assistant deputy coroner for the coroner's district constituted by paragraph (1) above.

3.—(1) On 1st April 1997, any process issued, order made, direction given, inquest begun or other thing done by or to the coroner for the existing South Durham Coroner's District shall be deemed to have been issued, made, given, begun or done by or to the coroner for the coroner's district constituted by article 2(1) above.

(2) All documents, exhibits, registers and other things in the custody of the coroner for the existing South Durham Coroner's District in connection with inquests or post-mortem investigations shall be transferred to the coroner for the coroner's district constituted by article 2(1) above.

(3) In this article "coroner" includes any deputy coroner or assistant deputy coroner.

Add: The East Sussex (Coroners) Order 1997, S.I. 1997 No. 488. **A2–133D**

The East Sussex (Coroners) Order 1997

(1997 No. 488)

1. This Order may be cited as the East Sussex (Coroners) Order 1997 and shall come into force on 1st April 1997.

2.—(1) The Eastern East Sussex Coroner's District and the Western East Sussex Coroner's District shall be abolished.

(2) The person who, at 31st March 1997, is the coroner for the existing Eastern East Sussex Coroner's District shall be deemed on 1st April 1997 to be appointed coroner for the County of East Sussex.

(3) Any person who, at 31st March 1997, is a deputy or assistant deputy coroner for the existing Eastern East Sussex Coroner's District shall be deemed on 1st April 1997 to be appointed deputy or, as the case may be, assistant deputy coroner for the County of East Sussex.

3.—(1) On 1st April 1997, any process issued, order made, direction given, inquest begun or other thing done by or to the coroner for the existing Eastern East Sussex Coroner's District or the coroner for the existing Western East Sussex Coroner's District shall be deemed to have been issued, made, given, begun or done by or to the coroner for the County of East Sussex.

(2) All documents, exhibits, registers and other things in the custody of the coroner for the existing Eastern East Sussex Coroner's District or the coroner for the Western East Sussex Coroner's District in connection with inquests or post-mortem investigations shall be transferred to the coroner for the County of East Sussex.

(3) In this article "coroner" includes any deputy coroner or assistant deputy coroner.

A2–133E Add: The Hampshire (Coroners) Order 1997, S.I. 1997 No. 489.

The Hampshire (Coroners) Order 1997

(1997 No. 489)

1. This Order may be cited as the Hampshire (Coroners) Order 1997 and shall come into force on 1st April 1997.

(2) In this Order "the 1988 Act" means the Coroners Act 1988.

2.—(1) There shall be a single coroner's district, called the Portsmouth and South East Hampshire Coroner's District, for the County of Portsmouth (which county comes into existence on 1st April 1997 by virtue of article 8(2) of the Hampshire (Cities of Portsmouth and Southampton) (Structural Change) Order 1995) and for so much of the County of Hampshire as is not included in the Central Hampshire, North East Hampshire or existing Southampton and New Forest Coroner's Districts.

(2) The Council of the County of Hampshire shall be the relevant council within the meaning of section 1(1A) of the 1988 Act for the coroner's district constituted by paragraph (1) above.

(3) The person who, at 31st March 1997, is the coroner for the existing Portsmouth and South East Hampshire Coroner's District shall be deemed on 1st April 1997 to be appointed coroner for the coroner's district constituted by paragraph (1) above.

(4) Any person who, at 31st March 1997, is a deputy or assistant deputy coroner for the existing Portsmouth and South East Hampshire Coroner's District shall be deemed on 1st April 1997 to be appointed deputy or, as the case may be, assistant deputy coroner for the coroner's district constituted by paragraph (1) above.

3.—(1) There shall be a single coroner's district, called the Southampton and New Forest Coroner's District, for the County of Southampton (which county comes into existence on 1st April 1997 by virtue of article 8(3) of the Hampshire (Cities of Portsmouth and Southampton) (Structural Change) Order 1995) and for so much of the County of Hampshire as is not included in the Central Hampshire, North East Hampshire or existing Portsmouth and South East Hampshire Coroner's Districts.

(2) The Council of the County of Hampshire shall be the relevant council within the meaning of section 1(1A) of the 1988 Act for the coroner's district constituted by paragraph (1) above.

(3) The person who, at 31st March 1997, is the coroner for the existing Southampton and New Forest Coroner's District shall be deemed on 1st April 1997 to be appointed coroner for the coroner's district constituted by paragraph (1) above.

(4) Any person who, at 31st March 1997, is a deputy or assistant deputy coroner for the existing Southampton and New Forest Coroner's District shall be deemed on 1st April 1997 to be appointed deputy or, as the case may be, assistant deputy coroner for the coroner's district constituted by paragraph (1) above.

4.—(1) On 1st April 1997, any process issued, order made, direction given, inquest begun or other thing done by or to the coroner for an existing coroner's district shall be deemed to have been issued, made, given, begun or done by or to the coroner for the relevant new coroner's district.

(2) All documents, exhibits, registers and other things in the custody of the coroner for an existing coroner's district in connection with inquests or post-mortem investigations shall be transferred to the coroner for the relevant new coroner's district.

(3) In paragraphs (1) and (2) above—

(a) the coroner's district constituted by article 2(1) above is the relevant new coroner's district for the existing Portsmouth and South East Hampshire Coroner's District; and

(b) the coroner's district constituted by article 3(1) above is the relevant new coroner's district for the existing Southampton and New Forest Coroner's district.

(4) In this article "coroner" includes any deputy coroner or assistant deputy coroner.

Add: The Humberside (Coroners) Order 1996, S.I. 1996 No. 658 (as amended by S.I. 1996 No. 787). **A2–133F**

The Humberside (Coroners) Order 1996

(1996 No. 658)

1.—(1) This Order may be cited as the Humberside (Coroners) Order 1996 and shall come into force on 1st April 1996.

(2) In this Order "the 1988 Act" means the Coroners Act 1988.

2.—(1) There shall be a single coroner's district, called the East Riding and Hull Coroner's District, for the Counties of the East Riding of Yorkshire and the City of Kingston upon Hull (which counties come into existence on 1st April 1996 by virtue of article 5(1) of the Humberside (Structural Change) Order 1995).

(2) The Council of the City of Kingston upon Hull shall be the relevant council within the meaning of section 1(1A) of the 1988 Act for the coroner's district constituted by paragraph (1) above.

3.—(1) There shall be a single coroner's district, called the North Lincolnshire and Grimsby Coroner's District, for the Counties of North Lincolnshire and North East Lincolnshire (which counties come into existence on 1st April 1996 by virtue of article 5(1) of the Humberside (Structural Change) Order 1995).

(2) The Council of the District of [North East Lincolnshire]**(e)** shall be the relevant council within the meaning of section 1(1A) of the 1988 Act for the coroner's district constituted by paragraph (1) above.

(e) Words inserted by S.I. 1996 No. 787.

4. On 1st April 1996, all rights and liabilities (including those in connection with legal proceedings) of the Humberside County Council, in its capacity prior to that date as the relevant council for the purposes of the 1988 Act for coroners—

(a) in the existing North Humberside and Scunthorpe Coroner's District of the County of Humberside shall be transferred to City of Kingston upon Hull Council in its capacity as the relevant council for those purposes for coroners in the coroner's district constituted by article 2(1) above; and

(b) in the existing Grimsby Coroner's District of the County of Humberside shall be transferred to [North East Lincolnshire]**(f)** District Council in its capacity as the relevant council for those purposes for coroners in the coroner's district constituted by article 3(1) above.

5.—(1) On 1st April 1996, any process issued, order made, direction given, inquest begun or other thing done by or to the coroner for an existing coroner's district shall be deemed to have been issued, made, given, begun or done by or to the coroner for the relevant new coroner's district.

(2) All documents, exhibits, registers and other things in the custody of the coroner for an existing coroner's district in connection with inquests or post-mortem investigations shall be transferred to the coroner for the relevant new coroner's district.

(3) In paragraphs (1) and (2) above the relevant new coroner's district is—

(a) the East Riding and Hull Coroner's District as respects the existing North Humberside and Scunthorpe Coroner's District; and

(b) the North Lincolnshire and Grimsby Coroner's District as respects the existing Grimsby Coroner's District.

(4) In this article "coroner" includes any deputy coroner or assistant deputy coroner.

A2–137A Add: The Kent (Coroners' Districts) (Amendment) Order 1996, S.I. 1996 No. 445.

The Kent (Coroners' Districts) (Amendment) Order 1996

(1996 No. 445)

Citation

A2–137A/1 **1.** This Order may be cited as the Kent (Coroners' Districts) (Amendment) Order 1996 and shall be read as one with the Kent (Coroners' Districts) Order 1974.

Commencement and application

A2–137A/2 **2.**—(1) This Order shall come into force on 15th April 1996.

(2) This Order shall not have effect in relation to any inquest begun before the day on which it comes into force or to any post-mortem examination which, before that day, a coroner has directed or requested a medical practitioner to make.

Alteration of Kent coroners' districts

A2–137A/3 **3.**—(1) The existing North Kent coroner's district of the county of Kent shall be abolished.

(2) The existing West Kent coroner's district, Maidstone coroner's district and Canterbury and Dover coroner's district shall be altered by transferring the areas specified in column 1 of the Schedule to this Order from the coroners' districts named in column 2 of the Schedule to the coroners' districts named in column 3 of the Schedule.

(f) *ibid.*

Renaming of Kent coroners' districts

4.—(1) The existing West Kent coroner's district shall be renamed as the North West Kent coroner's district. **A2–137A/4**

(2) The existing Maidstone coroner's district shall be renamed as the Mid Kent and Medway coroner's district.

(3) The existing Canterbury and Dover coroner's district shall be renamed as the East Kent coroner's district.

SCHEDULE

1. Area now comprised in Coroner's District named in Column 2 and to be transferred to Coroner's District named in Column 3	2. Coroner's District in which the area specified in Column 1 is now comprised	3. Coroner's District to which the area specified in Column 1 is to be transferred
The District of Dartford and the District of Gravesham	North Kent District	West Kent District
In the District of Tonbridge and Malling, the parishes of Wouldham, Burham, Aylesford, Snodland, Birling, East Malling and Larkfield, Ditton, Leybourne, Ryarsh, Trottiscliffe, Addington, Offham, West Malling, Mereworth, Wateringbury and East Peckham	West Kent District	Maidstone District
The City of Rochester Upon Medway, the District of Gillingham, and the District of Swale with the exception of Faversham and the parishes of Teynham, Lynsted, Doddington, Newnham, Norton and Buckland, Stone, Luddenham, Oare, Ospringe, Eastling, Stalisfield, Throwley, Sheldwich Badlesmere and Leaveland, Selling, Boughton Under Blean, Graveney with Goodnestone, Hernhill, Dunkirk	North Kent District	Maidstone District
In the District of Swale, Faversham and the parishes of Teynham, Lynsted, Doddington, Newnham, Norton and Buckland, Stone, Luddenhamn, Oare, Ospringe, Eastling, Stalisfield, Throwley, Sheldwich Badlesmere and Leaveland, Selling, Boughton under Blean, Graveney with Goodnestone, Hernhill, Dunkirk	North Kent District	Canterbury and Dover District

A2–137B Add: The Leicestershire (Coroners) Order 1997, S.I. 1997 No. 490.

The Leicestershire (Coroners) Order 1997

(1997 No. 490)

1.—(1) This Order may be cited as the Leicestershire (Coroners) Order 1997 and shall come into force on 1st April 1997.

(2) In this Order "the 1988 Act" means the Coroners Act 1988.

2.—(1) There shall be a single coroner's district, called the Leicester City and South Leicestershire Coroner's District, for the County of Leicester (which county comes into existence on 1st April 1997 by virtue of article 8(2) of the Leicestershire (City of Leicester and District of Rutland) (Structural Change) Order 1996 and for so much of the County of Leicestershire as is not included in the existing Northern Leicestershire Coroner's District.

(2) The Council of the City of Leicester shall be the relevant council within the meaning of section 1(1A) of the 1988 Act for the coroner's district constituted by paragraph (1) above.

(3) The person who, at 31st March 1997, is the coroner for the existing Leicester City and South Leicestershire Coroner's District shall be deemed on 1st April 1997 to be appointed coroner for the coroner's district constituted by paragraph (1) above.

(4) Any agreement between the person to whom paragraph (3) above applies and Leicestershire County Council (as the relevant council for the purposes of section 1 of the 1988 Act prior to 1st April 1997) as to his salary and pension as a coroner shall be deemed on and after 1st April 1997 to have effect as if originally made between him and Leicester City Council.

(5) Any person who, at 31st March 1997, is a deputy or assistant deputy coroner for the existing Leicester City and South Leicestershire Coroner's District shall be deemed on 1st April 1997 to be appointed deputy or, as the case may be, assistant deputy coroner for the coroner's district constituted by paragraph (1) above.

3.—(1) There shall be a single coroner's district, called the Rutland and North Leicestershire Coroner's District, for the County of Rutland (which county comes into existence on 1st April 1997 by virtue of article 8(3) of the Leicestershire (City of Leicester and District of Rutland) (Structural Change) Order 1996) and for so much of the County of Leicestershire as is not included in the existing Leicester City and South Leicestershire Coroner's District.

(2) The Council of the County of Leicestershire shall be the relevant council within the meaning of section 1(1A) of the 1988 Act for the coroner's district constituted by paragraph (1) above.

(3) The person who, at 31st March 1997, is the coroner for the existing Northern Leicestershire Coroner's District shall be deemed on 1st April 1997 to be appointed coroner for the coroner's district constituted by paragraph (1) above.

(4) Any person who, at 31st March 1997, is a deputy or assistant deputy coroner for the existing Northern Leicestershire Coroner's District shall be deemed on 1st April 1997 to be appointed deputy or, as the case may be, assistant deputy coroner for the coroner's district constituted by paragraph (1) above.

4.—(1) On 1st April 1997, any process issued, order made, direction given, inquest begun or other thing done by or to the coroner for an existing coroner's district shall be deemed to have been issued, made, given, begun or done by or to the coroner for the relevant new coroner's district.

(2) All documents, exhibits, registers and other things in the custody of the coroner for an existing coroner's district in connection with inquests or post-mortem investigations shall be transferred to the coroner for the relevant new coroner's district.

(3) In paragraphs (1) and (2) above the relevant new coroner's district is—

(a) the coroner's district constituted by article 2(1) above as respects the existing Leicester City and South Leicestershire Coroner's District; and

(b) the coroner's district constituted by article 3(1) above as respects the existing Northern Leicestershire Coroner's District.

(4) In this article "coroner" includes any deputy coroner or assistant deputy coroner.

Add: The Local Government Reorganisation (Compensation for Loss of Remuneration) Regulations 1995, S.I. 1995 No. 2837. **A2–137C**

The Local Government Reorganisation (Compensation for Loss of Remuneration) Regulations 1995

(1995 No. 2837)

Citation and commencement

1. These Regulations may be cited as the Local Government Reorganisation (Compensation for Loss of Remuneration) Regulations 1995 and shall come into force on 28th November 1995. **A2–137C/1**

Interpretation

2.—(1) In these Regulations— **A2–137C/2**

"eligible person" means a person entitled to compensation under these Regulations;

"prescribed period" means—

(a) in Wales, the period from 4 May 1995 to 30 September 1997;

(b) in the Isle of Wight, the period from 1 April 1995 to 30 September 1996; and

(c) in any other local government area in England to which an order made under section 17 of the 1992 Act applies, a period commencing with the date provided for in that order for an election to a unitary authority or authorities established by that order, and ending on a date eighteen months after that reorganisation date;

"registration officer" means any superintendent registrar and registrar of births and deaths appointed under section 6(1) of the 1953 Act and any deputy superintendent registrar or deputy registrar of births and deaths appointed under section 8(1) of that Act;

"relevant compensation period" means any period of 36 months beginning on the date on which an eligible person suffers a reduction or further reduction in remuneration to which regulation 3 applies;

"relevant contract" means a contract under which a person works for another whether under a contract of service or apprenticeship or otherwise, but does not include a contract for services;

"relevant employment" means employment under a relevant contract (or an office held by virtue of such employment)—

(a) in England with a district council or county council which is the subject of a structural change or boundary change under an order made under section 17 of the 1992 Act;

(b) in Wales—

(i) with a district council, county council, or joint board which ceases to exist by virtue of the 1994 Act; or

(ii) with the Residuary Body for Wales, a county borough council or a county council established under the 1994 Act,

and "relevant employer" is to be construed accordingly;

"remuneration" means—

(a) all the salary, wages, fees calculated as in paragraph (b) below and other payments made to an eligible person by an employer for his own use and the money value of any accommodation, vehicle or other allowances in kind arising from his employment so far as they are for the person's private use, but shall not include—

(i) any payment in respect of non contractual overtime, or non contractual bonus,

(ii) any payment made in consequence of the undertaking of additional duties attributable, in England, to an order made under section 17 of the 1992 Act, or, in Wales, to any provision made by or under the 1994 Act,

(iii) any allowance payable to him to cover the cost of providing office accommodation or clerical or other assistance,

(iv) any travelling or subsistence allowance, or other moneys to be spent, or to cover expenses incurred by him for the purposes of his employment,

(v) any payment as compensation for loss of holiday entitlement,

(vi) any payment in lieu of notice terminating his employment,

(vii) any compensation payable to him under these Regulations;

(b) for the purposes of paragraph (a) above, fees shall be calculated by dividing by five the total earned during the period of five years ending with the date on which the entitlement to compensation under these Regulations arises or, where the relevant employment (or office held by virtue of that employment) subsists for a shorter period, by dividing the total earned by a factor equal to the length in years and parts of a year of that employment (or office);

"reorganisation date" means—

(a) in England, the date on which a structural change or a boundary change (or both) takes effect, and

(b) in Wales, 1st April 1996;

"the 1953 Act" means the Registration Service Act 1953;

"the 1992 Act" means the Local Government Act 1992;

"the 1994 Act" means the Local Government (Wales) Act 1994.

[(2) For the purposes of these Regulations—

(a) any registration officer shall be deemed to be an officer in employment under a relevant contract with the county council or county borough council which made the scheme under section 14 of the 1953 Act for the district or sub-district in or for which the registration officer holds office; and

(b) any coroner shall be deemed to be an officer in employment under a relevant contract with the relevant council (within the meaning of the Coroners Act 1988) by which he was appointed,

and any reference in these Regulations—

(i) to "employment", "employer" or "employed" shall be construed accordingly; and

(ii) to a "contract of employment" or "contract" shall be construed as a reference to the terms and conditions of the appointment of registration officer or coroner, as the case may be.]**(a)**

(a) Words inserted by the Local Government Reorganisation (Compensation for Loss of Remuneration) (Amendment) Regulations 1996, S.I. 1996 No. 660.

Persons to whom these Regulations apply

3.—(1) Subject to regulation 4, any person falling within the cases specified in paragraphs (2) to (4) below is entitled to compensation under these Regulations. **A2–137C/3**

(2) This paragraph applies to a person—

(a) whose relevant employment terminates on a date falling within the prescribed period (the "former employment");

(b) who, since the termination of his former employment has not been in alternative employment and who returns within the prescribed period to relevant employment (the "new employment")—

(i) in England, with a relevant employer affected by a structural change or boundary change under the same section 17 order as that by which his former relevant employer was affected, or

(ii) in Wales, with any relevant employer established under the 1994 Act;

(c) whose commencing annual rate of remuneration in his new employment is lower than the annual rate he was paid at the termination of his former employment; and

(d) who satisfies the qualifying condition mentioned in paragraph (5) below.

(3) This paragraph applies to a person to whom paragraph (2) does not apply, but who—

(a) was in relevant employment—

(i) in England at the beginning of the prescribed period, who continues in that employment and whose annual rate of remuneration is reduced during that period, or

(ii) in England and Wales at the beginning of the prescribed period whose relevant contract is transferred by an order made under the 1992 Act, by virtue of any provision made by or under the 1994 Act, or otherwise by operation of law, and whose annual rate of remuneration is reduced by the relevant employer to whom that contract is transferred, and

(b) who satisfies the qualifying condition mentioned in paragraph (5) below.

(4) This paragraph applies to a person to whom either paragraph (2) or (3) above has applied, who suffers a further reduction in remuneration during the prescribed period whilst in relevant employment and who satisfies the qualifying condition mentioned in paragraph (5) below.

(5) For the purposes of paragraphs (2) to (4) above, a person satisfies the qualifying condition where the reduction in his remuneration is attributable—

(a) in England to an order made under section 17 of the 1992 Act, and

(b) in Wales to any provision made by or under the 1994 Act.

4.—(1) A person shall not be entitled to compensation under these Regulations if—

(a) he is a teacher subject to the Teachers Superannuation (Consolidation) Regulations 1988;

(b) he is aged 65 or over on the date on which the relevant compensation period commences;

(c) he is entitled to compensation under the Local Government (Compensation for Premature Retirement) Regulations 1982;

(d) he is entitled to compensation under Part II or III of the Local Government (Compensation for Redundancy) Regulations 1994, or Part VI of the Employment Protection (Consolidation) Act 1978;

(e) he is entitled to the immediate payment of benefits under the Local Government Pension Scheme Regulations 1995, or under the statutory instruments revoked by those Regulations;

(f) section 43(4) of the 1994 Act applies to him;

(g) he was not in relevant employment on a date falling twelve months before the reorganisation date;

(h) he can be required by his employer in accordance with his contract of employment to work variable hours and his reduction in remuneration is solely attributable to his employer requiring him to work fewer hours.

[(2) Sub-paragraph (b) in paragraph (1) above shall not apply to a coroner who is aged under 70 on the date on which the relevant compensation period commences.]**(b)**

Amount of compensation in respect of loss or diminution of remuneration

A2–137C/4 **5.**—(1) A relevant employer shall pay an eligible person an amount by way of compensation equal to three times the difference—

(a) in a case to which regulation 3(2) applies, between the annual rate of remuneration at the termination of his former employment and the commencing annual rate of remuneration of his new employment; or

(b) in a case to which regulation 3(3) applies, between the annual rate of remuneration before and after the reduction in question; or

(c) in a case to which regulation 3(4) applies, between the annual rate of remuneration before and after the further reduction in question.

(2) The amount of any compensation payable in accordance with paragraph (1) above shall be recalculated on each occasion during the relevant compensation period when the annual rate of remuneration for the relevant employment is increased and shall cease to be payable at any time during which the annual rate of remuneration for the new employment equals or exceeds that for the former employment or, as the case may be, the rate before the reduction or further reduction in question.

(3) The relevant employer shall calculate the amount of any compensation payable in accordance with paragraph (1) and any change in the compensation payable in accordance with paragraph (2).

(4) Any change in the amount of any compensation payable in accordance with paragraph (2) above shall not affect the entitlement to any instalment payable before that date.

Payment of compensation

A2–137C/5 **6.**—(1) Subject to regulations 5(2) to (4) and regulation 8 the amount of compensation payable to an eligible person shall be paid in 36 monthly instalments of which the first shall be paid as soon as practicable after the initial calculation under regulation 5(3).

(2) A relevant employer may during a relevant compensation period at such intervals as it thinks fit make interim payments, or payments on account of any instalment of compensation to which an eligible person has become entitled under these Regulations before a calculation is made under regulation 5(3).

(3) If the total of any instalments paid to an eligible person under paragraph (1) above exceeds or falls short of the total amount of compensation to which a person is entitled at the end of the relevant compensation period, the excess or shortfall is to be repaid by the eligible person, or as the case may be, paid by the relevant employer at the end of that period.

(4) If at any time during the relevant compensation period an eligible person ceases to be employed by one relevant employer and becomes employed by another, that person shall inform his new employer in writing of his entitlement to compensation under these Regulations and the new employer shall, subject to regulations 5(2) to (4) and regulation

(b) *ibid.*

8, be liable to pay any remaining instalments of compensation required to be paid in accordance with regulation 5 and paragraphs (1) to (3) above.

Notification of compensation

7.—(1) A relevant employer shall, after making the necessary calculation in accordance with regulation 5(3), give an eligible person written notice of the amount of compensation payable in accordance with these Regulations. **A2–137C/6**

(2) Written notice shall be given in accordance with paragraph (1) above not later than the expiry of three months from—

(a) the date on which the relevant compensation period commences,

(b) the date on which these Regulations come into force, whichever of those dates is the later.

Cessation of relevant employment

8.—(1) If an eligible person— **A2–137C/7**

(a) ceases to be employed in relevant employment in the circumstances mentioned in paragraph (2) below,

(b) subject to paragraph (1A) below reaches the age of 65 during the relevant compensation period, or

(c) dies,

he shall cease to be entitled to any instalments of compensation payable after that event.

[(1A) Sub-paragraph (b) in paragraph (1) above shall apply to an eligible person who is a coroner as if for the number "65" there were substituted the number "70"]**(c)**.

(2) The circumstances mentioned in paragraph (1) are that before the expiry of the compensation period an eligible person—

(a) becomes entitled to compensation under the Local Government (Compensation for Premature Retirement) Regulations 1982;

(b) becomes entitled to compensation under Part II or III of the Local Government (Compensation for Redundancy) Regulations 1994 or Part VI of the Employment Protection (Consolidation) Act 1978;

(c) becomes entitled to the immediate payment of benefits under the Local Government Pension Scheme Regulations 1995; or

(d) voluntarily resigns from his employment or is dismissed by his employer.

Add: The North Yorkshire (Coroners' Districts) Order 1997, S.I. 1997 No. 1532. **A2–137D**

The North Yorkshire (Coroners' Districts) Order 1997

(1997 No. 1532)

Citation

1. This Order may be cited as the North Yorkshire (Coroners' Districts) Order 1997. **A2–137D/1**

(c) *ibid.*

Commencement and application

A2–137D/2 **2.**—(1) This Order shall come into force on 1st August 1997.

(2) This Order shall not have effect in relation to any inquest before the day on which it comes into force or to any post-mortem examination which, before that day, a coroner has directed or requested a medical practitioner to make.

Alteration of coroners' districts

A2–137D/3 **3.**—(1) The existing Claro coroner's district, North Eastern coroner's district, Scarborough and Ryedale coroner's district and Western coroner's district of the county of North Yorkshire shall be abolished.

(2) From the area comprising the coroners' districts mentioned in paragraph (1) above there shall be formed the two coroners' districts named in column 1 of the Schedule to this Order which shall consist of the areas specified in column 2 of the Schedule.

SCHEDULE **Article 2**

1. Name of Coroner's District	2. Area comprised in Coroner's District named in column 1
Eastern District	The districts of Hambleton, Ryedale and Scarborough
Western District	The districts of Craven, Harrogate, Richmondshire and Selby

A2–174 The Railways (Notice of Accidents) Order 1986 was repealed by the Reporting of Injuries, Diseases and Dangerous Occurrences Regulations 1995, S.I. 1995 No. 3163, reg. 15 and Sched. 8, Part I, as from April 1, 1996.

A2–237A The Registration of Births and Deaths Regulations 1987 and the Registration of Births and Deaths (Welsh Language) Regulations 1987 have been further amended by S.I. 1997 No. 844.

The Registration of Births and Deaths (Amendment) Regulations 1997

(1997 No. 844)

Citation, commencement and interpretation

A2–237A/1 **1.**—(1) These Regulations may be cited as the Registration of Births and Deaths (Amendment) Regulations 1997 and shall come into force on 1st April 1997.

(2) In these Regulations, unless the context otherwise requires—

"the principal Regulations" means the Registration of Births and Deaths Regulations 1987; and

"the Welsh Language Regulations" means the Registration of Births and Deaths (Welsh Language) Regulations 1987.

Amendment of provisions relating to the registration of births

A2–237A/2 **2.**—(1) The provisions of Parts III (registration of live-births) and VIII (registration of still-births) of the principal Regulations shall be amended in accordance with the following provisions of this regulation.

(2) In regulation 13 (declaration and registration under section 9 of the Act) at the beginning of paragraph (1) there shall be inserted the words "In relation to a live-birth,".

(3) In regulation 33 (reference to coroner) in paragraph (1) for the words "a registrar" there shall be substituted the words "the relevant registrar".

(4) After regulation 34 there shall be inserted the following regulation—

"Declaration and registration of a still-birth under section 9 of the Act

34A.—(1) In relation to a still-birth, the officer before whom a declaration for the purposes of section 9(1) of the Act (giving of information to a person other than the registrar may be made shall be any registrar) other than the relevant registrar.

(2) The officer before whom the declaration is to be made shall—

(a) enter in the declaration the particulars required to be registered concerning the still-birth, using an approved form for the purpose;

(b) show or read the particulars entered on the form to the informant and correct any error or omission, requiring the informant to initial any amendment and then to sign the declaration;

(c) attest the declaration himself; and

(d) send the declaration and either the certificate in form 10 or the declaration in form 11 to the relevant registrar in accordance with section 11(1B)(b) of the Act.

(3) Except in a case to which regulation 33 applies, where it appears to the relevant registrar that the particulars contained in the declaration are in any material respect not proper to be registered, he shall return the declaration to the officer before whom it was attested together with a note of the matters in which it appears to need amendment, and—

(a) that officer shall then in the presence of the declarant amend any error by striking out any incorrect particulars and inserting the correct particulars;

(b) any amendment so made shall be initialled by the declarant and the declaration shall be returned to the relevant registrar.

(4) On receiving the declaration and either the certificate in form 10 or the declaration in form 11 the registrar shall, subject to paragraph (3), enter the particulars of the birth in the register in the following manner—

(a) in spaces 1 and 3 to 13 of form 9, he shall enter the particulars as appearing in the corresponding spaces of the declaration, except that where any particulars have been corrected in pursuance of paragraph (3) he shall enter in the register only the particulars as corrected, omitting any incorrect particular which has been struck out and the initials of the declarant;

(b) in space 2 of form 9, he shall enter the cause of death and nature of the evidence that the child was still-born—

(i) if he has received a certificate in form 10, as they appear in that certificate; or

(ii) if he has received a declaration in form 11, as they appear in the corresponding spaces of the declaration for the purposes of section 9(1) of the Act, except that where those particulars have been corrected in pursuance of paragraph (3) he shall enter in the register only the particulars as corrected, omitting any incorrect particular which has been struck out and the initials of the declarant.

(c) in space 14 of form 9—

(i) he shall enter the name of the declarant in the form in which he signed the declaration and shall add the words "by declaration dated . . . ", inserting the date on which the declaration was made and signed;

(ii) if, pursuant to section 9(4) of the Act, a request made under paragraph (b) or (c) of section 10(1) of the Act was included in the declaration, he shall after the words required by head (i) make the same addition as, on completion of registration under regulation 10, would be required under (as the case may be) head (ii) or (iii) of paragraph (1)(b) of that regulation;

(d) in space 15 of form 9 he shall enter the date on which the entry is made; and

(e) in space 16 of form 9 he shall sign the entry, adding his official description.".

(5) In regulation 35 (registration on coroner's notification where no inquest is held) in paragraph (1) after the words "in accordance with Regulation 34(2)" there shall be inserted the words "or, if a declaration is made for the purposes of section 9(1) of the Act, in accordance with regulation 34A(4)".

Amendment of provisions relating to the registration of deaths

A2–237A/3 **3.**—(1) The provisions of Part X (registration of deaths) of the principal Regulations shall be amended in accordance with the following provisions of this regulation.

(2) After regulation 42 there shall be inserted the following regulation—

"Declaration and registration under section 23A of the Act

42A.—(1) The officer before whom a declaration for the purposes of section 23A of the Act (giving of information concerning a death to a person other than the registrar) may be made shall be any registrar other than the relevant registrar.

(2) The officer before whom the declaration is to be made shall—

(a) enter in the declaration the particulars required to be registered concerning the death, using an approved form for the purpose;

(b) show or read the particulars entered on the form to the informant and correct any error or omission, requiring the informant to initial any amendment and then to sign the declaration;

(c) attest the declaration himself; and

(d) send the declaration to the relevant registrar in accordance with section 23A(3) of the Act.

(3) Except in a case to which regulation 41 applies, where it appears to the relevant registrar that the particulars contained in the declaration are in any material respect not proper to be registered, he shall return the declaration to the officer before whom it was attested together with a note of the matters in which it appears to need amendment, and—

(a) that officer shall then in the presence of the declarant amend any error by striking out any incorrect particulars and inserting the correct particulars;

(b) any amendment so made shall be initialled by the declarant and the declaration shall be returned to the relevant registrar.

(4) On receiving the declaration the registrar shall, subject to paragraph (3), enter the particulars of the death in the register in the following manner—

(a) in spaces 1 to 7 of form 13, he shall enter the particulars as appearing in the corresponding spaces of the declaration, except that where any particulars have been corrected in pursuance of paragraph (3) he shall enter in the register only the particulars as corrected, omitting any incorrect particular which has been struck out and the initials of the declarant;

(b) in space 8 of form 13 he shall enter the cause of death as it appears in the certificate of cause of death delivered to the registrar under section 22(1) of the Act;

(c) in space 9 of form 13 he shall enter the name of the declarant in the form in which he signed the declaration and shall add the words 'by declaration dated . . . ', inserting the date on which the declaration was made and signed;

(d) in space 10 of form 13 he shall enter the date on which the entry is made; and

(e) in space 11 of form 13 he shall sign the entry, adding his official description".

(3) In regulation 43 (registration where inquest is not held) in paragraph (1) after the words "in accordance with Regulation 42(2) to (7)" there shall be inserted "or, if a declaration is made for the purposes of section 23A of the Act, in accordance with Regulation 42A(4)".

(4) After regulation 44 there shall be inserted the following regulation—

"Registration after receipt of declaration and coroner's notification of cause of death

44A. Where the registrar receives a notification as mentioned in regulation 43(2) in respect of a death in respect of which a declaration has been made for the purposes of section 23A of the Act, but that death has not yet been registered, he shall register that death in accordance with regulation 42A and shall enter in the margin of the entry the particulars required by regulation 44(a).".

(5) In regulation 47 (registration after twelve months) at the end of paragraph (3) there shall be inserted the words "or shall enter in the register the particulars of death given in a declaration made for the purposes of section 23A of the Act, in accordance with regulation 42A".

Amendment of general provisions

4.—(1) Parts II (general provisions as to registration) and XII (correction of errors) of the principal Regulations shall be amended in accordance with the following provisions of this regulation. **A2–237A/4**

(2) In regulation 3 (preparation of draft particulars) in paragraph (2) for the words "Regulation 11, 12 or 13", there shall be substituted the words "Regulation 11, 12, 13, 34A or 42A,".

(3) In regulation 55 (correction of minor clerical errors after completion) in paragraph (2)—

(a) in sub-paragraph (c) for the words "or 17(2)(b)(i)" there shall be substituted the words "17(2)(b)(i) or 34A(4)(c)"; and

(b) at the end of sub-paragraph (f)(i) there shall be inserted the words ", 34A or 42A".

Amendment of the Registration of Births and Deaths (Welsh Language) Regulations 1987

5.—(1) The Welsh Language Regulations shall be amended in accordance with the following provisions of this regulation. **A2–237A/5**

(2) In regulation 5 (registration of still-births occurring in Wales) for paragraph (2) there shall be substituted the following paragraphs—

"(2) Subject to paragraph (2A), where a qualified informant, giving information relating to the registration of a still-birth which occurred in Wales, elects for the particulars required by Part VIII of the principal Regulations to be entered in Welsh as well as in English, the registrar shall enter those particulars accordingly.

(2A) Paragraph (2) of this regulation shall apply only where—

(a) the informant gives the requisite information either—

(i) personally to the relevant registrar; or

(ii) by declaration under section 9 of the Act, before a registrar in Wales; and

(b) the informant gives such information in Welsh and the officer to or before whom he gives it can understand and write Welsh.".

(3) In regulation 6 (registration of deaths occurring in Wales) for paragraph (3) there shall be substituted the following paragraphs—

"(3) Subject to paragraphs (3A) and (4), where a qualified informant giving information relating to the registration of a death which occurred in Wales, elects for the particulars required by Part X of the principal Regulations to be entered in Welsh as well as in English, the registrar shall enter those particulars accordingly.

(3A) Paragraph (3) shall apply only where—

(a) the informant gives the requisite information either—

(i) personally, to the relevant registrar; or

(ii) by declaration under section 23A of the Act, before a registrar in Wales; and

(b) the informant gives the requisite information in Welsh and the officer to or before whom he gives it can understand and write Welsh.".

A2–238 The Reporting of Injuries, Diseases and Dangerous Occurrences Regulations 1985, were repealed by RIDDOR 1995, S.I. 1995 No. 3163, reg. 15(1) and Sched. 8 Part I.

A2–279/1 Add: The Reporting of Injuries, Diseases and Dangerous Occurrences Regulations 1995, S.I. 1995 No. 3163, regs. 1–6, 8, 10, 13, 14, Scheds. 1–3, 5, 7.

Reporting of Injuries, Diseases and Dangerous Occurrences Regulations 1995

(1995 No. 3163)

Citation and commencement

A2–279/2 **1.** These Regulations may be cited as the Reporting of Injuries, Diseases and Dangerous Occurrences Regulations 1995 and shall come into force on 1 April 1996.

Interpretation

A2–279/3 **2.**—(1) In these Regulations, unless the context otherwise requires—

"the 1995 Order" means the Health and Safety at Work etc. Act 1974 (Application outside Great Britain) Order 1995;

"accident" includes

(a) an act of non-consensual physical violence done to a person at work; and

(b) an act of suicide which occurs on, or in the course of the operation of, a relevant transport system;

"approved" means approved for the time being in writing for the purposes of these Regulations by the Executive and published in such form as the Executive considers appropriate;

"biological agent" has the meaning assigned to it by regulation 2(1) of the Control of Substances Hazardous to Health Regulations 1994;

"construction site" means any place where there are carried out building operations or works of engineering construction such that those operations or works fall within section 127(1) of the Factories Act 1961,

"dangerous occurrence" means an occurrence which arises out of or in connection with work and is of a class specified in—

(a) paragraphs 1–17 of Part I of Schedule 2;

(b) paragraphs 18–21 of Part I of Schedule 2 and takes place elsewhere that at an offshore workplace;

(c) paragraphs 22–40 of Part II of Schedule 2 and takes place at a mine;

(d) paragraphs 41–48 of Part III of Schedule 2 and takes place at a quarry;

(e) paragraphs 49–72 of Part IV of Schedule 2 and takes place where a relevant transport system is operated (other than at a factory, dock, construction site, mine or quarry); or

(f) paragraphs 73–83 of Part V of Schedule 2 and takes place at an offshore workplace;

"disease" includes a medical condition;

"diving contractor" and "diving operation" have the meaning assigned to them by the Diving Operations at Work Regulations 1981;

"dock" means any place to which section 125(1) of the Factories Act 1961 applies;

"the Executive" means the Health and Safety Executive;

"factory" has the meaning assigned to it by section 175 of the Factories Act 1961;

"guided transport system" means a system using a mode of guided transport prescribed under regulation 3 of the Railways and Other Transport Systems (Approval of Works, Plant and Equipment) Regulations 1994;

"major injury" means an injury or condition specified in Schedule 1;

"mine" or "quarry" means a mine or, as the case may be, a quarry within the meaning of section 180 of the Mines and Quarries Act 1954 and for the purposes of these Regulations includes a closed tip within the meaning of section 2(2)(b) of the Mines and Quarries (Tips) Act 1969 which is associated with that mine or that quarry;

"offshore installation" has the meaning assigned to it by article 4(2) of the 1995 Order but excluding the fixed structures specified in article 4(2)(a) of that Order;

"offshore workplace" means any place where activities are carried on or any premises such that prescribed provisions of the 1974 Act are applied to those activities or premises by virtue of articles 4, 5 or 6 of the 1995 Order, and for this purpose those articles shall be deemed to apply to activities or premises within Great Britain which are in tidal waters or on the foreshore or other land intermittently covered by such waters as they apply to activities and premises within territorial waters or a designated area;

"operator", in relation to a vehicle to which paragraph 16 or 17 of Part I of Schedule 2 applies, means—

(a) a person who holds an operator's licence (granted under Part V of the Transport Act 1968 for the use of that vehicle for the carriage of goods on a road; except that where by virtue of regulation 32(1) to (3) of the Goods Vehicles (Operators' Licences, Qualifications and Fees) Regulations 1984 the vehicle is included in a licence held by a holding company and that company is not operating the vehicle at the relevant time, the "operator" shall be the subsidiary company specified in the application made under the said regulation 32(1) or, if more than one subsidiary company is so specified, whichever one is operating the vehicle at the relevant time, and in this sub-paragraph "holding company" and "subsidiary company" have the same meanings as in the said Regulations of 1984; or

(b) where no such licence is held—

(i) (in the case of a vehicle which is not registered in the United Kingdom) the driver of the vehicle, or

(ii) (in the case of any other vehicle) the keeper of the vehicle; and for this purpose, where the vehicle is on hire or lease to any person, that person shall be treated as its keeper;

but where an employee who would otherwise be the operator of a vehicle in accordance with sub-paragraph (b)(i) above uses that vehicle for the carriage of any dangerous substance on behalf of his employer, that employer shall (notwithstanding that sub-paragraph) be regarded as the operator of the vehicle concerned;

"owner" means—

(a) in relation to a mine or quarry, the person who is for the time being entitled to work it;
(b) in relation to a pipeline, the person who is for the time being entitled to control the flow of anything through that pipeline or through that pipeline once it is commissioned;

"passenger train" means a train carrying passengers or made available for the carriage of passengers;

"pipeline" and "pipeline works" have the meaning assigned to them by article 6(2) of the 1995 Order;

"railway" has the meaning assigned to it by section 67 of the Transport and Works Act 1992;

"relevant transport system" means a railway, tramway, trolley vehicle system or guided transport system;

"responsible person" means—
(a) in the case of—
  (i) a mine, the manager of that mine;
  (ii) a quarry, the owner of that quarry;
  (iii) a closed tip, the owner of the mine or quarry with which that tip is associated;
  (iv) an offshore installation (otherwise than in the case of a disease reportable under regulation 5), the duty holder for the purposes of the Offshore Installations and Pipeline Works (Management and Administration) Regulations 1995 provided that for the purposes of this provision regulation 3(2)(c) of those Regulations shall be deemed not to apply;
  (v) a dangerous occurrence at a pipeline (being an accident to which paragraph 14(a)–(f) of Part I of Schedule 2 applies), the owner of that pipeline;
  (vi) a dangerous occurrence at a well, the person appointed by a concession owner to execute any function of organising or supervising any operation to be carried out by the well or, where no such person has been appointed, the concession owner (and for this purpose "concession owner" means the person who at any time has the right to exploit or explore mineral resources in any area, or to store gas in any area and to recover gas so stored if, at any time, the well is, or is to be, used in the exercise of that right);
  (vii) a diving operation (otherwise than in the case of a disease reportable under regulation 5), the diving contractor;
  (viii) a vehicle to which paragraph 16 or 17 of Part I of Schedule 2 applies, the operator of the vehicle;
(b) (where sub-paragraph (a) above does not apply) in the case of the death of or other injury to an employee reportable under regulation 3 or of a disease suffered by an employee reportable under regulation 5, his employer; and
(c) in any other case, the person for the time being having control of the premises in connection with the carrying on by him of any trade, business or other undertaking (whether for profit or not) at which, or in connection with the work at which, the accident or dangerous occurrences reportable under regulation 3, or case of disease reportable under regulation 5, happened;

"road" has the meaning assigned to it by section 192(1) of the Road Traffic Act 1988;

"road vehicle" means any vehicle, other than a train, on a road;

"running line" means any line which is not a siding and is ordinarily used for the passage of trains;

"train" includes a reference to a locomotive, tramcar or other power unit and to a vehicle used on a relevant transport system;

"tramway" has the meaning assigned to it by section 67 of the Transport and Works Act 1992;

"trolley vehicle system" has the meaning assigned to it by section 67 of the Transport and Works Act 1992;

"well" includes any structures and devices on top of a well;

(2) In these Regulations, unless the context otherwise requires, any reference to—

(a) a numbered regulation or Schedule is a reference to the regulation or Schedule in these Regulations so numbered;

(b) a numbered paragraph is a reference to the paragraph so numbered in the regulation or Schedule in which that reference appears; and

(c) an accident or a dangerous occurrence which arises out of or in connection with work shall include a reference to an accident, or as the case may be, a dangerous occurrence attributable to the manner of conducting an undertaking, the plant or substances used for the purposes of an undertaking and the condition of the premises so used or any part of them.

(3) For the purposes of these Regulations, a person who is at an offshore workplace shall be deemed to be at work at all times when he is at that workplace in connection with his work.

Notification and reporting of injuries and dangerous occurrences

3.—(1) Subject to regulation 10, where— **A2–279/4**

(a) any person dies as a result of an accident arising out of or in connection with work;

(b) any person at work suffers a major injury as a result of an accident arising out of or in connection with work;

(c) any person not at work suffers an injury as a result of an accident arising out of or in connection with work and that person is taken from the site of the accident to a hospital for treatment in respect of that injury;

(d) any person not at work suffers a major injury as a result of an accident arising out of or in connection with work at a hospital; or

(e) there is a dangerous occurrence,

the responsible person shall—

(i) forthwith notify the relevant enforcing authority thereof by the quickest practicable means; and

(ii) within 10 days send a report thereof to the relevant enforcing authority on a form approved for the purposes of this sub-paragraph, unless within that period he makes a report thereof to the Executive by some other means so approved.

(2) Subject to regulation 10, where a person at work is incapacitated for work of a kind which he might reasonably be expected to do, either under his contract of employment, or, if there is no such contract, in the normal course of his work, for more than three consecutive days (excluding the day of the accident but including any days which would not have been working days) because of an injury resulting from an accident arising out of or in connection with work (other than one reportable under paragraph (1)), the responsible person shall as soon as practicable and, in any event, within 10 days of the accident send a report thereof to the relevant enforcing authority on a form approved for the purposes of this regulation, unless within that period he makes a report thereof to the Executive by some other means so approved.

Reporting of the death of an employee

4. Subject to regulation 10, where an employee, as a result of an accident at work, has suffered an injury reportable under regulation 3 which is a cause of his death within one year of the date of that accident, the employer shall inform the relevant enforcing authority in writing of the death as soon as it comes to his knowledge, whether or not the accident has been reported under regulation 3. **A2–279/5**

Reporting of cases of disease

A2–279/6 **5.**—(1) Subject to paragraphs (2) and (3) and to regulation 10, where—

(a) a person at work suffers from any of the occupational diseases specified in column 1 of Part I of Schedule 3 and his work involves one of the activities specified in the corresponding entry in column 2 of that Part; or

(b) a person at an offshore workplace suffers from any of the diseases specified in Part II of Schedule 3,

the responsible person shall forthwith send a report thereof to the relevant enforcing authority on a form approved for the purposes of this regulation, unless he forthwith makes a report thereof to the Executive by some other means so approved.

(2) Paragraph (1) shall apply only if—

(a) in the case of an employee, the responsible person has received a written statement prepared by a registered medical practitioner diagnosing the disease as one of those specified in Schedule 3; or

(b) in the case of a self-employed person, that person has been informed, by a registered medical practitioner, that he is suffering from a disease so specified.

(3) In the case of a self-employed person, it shall be a sufficient compliance with paragraph (1) if that person makes arrangements for the report to be sent to the relevant enforcing authority by some other person.

Reporting of gas incidents

A2–279/7 **6.**—(1) Whenever a conveyor of flammable gas through a fixed pipe distribution system, or a filler, importer or supplier (other than by means of retail trade) of a refillable container containing liquefied petroleum gas receives notification of any death or any major injury which has arisen out of or in connection with the gas distributed, filled, imported or supplied, as the case may be, by that person, he shall forthwith notify the Executive of the incident, and shall within 14 days send a report of it to the Executive on a form approved for the purposes of this regulation.

(2) Whenever an employer or self-employed person who is a member of a class of persons approved by the Executive for the purposes of paragraph (3) of regulation 3 of the Gas Safety (Installation and Use) Regulations 1994 has in his possession sufficient information for it to be reasonable for him to decide that a gas fitting as defined in the said Regulations or any flue or ventilation used in connection with that fitting, by reason of its design, construction, manner of installation, modification or servicing, is or has been likely to cause death, or any major injury by reason of—

(a) accidental leakage of gas;

(b) inadequate combustion of gas; or

(c) inadequate removal of the products of combustion of gas,

he shall within 14 days send a report of it to the Executive on a form approved for the purposes of this regulation, unless he has previously reported such information.

Additional provisions relating to mines and quarries

8. The provisions of Schedule 5 (which contains additional provisions relating to mines and quarries) shall have effect.

Additional provisions relating to offshore workplaces

9. The provisions of Schedule 6 (which contains additional provisions relating to offshore workplaces) shall have effect.

Restrictions on the application of regulations 3, 4 and 5

10.—(1) The requirements of regulation 3 relating to the death or injury of a person as a result of an accident shall not apply to an accident causing death or injury to a person arising out of the conduct of any operation on, or any examination or other medical treatment of, that person which is administered by, or conducted under the supervision of, a registered medical practitioner or a registered dentist (and for the purposes of this paragraph a registered dentist has the meaning assigned to it by section 53(1) of the Dentists Act 1984.

(2) The requirements of regulations 3 and 4 relating to the death or injury of a person as a result of an accident, shall apply to an accident arising out of or in connection with the movement of a vehicle on a road only if that person—

- (a) was killed or suffered an injury as a result of exposure to a substance being conveyed by the vehicle; or
- (b) was either himself engaged in, or was killed or suffered an injury as a result of the activities of another person who was at the time of the accident engaged in, work connected with the loading or unloading of any article or substance onto or off the vehicle; or
- (c) was either himself engaged in, or was killed or suffered an injury as a result of the activities of another person who was at the time of the accident engaged in, work on or alongside a road, being work concerned with the construction, demolition, alteration, repair or maintenance of—
  - (i) the road or the markings or equipment thereon;
  - (ii) the verges, fences, hedges or other boundaries of the road;
  - (iii) pipes or cables on, under, over or adjacent to the road; or
  - (iv) buildings or structures adjacent to or over the road; or
- (d) was killed or suffered an injury as a result of an accident involving a train.

(3) The requirements of regulations 3, 4 and 5 relating to any death, injury or case of disease shall not apply to a member of the armed forces of the Crown or of a visiting force who was on duty at the relevant time (and for the purposes of this paragraph a visiting force has the meaning assigned to it by section 12(1) of the Visiting Forces Act 1952.

(4) Regulations 3, 4 and 5 shall not apply otherwise than in respect of offshore workplaces to anything which is required to be notified under any of the enactments or instruments specified in Schedule 7.

(5) Regulation 3(1)(i) shall not apply to a self-employed person who is injured at premises of which he is the owner or occupier, but regulation 3(1)(ii) shall apply to such a self-employed person (other than in the case of death) and it shall be sufficient compliance with that sub-paragraph if that self-employed person makes arrangements for the report to be sent to the relevant enforcing authority by some other person.

Certificates of exemption

13.—(1) Subject to paragraph (2) and to any of the provisions imposed by the Communities in respect of the encouragement of improvements in the safety and health of workers at work, the Executive may, by a certificate in writing, exempt any person or class of persons from any requirement imposed by these Regulations and any such exemption may be granted subject to conditions and with or without limit of time and may be revoked by a certificate in writing at any time. **A2–279/8**

(2) The Executive shall not grant any such exemption unless, having regard to the circumstances of the case and, in particular, to—

- (a) the conditions, if any, which it proposes to attach to the exemption; and
- (b) any other requirements imposed by or under any enactments which apply to the case,

it is satisfied that the health and safety of persons who are likely to be affected by the exemption will not be prejudiced in consequence of it.

Repeal and amendment of provisions in the Regulation of Railways Act 1871, the Railway Employment (Prevention of Accidents) Act 1900 and the Transport and Works Act 1992

A2–279/9 **14.**—(1) Section 6 (Companies to make returns of accidents to Board of Trade) of the Regulations of Railways Act 1871, section 13(2) of the Railway Employment (Prevention of Accidents) Act 1900 and sections 43 (Accidents etc.) and 44 (Accidents etc: consequential amendments) of the Transport and Works Act 1992 are hereby repealed.

(2) The Regulation of Railways Act 1871 shall be amended as follows–

(a) in section 2 (Interpretation) there shall be added at the end of the words "The term 'relevant transport system' has the meaning assigned to it by regulation 2 of the Reporting of Injuries, Diseases and Dangerous Occurrences Regulations 1995.";

(b) in section 7 (Inquiry into accidents and formal investigation in serious cases) for the words "accident, of which notice is for the time being required by or in pursuance of this Act to be sent to the Board of Trade" there shall be substituted the words "accident or occurrence which arises from the operation of a relevant transport system and which is required to be reported by regulation 3(1) of the Reporting of Injuries, Diseases and Dangerous Occurrences Regulations 1995";

(c) in section 7, after the word "accident", in each place where it subsequently occurs, there shall be added the words "or occurrence";

(d) in section 8 (Appointment of an assessor to coroner) for the words "accident, of which notice for the time being is required by or in pursuance of this Act to be sent to the Board of Trade" there shall be substituted the words "accident or occurrence—

(i) which arises from the operation of a relevant transport system, and

(ii) which is required to be reported under regulation 3(1) of the Reporting of Injuries, Diseases and Dangerous Occurrences Regulations 1995,"; and

(e) in section 8, after the word "accident", in the second place where it occurs, there shall be inserted the words "or occurrence".

A2–279/10 SCHEDULE 1 **Regulation 2(1)**

MAJOR INJURIES

1. Any fracture, other than to the fingers, thumbs or toes.
2. Any amputation.
3. Dislocation of the shoulder, hip, knee or spine.
4. Loss of sight (whether temporary or permanent).
5. A chemical or hot metal burn to the eye or any penetrating injury to the eye.
6. Any injury resulting from an electric shock or electrical burn (including any electrical burn caused by arcing or arcing products) leading to unconsciousness or requiring resuscitation or admittance to hospital for more than 24 hours.
7. Any other injury—

(a) leading to hypothermia, heat-induced illness or to unconsciousness,

(b) requiring resuscitation, or

(c) requiring admittance to hospital for more than 24 hours.

8. Loss of consciousness caused by asphyxia or by exposure to a harmful substance or biological agent.

9. Either of the following conditions which result from the absorption of any substance by inhalation, ingestion or through the skin—
(a) acute illness requiring medical treatment; or
(b) loss of consciousness.

10. Acute illness which requires medical treatment where there is reason to believe that this resulted from exposure to a biological agent or its toxins or infected material.

SCHEDULE 2 **Regulation 2(1)**

DANGEROUS OCCURRENCES

PART I

GENERAL

Lifting machinery, etc.

1. The collapse of, the overturning of, or the failure of any load-bearing part of any— **A2–279/11**
(a) lift or hoist;
(b) crane or derrick;
(c) mobile powered access platform;
(d) access cradle or window-cleaning cradle;
(e) excavator;
(f) pile-driving frame or rig having an overall height, when operating, or move than 7 metres; or
(g) fork lift truck.

Pressure systems

2. The failure of any closed vessel (including a boiler or boiler tube) or of any associated pipework, in which the internal pressure was above or below atmospheric pressure, where the failure has the potential to cause the death of any person. **A2–279/12**

Freight containers

3.—(1) The failure of any freight container in any of its load-bearing parts while it is being raised, lowered or suspended. **A2–279/13**

(2) In this paragraph, "freight container" means a container as defined in regulation 2(1) of the Freight Containers (Safety Convention) Regulations 1984.

Overhead electric lines

4. Any unintentional incident in which plant or equipment either— **A2–279/14**
(a) comes into contact with an uninsulated overhead electric line in which the voltage exceeds 200 volts; or
(b) causes an electrical discharge from such an electric line by coming into close proximity to it.

Electrical short circuit

5. Electrical short circuit or overload attended by fire or explosion which results in the stoppage of the plant involved for more than 24 hours or which has the potential to cause the death of any person. **A2–279/15**

Explosives

A2–279/16 **6.**—(1) Any of the following incidents involving explosives—

(a) the unintentional explosion or ignition of explosives other than one—

(i) caused by the unintentional discharge of a weapon where, apart from that unintentional discharge, the weapon and explosives functioned as they were designed to do; or

(ii) where a fail-safe device or safe system of work functioned so as to prevent any person from being injured in consequence of the explosion or ignition;

(b) a misfire (other than one at a mine or quarry or inside a well or one involving a weapon) except where a fail-safe device or safe system of work functioned so as to prevent any person from being endangered in consequence of the misfire;

(c) the failure of the shots in any demolition operation to cause the intended extent of collapse or direction of fall of a building or structure;

(d) the projection of material (other than at a quarry) beyond the boundary of the site on which the explosives are being used or beyond the danger zone in circumstances such that any person was or might have been injured thereby;

(e) any injury to a person (other than at a mine or quarry or one otherwise reportable under these Regulations) involving first-aid or medical treatment resulting from the explosion or discharge of any explosives or detonator.

(2) In this paragraph "explosives" means any explosive of a type which would, were it being transported, be assigned to Class I within the meaning of the Clarification and Labelling of Explosives Regulations 1983 and "danger zone" means the area from which persons have been excluded or forbidden to enter to avoid being endangered by any explosion or ignition of explosives.

Biological agents

A2–279/17 **7.** Any accident or incident which resulted or could have resulted in the release or escape of a biological agent likely to cause severe human infection or illness.

Malfunction of radiation generators, etc.

A2–279/18 **8.**—(1) Any incident in which—

(a) the malfunction of a radiation generator or its ancillary equipment used in fixed or mobile industrial radiography, the irradiation of food or the processing of products by irradiation, causes it to fail to de-energise at the end of the intended exposure period; or

(b) the malfunction of equipment used in fixed or mobile industrial radiography or gamma irradiation causes a radioactive source to fail to return to its safe position by the normal means at the end of the intended exposure period.

(2) In this paragraph, "radiation generator" has the same meaning as in regulation 2 of the Ionising Radiations Regulations 1985.

Breathing apparatus

A2–279/19 **9.**—(1) Any incident in which breathing apparatus malfunctions—

(a) while in use, or

(b) during testing immediately prior to use in such a way that had the malfunction occurred while the apparatus was in use it would have posed a danger to the health or safety of the user.

(2) This paragraph shall not apply to breathing apparatus while it is being—

(a) used in a mine; or
(b) maintained or tested as part of a routine maintenance procedure.

Diving operations

10. Any of the following incidents in relation to a diving operation— **A2–279/20**
(a) the failure or the endangering of—
(i) any lifting equipment associated with the diving operation, or
(ii) life support equipment, including control panels, hoses and breathing apparatus, which puts a diver at risk;
(b) any damage to, or endangering of, the dive platform, or any failure of the dive platform to remain on station, which puts a diver at risk;
(c) the trapping of a diver;
(d) any explosion in the vicinity of a diver; or
(e) any uncontrolled ascent or any omitted decompression which puts a diver at risk.

Collapse of scaffolding

11. The complete or partial collapse of— **A2–279/21**
(a) any scaffold which is—
(i) more than 5 metres in height which results in a substantial part of the scaffold falling or overturning; or
(ii) erected over or adjacent to water in circumstances such that there would be a risk of drowning to a person falling from the scaffold into the water; or
(b) the suspension arrangements (including any outrigger) of any slung or suspended scaffold which causes a working platform or cradle to fall.

Train collisions

12. Any unintended collision of a train with any other train or vehicle, other than one reportable under Part IV of this Schedule, which caused, or might have caused, the death of, or major injury to, any person. **A2–279/22**

Wells

13. Any of the following incidents in relation to a well (other than a well sunk for the purpose of the abstraction of water)— **A2–279/23**
(a) a blow-out (that is to say an uncontrolled flow of well-fluids from a well);
(b) the coming into operation of a blow-out prevention or diversion system to control a flow from a well where normal control procedures fail;
(c) the detection of hydrogen sulphide in the course of operations at a well or in samples of well-fluids from a well where the presence of hydrogen sulphide in the reservoir being drawn on by the well was not anticipated by the responsible person before that detection;
(d) the taking of precautionary measures additional to any contained in the original drilling programme following failure to maintain a planned minimum separation distance between wells drilled from a particular installation; or
(e) the mechanical failure of any safety critical element of a well (and for this purpose the safety critical element of a well is any part of a well whose failure would cause or contribute to, or whose purpose is to prevent or limit the effect of, the unintentional release of fluids from a well or a reservoir being drawn on by a well).

Pipelines or pipeline works

A2–279/24 **14.** The following incidents in respect of a pipeline or pipeline works—

(a) the uncontrolled or accidental escape of anything from, or inrush of anything into, a pipeline which has the potential to cause the death of, major injury or damage to the health of any person or which results in the pipeline being shut down for more than 24 hours;

(b) the unintentional ignition of anything in a pipeline or of anything which, immediately before it was ignited, was in a pipeline;

(c) any damage to any part of a pipeline which has the potential to cause the death of, major injury or damage to the health of any person or which results in the pipeline being shut down for more than 24 hours;

(d) any substantial and unintentional change in the position of a pipeline requiring immediate attention to safeguard the integrity or safety of a pipeline;

(e) any unintentional change in the subsoil or seabed in the vicinity of a pipeline which has the potential to affect the integrity or safety of a pipeline;

(f) any failure of any pipeline isolation device, equipment or system which has the potential to cause the death of, major injury or damage to the health of any person or which results in the pipeline being shut down for more than 24 hours; or

(g) any failure of equipment involved with pipeline works which has the potential to cause the death of, major injury or damage to the health of any person.

Fairground equipment

A2–279/25 **15.** The following incidents on fairground equipment in use or under test—

(a) the failure of any load-bearing part;

(b) the failure of any part designed to support or restrain passengers; or

(c) the derailment or the unintended collision of cars or trains.

Carriage of dangerous substances by road

A2–279/26 **16.**—(1) Any incident involving a road tanker or tank container used for the carriage of a dangerous substance in which—

(a) the road tanker or vehicle carrying the tank container overturns (including turning onto its side);

(b) the tank carrying the dangerous substance is seriously damaged;

(c) there is an uncontrolled release or escape of the dangerous substance being carried; or

(d) there is a fire involving the dangerous substance being carried.

(2) In this paragraph, "carriage", "dangerous substance", "road tanker" and "tank container" have the same meanings as in regulation 2(1) of the Road Traffic (Carriage of Dangerous Substances in Road Tankers and Tank Containers) Regulations 1992.

17.—(1) Any incident involving a vehicle used for the carriage of a dangerous substance, other than a vehicle to which paragraph 16 applies, where there is—

(a) an uncontrolled release or escape of the dangerous substance being carried in such a quantity as to have the potential to cause the death of, or major injury to, any person; or

(b) a fire which involves the dangerous substance being carried.

(2) In this paragraph, "carriage" and "dangerous substance" have the same meaning as in regulation 2(1) of the Road Traffic (Carriage of Dangerous Substances in Packages etc.) Regulations 1992.

DANGEROUS OCCURRENCES WHICH ARE REPORTABLE EXCEPT IN RELATION TO OFFSHORE WORKPLACES

Collapse of building or structure

18. Any unintended collapse or partial collapse of— **A2–279/27**

(a) any building or structure (whether above or below ground) under construction, reconstruction, alteration or demolition which involves a fall of more than 5 tonnes of material;

(b) any floor or wall of any building (whether above or below ground) used as a place of work; or

(c) any false-work.

Explosion or fire

19. An explosion or fire occurring in any plant or premises which results in the stoppage of that plant or as the case may be the suspension of normal work in those premises for more than 24 hours, where the explosion or fire was due to the ignition of any material. **A2–279/28**

Escape of flammable substances

20.—(1) The sudden, uncontrolled release— **A2–279/29**

(a) inside a building—

(i) of 100 kilograms or more of a flammable liquid,

(ii) of 10 kilograms or more of a flammable liquid at a temperature above its normal boiling point, or

(iii) of 10 kilograms or more of a flammable gas; or

(b) in the open air, of 500 kilograms or more of any of the substances referred to in sub-paragraph (a) above.

(2) In this paragraph, "flammable liquid" and "flammable gas" mean respectively a liquid and a gas so classified in accordance with regulation 5(2), (3) or (5) of the Chemicals (Hazard Information and Packaging for Supply) Regulations 1994.

Escape of substances

21. The accidental release or escape of any substance in a quantity sufficient to cause the death, major injury or any other damage to the health of any person.

PART II

DANGEROUS OCCURRENCES WHICH ARE REPORTABLE IN RELATION TO MINES

Fire or ignition of gas

22. The ignition, below ground, of any gas (other than gas in a safety lamp) or of any dust. **A2–279/30**

23. The accidental ignition of any gas in part of a firedamp drainage system on the surface or in an exhauster house.

24. The outbreak of any fire below ground.

25. An incident where any person in consequence of any smoke or any other indication that a fire may have broken out below ground has been caused to leave any place pursuant to either Regulation 11(1) of the Coal and Other Mines (Fire and Rescue) Regulations 1956 or section 79 of the Mines and Quarries Act 1954.

26. The outbreak of any fire on the surface which endangers the operation of any winding or haulage apparatus installed at a shaft or unwalkable outlet or of any mechanically operated apparatus for producing ventilation below ground.

Escape of gas

A2–279/31 **27.** Any violent outburst of gas together with coal or other solid matter into the mine workings except when such outburst is caused intentionally.

Failure of plant or equipment

A2–279/31A **28.** The breakage of any rope, chain, coupling, balance rope, guide rope, suspension gear or other gear used for or in connection with the carrying of persons through any shaft or staple shaft.

29. The breakage or unintentional uncoupling of any rope, chain, coupling, rope tensioning system or other gear used for or in connection with the transport of persons below ground, or breakage of any belt, rope or other gear used for or in connection with a belt conveyor designated by the mine manager as a man-riding conveyor.

30. An incident where any conveyance being used for the carriage of persons is overwound; or any conveyance not being so used is overwound and becomes detached from its winding rope; or any conveyance operated by means of the friction of a rope on a winding sheave is brought to rest by the apparatus provided in the headframe of the shaft or in the part of the shaft below the lowest landing for the time being in use, being apparatus provided for bringing the conveyance to rest in the event of its being overwound.

31. The stoppage of any ventilating apparatus (other than an auxiliary fan) which causes a substantial reduction in ventilation of the mine lasting for a period exceeding 30 minutes, except when for the purpose of planned maintenance.

32. The collapse of any headframe, winding engine house, fan house or storage bunker.

Breathing apparatus

A2–279/32 **33.** At any mine an incident where—

(a) breathing apparatus or a smoke helmet or other apparatus serving the same purpose or a self-rescuer, while being used, fails to function safely or develops a defect likely to affect its safe working; or

(b) immediately after using and arising out of the use of breathing apparatus or a smoke helmet or other apparatus serving the same purpose or a self-rescuer, any person receives first-aid or medical treatment by reason of his unfitness or suspected unfitness at the mine.

Injury by explosion of blasting material etc.

A2–279/33 **34.** An incident in which any person suffers an injury (not being a major injury or one reportable under regulation 3(2)) which results from an explosion or discharge of any blasting material or device within the meaning of section 69(4) of the Mines and Quarries Act 1954 for which he receives first-aid or medical treatment at the mine.

Use of emergency escape apparatus

A2–279/34 **35.** An incident where any apparatus is used (other than for the purpose of training and practice) which has been provided at the mine in accordance with regulation 4 of the Mines (Safety of Exit) Regulations 1988 or where persons leave the mine when apparatus and equipment normally used by persons to leave the mine is unavailable.

Inrush of gas or water

36. Any inrush of noxious or flammable gas from old workings. **A2–279/35**
37. Any inrush of water or material which flows when wet from any source.

Insecure tip

38. Any movement of material or any fire or any other event which indicates that a tip to which Part I of the Mines and Quarries (Tips) Act 1969 applies, is or is likely to become insecure. **A2–279/36**

Locomotives

39. Any incident where an underground locomotive when not used for testing purposes is brought to rest by means other than its safety circuit protective devices or normal service brakes. **A2–279/37**

Falls of ground

40. Any fall of ground, not being part of the normal operations at a mine, which results from a failure of an underground support system and prevents persons travelling through the area affected by the fall or which otherwise exposes them to danger. **A2–279/38**

PART III

DANGEROUS OCCURRENCES WHICH ARE REPORTABLE IN RELATION TO QUARRIES

Collapse of storage bunkers

41. The collapse of any storage bunker. **A2–279/39**

Sinking of craft

42. The sinking of any water-borne craft or hovercraft. **A2–279/40**

Injuries

43.—(1) An incident in which any person suffers an injury (not otherwise reportable under these Regulations, which results from an explosion or from the discharge of any explosives for which he receives first-aid or medical treatment at the quarry. **A2–279/41**

(2) In this paragraph, "explosives" has the same meaning as in regulation 2(1) of the Quarries (Explosives) Regulations 1988.

Projection of substances outside quarry

44. Any incident in which any substance is ascertained to have been projected beyond a quarry boundary as a result of blasting operations in circumstances in which any person was or might have been endangered. **A2–279/42**

Misfires

45. Any misfire, as defined by regulation 2(1) of the Quarries (Explosives) Regulations 1988. **A2–279/43**

Insecure tips

46. Any event (including any movement of material or any fire) which indicates that a tip, to which Part I of the Mines and Quarries (Tips) Act 1969 applies, is or is likely to become insecure. **A2–279/44**

Movement of slopes or faces

A2–279/45 **47.** Any movement or failure of an excavated slope or face which—

(a) has the potential to cause the death of any person; or

(b) adversely affects any building, contiguous land, transport system, footpath, public utility or service, watercourse, reservoir or area of public access.

Explosions or fires in vehicles or plant

A2–279/46 **48.**—(1) Any explosion or fire occurring in any large vehicle or mobile plant which results in the stoppage of that vehicle or plant for more than 24 hours and which affects—

(a) any place where persons normally work; or

(b) the route or egress from such a place.

(2) In this paragraph, "large vehicle or mobile plant" means—

(a) a dump truck having a load capacity of at least 50 tonnes; or

(b) an excavator having a bucket capacity of at least 5 cubic metres.

PART IV

DANGEROUS OCCURRENCES WHICH ARE REPORTABLE IN RESPECT OF RELEVANT TRANSPORT SYSTEMS

Accidents to passenger trains

A2–279/47 **49.** Any collision in which a passenger train collides with another train.

50. Any case where a passenger train or any part of such a train unintentionally leaves the rails.

Accidents not involving passenger trains

A2–279/48 **51.** Any collision between trains, other than one between a passenger train and another train, on a running line where any train sustains damage as a result of the collision, and any such collision in a siding which results in a running line being obstructed.

52. Any derailment, of a train other than a passenger train, on a running line, except a derailment which occurs during shunting operations and does not obstruct any other running line.

53. Any derailment, of a train other than a passenger train, in a siding which results in a running line being obstructed.

Accidents involving any kind of train

A2–279/49 **54.** Any case of a train striking a buffer stop, other than in a siding, where damage is caused to the train.

55. Any case of a train striking any cattle or horse, whether or not damage is caused to the train, or striking any other animal if, in consequence, damage (including damage to the windows of the driver's cab but excluding other damage consisting solely in the breakage of glass) is caused to the train necessitating immediate temporary or permanent repair.

56. Any case of a train on a running line striking or being struck by any object which causes damage (including damage to the windows of the driver's cab but excluding other damage consisting solely in the breakage of glass) necessitating immediate temporary or permanent repair or which might have been liable to derail the train.

57. Any case of a train, other than one on a railway, striking or being struck by a road vehicle.

58. Any case of a passenger train, or any other train not fitted with continuous self-applying brakes, becoming unintentionally divided.

59.—(1) Any of the following classes of accident which occurs or is discovered whilst the train is on a running line—

(a) the failure of an axle;

(b) the failure of a wheel or tyre, including a tyre loose on its wheel;

(c) the failure of a rope or the fastenings thereof or of the winding plant or equipment involved in working an incline;

(d) any fire, severe electrical arcing or fusing in or on any part of a passenger train or a train carrying dangerous goods;

(e) in the case of any train other than a passenger train, any severe electrical arcing or fusing, or any fire which was extinguished by a fire-fighting service; or

(f) any other failure of any part of a train which is likely to cause an accident to that or any other train or to kill or injure any person.

(2) In this paragraph "dangerous goods" has the same meaning as in regulation 1(2) of the Carriage of Dangerous Goods by Rail Regulations 1994.

Accidents and incidents at level crossings

60. Any case of a train striking a road vehicle or gate at a level crossing. **A2–279/50**

61. Any case of a train running onto a level crossing when not authorised to do so.

62. A failure of the equipment at a level crossing which could endanger users of the road or path crossing the railway.

Accidents involving the permanent way and other works on or connected with a relevant transport system

63. The failure of a rail in a running line or of a rack rail, which results in— **A2–279/51**

(a) a complete fracture of the rail through its cross-section; or

(b) in a piece becoming detached from the rail which necessitates an immediate stoppage of traffic or the immediate imposition of a speed restriction lower than that currently in force.

64. A buckle of a running line which necessitates an immediate stoppage of traffic or the immediate imposition of a speed restriction lower than that currently in force.

65. Any case of an aircraft or a vehicle of any kind landing on, running into or coming to rest foul of the line, or damaging the line, which causes damage which obstructs the line or which damages any railway equipment at a level crossing.

66. The runaway of an escalator, lift or passenger conveyor.

67. Any fire or severe arcing or fusing which seriously affects the functioning of signalling equipment.

68. Any fire affecting the permanent way or works of a relevant transport system which necessitates the suspension of services over any line, or the closure of any part of a station or signal box or other premises, for a period—

(a) in the case of a fire affecting any part of a relevant transport system below ground, of more than 30 minutes, and

(b) in any other case, of more than 1 hour.

69. Any other fire which causes damage which has the potential to affect the running of a relevant transport system.

Accidents involving failure to the works on or connected with a relevant transport system

A2–279/52 **70.**—(1) The following classes of accident where they are likely either to cause an accident to a train or to endanger any person—

(a) the failure of a tunnel, bridge, viaduct, culvert, station, or other structure or any part thereof including the fixed electrical equipment of an electrified relevant transport system;

(b) any failure in the signalling system which endangers or which has the potential to endanger the safe passage of trains other than a failure of a traffic light controlling the movement of vehicles on a road;

(c) a slip of a cutting or of an embankment;

(d) flooding of the permanent way;

(e) the striking of a bridge by a vessel or by a road vehicle or its load; or

(f) the failure of any other portion of the permanent way or works not specified above.

Incidents of serious congestion

A2–279/53 **71.** Any case where planned procedures or arrangements have been activated in order to control risks arising from an incident of undue passenger congestion at a station unless that congestion has been relieved within a period of time allowed for by those procedures or arrangements.

Incidents of signals passed without authority

A2–279/54 **72.**—(1) Any case where a train, travelling on a running line or entering a running line from a siding, passes without authority a signal displaying a stop aspect unless—

(a) the stop aspect was not displayed in sufficient time for the driver to stop safely at the signal; or

(b) the line is equipped with automatic train protection equipment which is in operation.

(2) In this paragraph "automatic train protection equipment" means equipment which automatically controls the speed of a train, either by bringing it to a halt or reducing its speed, in the event that the train passes a signal without authority or exceeds a prescribed speed limit.

PART V

DANGEROUS OCCURRENCES WHICH ARE REPORTABLE IN RESPECT OF AN OFFSHORE WORKPLACE

Release of petroleum hydrocarbon

A2–279/55 **73.** Any unintentional release of petroleum hydrocarbon on or from an offshore installation which—

(a) results in—
    (i) a fire or explosion; or
    (ii) the taking of action to prevent or limit the consequences of a potential fire or explosion; or

(b) has the potential to cause death or major injury to any person.

Fire or explosion

A2–279/56 **74.** Any fire or explosion at an offshore installation, other than one to which paragraph 73 above applies, which results in the stoppage of plant or the suspension of normal work.

Release or escape of dangerous substances

75. The uncontrolled or unintentional release or escape of any substance (other than petroleum hydrocarbon) on or from an offshore installation which has the potential to cause the death of, major injury to or damage to the health of any person. **A2–279/57**

Collapses

76. Any unintended collapse of any offshore installation or any unintended collapse of any part thereof or any plant thereon which jeopardises the overall structural integrity of the installation. **A2–279/58**

Dangerous occurrences

77. Any of the following occurrences having the potential to cause death or major injury— **A2–279/59**

(a) the failure of equipment required to maintain a floating offshore installation on station;
(b) the dropping of any object on an offshore installation or on an attendant vessel or into the water adjacent to an installation or vessel; or
(c) damage to or on an offshore installation caused by adverse weather conditions.

Collisions

78. Any collision between a vessel or aircraft and an offshore installation which results in damage to the installation, the vessel or the aircraft. **A2–279/60**

79. Any occurrence with the potential for a collision between a vessel and an offshore installation where, had a collision occurred, it would have been liable to jeopardise the overall structural integrity of the offshore installation.

Subsidence or collapse of seabed

80. Any subsidence or local collapse of the seabed likely to affect the foundations of an offshore installation or the overall structural integrity of an offshore installation. **A2–279/61**

Loss of stability or buoyancy

81. Any incident involving loss or stability or buoyancy of a floating offshore installation. **A2–279/62**

Evacuation

82. Any evacuation (other than one arising out of an incident reportable under any other provision of these Regulations) of an offshore installation, in whole or part, in the interests of safety. **A2–279/63**

Falls into water

83. Any case of a person falling more than 2 metres into water (unless the fall results in death or injury required to be reported under sub-paragraphs (a)–(d) of regulation 3(1)). **A2–279/64**

SCHEDULE 3 **Regulation 5(1) and (2)**

REPORTABLE DISEASES

PART I

OCCUPATIONAL DISEASES

Column 1	Column 2
Diseases	**Activities**
Conditions due to physical agents and the physical demands of work	
1. Inflammation, ulceration or malignant disease of the skin due to ionising radiation 2. Malignant disease of the bones due to ionising radiation. 3. Blood dyscrasia due to ionising radiation.	Work with ionising radiation.
4. Cataract due to electromagnetic radiation.	Work involving exposure to electromagnetic radiation (including radiant heat).
5. Decompression illness. 6. Barotrauma resulting in lung or other organ damage. 7. Dysbaric osteonecrosis.	Work involving breathing gases at increased pressure (including diving).
8. Cramp of the hand or forearm due to repetitive movements.	Work involving prolonged periods of handwriting, typing or other repetitive movements of the fingers, hand or arm.
9. Subcutaneous cellulitis of the hand (*beat hand*).	Physically demanding work causing severe or prolonged friction or pressure on the hand.
10. Bursitis or subcutaneous cellulitis arising at or about the knee due to severe or prolonged external friction or pressure at or about the knee (*beat knee*).	Physically demanding work causing severe or prolonged friction or pressure at or about the knee.
11. Bursitis or subcutaneous cellulitis arising at or about the elbow due to severe or prolonged external friction or pressure at or about the elbow (*beat elbow*).	Physically demanding work causing severe or prolonged friction or pressure at or about the elbow.

Column 1	Column 2
Diseases	**Activities**
12. Traumatic inflammation of the tendons of the hand or forearm or of the associated tendon sheaths.	Physically demanding work, frequent or repeated movements, constrained postures or extremes of extension or flexion of the hand or wrist.
13. Carpal tunnel syndrome.	Work involving the use of hand-held vibrating tools.
14. Hand-arm vibration syndrome.	Work involving: (a) the use of chain saws, brush cutters or hand-held or hand-fed circular saws in forestry or woodworking; (b) the use of hand-held rotary tools in grinding material or in sanding or polishing metal; (c) the holding of material being ground or metal being sanded or polished by rotary tools; (d) the use of hand-held percussive metal-working tools or the holding of metal being worked upon by percussive tools in connection with riveting, caulking, chipping, hammering, fettling or swaging; (e) the use of hand-held powered percussive drills or hand-held powered percussive hammers in mining, quarrying or demolition, or on roads or footpaths (including road construction); or (f) the holding of material being worked upon by pounding machines in shoe manufacture.
Infections due to biological agents	
15. Anthrax.	(a) Work involving handling infected animals, their products or packaging containing infected material; or (b) work on infected sites.
16. Brucellosis.	Work involving contact with: (a) animals or their carcasses (including any parts thereof) infected by brucella or the untreated products of same; or (b) laboratory specimens or vaccines of or containing brucella.

Column 1	Column 2
Diseases	**Activities**
17. (a) Avian chlamydiosis.	Work involving contact with birds infected with chlamydia psittaci, or the remains or untreated products of such birds.
(b) Ovine chlamydiosis.	Work involving contact with sheep infected with chlamydia psittaci or the remains or untreated products of such sheep.
18. Hepatitis.	Work involving contact with: (a) human blood or human blood products; or (b) any source of viral hepatitis.
19. Legionellosis.	Work on or near cooling systems which are located in the workplace and use water; or work on hot water service systems located in the workplace which are likely to be a source of contamination.
20. Leptospirosis.	(a) Work in places which are or are liable to be infested by rats, field-mice, voles or other small mammals; (b) work at dog kennels or involving the care or handling of dogs; or (c) work involving contact with bovine animals or their meat products or pigs or their meat products.
21. Lyme disease.	Work involving exposure to ticks (including in particular work by forestry workers, rangers, dairy farmers, game keepers and other persons engaged in countryside management).
22. Q fever.	Work involving contact with animals, their remains or their untreated products.
23. Rabies.	Work involving handling or contact with infected animals.
24. Streptococcus suis.	Work involving contact with pigs infected with streptococcus suis, or with the carcasses, products or residues of pigs so affected.
25. Tetanus.	Work involving contact with soil likely to be contaminated by animals.

Column 1	Column 2
Diseases	**Activities**
26. Tuberculosis.	Work with persons, animals, human or animal remains or any other material which might be a source of infection.
27. Any infection reliably attributable to the performance of the work specified in the entry opposite hereto.	Work with micro-organisms; work with live or dead human beings in the course of providing any treatment or service or in conducting any investigation involving exposure to blood or body fluids; work with animals or any potentially infected material derived from any of the above.
Conditions due to substances	
28. Poisonings by any of the following: (a) acrylamide monomer; (b) arsenic or one of its compounds; (c) benzene or a homologue of benzene; (d) beryllium or one of its compounds; (e) cadmium or one of its compounds; (f) carbon disulphide; (g) diethylene dioxide (dioxan); (h) ethylene oxide; (i) lead or one of its compounds; (j) manganese or one of its compounds; (k) mercury or one of its compounds; (l) methyl bromide; (m) nitrochlorobenzene, or a nitro- or amino- or chloro-derivative of benzene or of a homologue of benzene; (n) oxides of nitrogen; (o) phosphorus or one of its compounds.	Any activity.
29. Cancer of a bronchus or lung.	(a) Work in or about a building where nickel is produced by decomposition of a gaseous nickel compound or where any industrial process which is ancillary or incidental to that process is carried on; or

Column 1	Column 2
Diseases	**Activities**
	(b) work involving exposure to bis(chloromethyl) ether or any electrolytic chromium processes (excluding passivation) which involve hexavalent chromium compounds, chromate production or zinc chromate pigment manufacture.
30. Primary carcinoma of the lung where there is accompanying evidence of silicosis.	Any occupation in: (a) glass manufacture; (b) sandstone tunnelling or quarrying; (c) the pottery industry; (d) metal ore mining; (e) slate quarrying or slate production; (f) clay mining; (g) the use of siliceous materials as abrasives; (h) foundry work; (i) granite tunnelling or quarrying; or (j) stone cutting or masonry.
31. Cancer of the urinary tract.	1. Work involving exposure to any of the following substances: (a) beta-naphthylamine or methylene-bis-orthochloroaniline; (b) diphenyl substituted by at least one nitro or primary amino group or by at least one nitro and primary amino group (including benzidine); (c) any of the substances mentioned in sub-paragraph (b) above if further ring substituted by halogeno, methyl or methoxy groups, but not by other groups; or (d) the salts of any of the substances mentioned in sub-paragraphs (a) to (c) above. 2. The manufacture of auramine or megenta.
32. Bladder cancer.	Work involving exposure to aluminium smelting using the Soderberg process.

Column 1	Column 2
Diseases	**Activities**
33. Angiosarcoma of the liver.	(a) Work in or about machinery or apparatus used for the polymerisation of vinyl chloride monomer, a process which, for the purposes of this sub-paragraph, comprises all operations up to and including the drying of the slurry produced by the polymerisation and the packaging of the dried product; or (b) work in a building or structure in which any part of the process referred to in the foregoing sub-paragraph takes place.
34. Peripheral neuropathy.	Work involving the use or handling of or exposure to the fumes of or vapour containing n-hexane or methyl n-butyl ketone.
35. Chrome ulceration of: (a) the nose or throat; or (b) the skin of the hands or forearm.	Work involving exposure to chromic acid or to any other chromium compound.
36. Folliculitis. 37. Acne. 38. Skin cancer.	Work involving exposure to mineral oil, tar, pitch or arsenic.
39. Pneumoconiosis (excluding asbestosis).	1. (a) The mining, quarrying or working of silica rock or the working of dried quartzose sand, any dry deposit or residue of silica or any dry admixture containing such materials (including any activity in which any of the aforesaid operations are carried out incidentally to the mining or quarrying of other minerals or to the manufacture of articles containing crushed or ground silica rock); or (b) the handling of any of the materials specified in the foregoing sub-paragraph in or incidentally to any of the operations mentioned therein or substantial exposure to the dust arising from such operations.

Column 1	Column 2
Diseases	**Activities**
	2. The breaking, crushing or grinding of flint, the working or handling of broken, crushed or ground flint or materials containing such flint or substantial exposure to the dust arising from any of such operations.
	3. Sand blasting by means of compressed air with the use of quartzose sand or crushed silica rock or flint or substantial exposure to the dust arising from such sand blasting.
	4. Work in a foundry or the performance of, or substantial exposure to the dust arising from, any of the following operations: (a) the freeing of steel castings from adherent siliceous substance or; (b) the freeing of metal castings from adherent siliceous substance: (i) by blasting with an abrasive propelled by compressed air, steam or a wheel, or (ii) by the use of power-driven tools
	5. The manufacture of china or earthenware (including sanitary earthenware, electrical earthenware and earthenware tiles) and any activity involving substantial exposure to the dust arising therefrom.
	6. The grinding of mineral graphite or substantial exposure to the dust arising from such grinding.
	7. The dressing of granite or any igneous rock by masons, the crushing of such materials or substantial exposure to the dust arising from such operations.
	8. The use or preparation for use of an abrasive wheel or substantial exposure to the dust arising therefrom.
	9. (a) Work underground in any mine in which one of the objects of the mining operations is the getting of any material;

Column 1	Column 2
Diseases	**Activities**
	(b) the working or handling above ground at any coal or tin mine or of any materials extracted therefrom or any operation incidental thereto; (c) the trimming of coal in any ship, barge, lighter, dock or harbour or at any wharf or quay; or (d) the sawing, splitting or dressing of slate or any operation incidental thereto.
	10. The manufacture or work incidental to the manufacture of carbon electrodes by an industrial undertaking for use in the electrolytic extraction of aluminium from aluminium oxide and any activity involving substantial exposure to the dust therefrom.
	11. Boiler scaling or substantial exposure to the dust arising therefrom.
40. Byssinosis.	The spinning or manipulation of raw or waste cotton or flax or the weaving of cotton or flax, carried out in each case in a room in a factory, together with any other work carried out in such a room.
41. Mesothelioma. 42. Lung Cancer. 43. Asbestosis.	(a) The working or handling of asbestos or any admixture of asbestos; (b) the manufacture or repair of asbestos textiles or other articles containing or composed of asbestos; (c) the cleaning of any machinery or plant used in any of the foregoing operations and of any chambers, fixtures and appliances for the collection of asbestos dust; or (d) substantial exposure to the dust arising from any of the foregoing operations.
44. Cancer of the nasal cavity or associated air sinuses.	1. (a) Work in or about a building where wooden furniture is manufactured; (b) work in a building used for the manufacture of footwear or components of footwear made wholly or partly of leather or fibre board; or

Column 1	Column 2
Diseases	**Activities**
	(c) work at a place used wholly or mainly for the repair of footwear made wholly or partly of leather or fibre board.
	2. Work in or about a factory building where nickel is produced by decomposition of a gaseous nickel compound or in any process which is ancillary or incidental thereto.
45. Occupational dermatitis.	Work involving exposure to any of the following agents: (a) epoxy resin systems; (b) formaldehyde and its resins; (c) metalworking fluids; (d) chromate (hexavalent and derived from trivalent chromium); (e) cement, plaster or concrete; (f) acrylates and methacrylates; (g) colophony (rosin) and its modified products; (h) glutaraldehyde; (i) mercaptobenzothiazole, thiurams, substituted paraphenylene-diamines and related rubber processing chemicals; (j) biocides, anti-bacterials, preservatives or disinfectants; (k) organic solvents; (l) antibiotics and other pharmaceuticals and therapeutic agents; (m) strong acids, strong alkalis, strong solutions (*e.g.* brine) and oxidising agents including domestic bleach or reducing agents; (n) hairdressing products including in particular dyes, shampoos, bleaches and permanent waving solutions; (o) soaps and detergents; (p) plants and plant-derived material including in particular the daffodil, tulip and chrysanthemum families, the parsley family (carrots, parsnips, parsley and celery), garlic and onion, hardwoods and the pine family; (q) fish, shell-fish or meat; (r) sugar or flour; or

Column 1	Column 2
Diseases	**Activities**
	(s) any other known irritant or sensitising agent including in particular any chemical bearing the warning "may cause sensitisation by skin contact" or "irritating to the skin".
46. Extrinsic alveolitis (including farmer's lung).	Exposure to moulds, fungal spores or heterologous proteins during work in: (a) agriculture, horticulture, forestry, cultivation of edible fungi or malt-working; (b) loading, unloading or handling mouldy vegetable matter or edible fungi whilst same is being stored; (c) caring for or handling birds; or (d) handling bagasse.
47. Occupational asthma.	Work involving exposure to any of the following agents: (a) isocyanates; (b) platinum salts; (c) fumes or dust arising from the manufacture, transport or use of hardening agents (including epoxy resin curing agents) based on phthalic anhydride, tetrachlorophthalic anhydride, trimellitic anhydride or triethylene-tetramine; (d) fumes arising from the use of rosin as a soldering flux; (e) proteolytic enzymes; (f) animals including insects and other arthropods used for the purposes of research or education or in laboratories; (g) dusts arising from the sowing, cultivation, harvesting, drying, handling, milling, transport or storage of barley, oats, rye, wheat or maize or the handling, milling, transport or storage of meal or flour made therefrom; (h) antibiotics; (i) cimetidine; (j) wood dust; (k) ispaghula; (l) castor bean dust; (m) ipecacuanha;

Column 1	Column 2
Diseases	**Activities**
	(n) azodicarbonamide; (o) animals including insects and other arthropods (whether in their larval forms or not) used for the purposes of pest control or fruit cultivation or the larval forms of animals used for the purposes of research or education or in laboratories; (p) glutaraldehyde; (q) persulphate salts or henna; (r) crustaceans or fish or products arising from these in the food processing industry; (s) reactive dyes; (t) soya bean; (u) tea dust; (v) green coffee bean dust; (w) fumes from stainless steel welding; (x) any other sensitising agent, including in particular any chemical bearing the warning "may cause sensitisation by inhalation".

PART II

DISEASES ADDITIONALLY REPORTABLE IN RESPECT OF OFFSHORE WORKPLACES

A2–279/66

48. Chickenpox.
49. Cholera.
50. Diphtheria.
51. Dysentery (amoebic or bacillary).
52. Acute encephalitis.
53. Erysipelas.
54. Food poisoning.
55. Legionellosis.
56. Malaria.
57. Measles.
58. Meningitis.
59. Meningococcal septicaemia (without meningitis).
60. Mumps.
61. Paratyphoid fever.
62. Plague.
63. Acute poliomyelitis.
64. Rabies.
65. Rubella.
66. Scarlet fever.
67. Tetanus.
68. Tuberculosis.
69. Typhoid fever.
70. Typhus.
71. Viral haemorrhagic fever.
72. Viral hepatitis.

SCHEDULE 5

Regulation 8

ADDITIONAL PROVISIONS RELATING TO MINES AND QUARRIES

A2–279/67 **1.** In this Schedule, unless the context otherwise requires—
"appropriate person" means—

(a) in the case of a coal mine, the responsible person or a person appointed in the management structure of that mine established pursuant to paragraph (1) of regulation 10 of the Management and Administration of Safety and Health at Mines Regulations 1993;
(b) in the case of any other mine, the responsible person;
(c) in the case of a quarry—
 (i) the responsible person, or
 (ii) (where there is a sole manager) that manager, or
 (iii) (where there are two or more managers) the manager of the part of the quarry where the accident or dangerous occurrence happened, or
 (iv) any person who is for the time being treated for the purposes of the Mines and Quarries Act 1954 as such a manager;

"nominated person" means the person (if any) who is for the time being nominated—
(a) in a case where there is an association or body representative of a majority of the total number of persons employed at a mine or quarry, by that association or body;
(b) in any other case, jointly by associations or bodies which are together representative of such a majority,

to receive on behalf of the persons so employed notices under this Schedule.

2. Where at a mine or a quarry any person, as a result of an accident arising out of or in connection with work, dies or suffers any major injury, or where there is a dangerous occurrence, the responsible person shall—
(a) forthwith notify the nominated person thereof by the quickest practicable means; and
(b) within 7 days send a report thereof to the nominated person on a form approved for the purposes of regulation 3.

3. Where there is a non-fatal injury to any person at a mine or quarry which is reported in accordance with paragraph 2, after which that person dies and his death is a result of the accident then as soon as it comes to his knowledge the responsible person shall give notice of the death to the nominated person.

4.—(1) Where there is an accident or dangerous occurrence in relation to which paragraph 2 applies no person shall disturb the place where it happened or tamper with anything at that place before—
(a) the expiration of 3 clear days after the matter to which paragraph 2 applies has been notified in accordance with these Regulations; or
(b) the place has been visited by an inspector and by workmen's inspectors exercising the powers conferred on them by section 123 of the Mines and Quarries Act 1954;

whichever is the sooner.

(2) Nothing in sub-paragraph (1) of this paragraph shall prohibit the doing of anything by or with the consent of an inspector.

(3) The requirements of sub-paragraph (1) of this paragraph shall not apply to an accident or to a dangerous occurrence if an appropriate person—
(a) has taken adequate steps to ascertain that disturbing the site—
 (i) is unlikely to prejudice any investigation by an inspector into the circumstances of the accident or dangerous occurrence, and
 (ii) is necessary to secure the safety of any person at the mine or quarry or to avoid disrupting the normal working thereof; and
(b) (except in the case of a non-fatal accident or a dangerous occurrence, where the nominated person or any person designated by that nominated person pursuant to this sub-paragraph cannot be contacted within a reasonable time) has notified the nominated person, or any person designated in writing by the nominated person to receive any such notification, of the proposed disturbance, and gives

such a person a reasonable opportunity to visit the site before it is disturbed; and

(c) has taken adequate steps to ensure that there is obtained such information as will enable a full and accurate plan to be prepared forthwith, which plan shall show the position of any equipment or other item relevant to the accident or dangerous occurrence immediately after it happened; and

(d) ensures that any equipment or other item relevant to the accident or dangerous occurrence is kept as it was immediately after the incident until an inspector agrees that it may be disposed of.

(4) The person who has taken the steps referred to in sub-paragraph (3)(c) of this paragraph shall ensure that the plan referred to in that sub-paragraph is signed by the person who prepared it and bears the date on which it was prepared, and that a copy of that plan is supplied on request to any inspector or to the nominated person.

SCHEDULE 7 **Regulation 10(4)**

ENACTMENTS OR INSTRUMENTS REQUIRING THE NOTIFICATION OF EVENTS WHICH ARE NOT REQUIRED TO BE NOTIFIED OR REPORTED UNDER THESE REGULATIONS

1 Title of Enactment or Instrument	**2 Reference**
The Explosives Act 1875.	1875 c. 17.
The Nuclear Installations Act 1965 and Orders and Regulations made or to be made thereunder.	1965 c. 57.
The Merchant Shipping Act 1988 and Orders and Regulations made or to be made thereunder.	1988 c. 12.
The Ionising Radiations Regulations 1985.	S.I. 1985/1333.
The Air Navigation (Investigation of Air Accidents involving Civil and Military Aircraft or Installations) Regulations 1986.	S.I. 1986/1953.
The Civil Aviation (Investigation of Air Accidents) Regulations 1989.	S.I. 1989/2062.

A2–323A The Social Security (Industrial Industries) (Prescribed Diseases) Regulations 1985 have been further amended by S.I. 1997 No. 810.

The Social Security (Industrial Injuries) (Miscellaneous Amendments) Regulations 1997

(1997 No. 810)

Amendment of Schedule 1 to the Prescribed Diseases Regulations

6.—(1) Part I of Schedule 1 to the Prescribed Diseases Regulations (list of prescribed diseases and the occupations for which they are prescribed), shall be amended in accordance with the following paragraphs of this regulation.

(2) In column 2 for the entry relating to disease D3 (diffuse mesothelioma) there shall be substituted the following entry—

"Exposure to asbestos, asbestos dust or any admixture of asbestos at a level above that commonly found in the environment at large.".

(3) In column 1 of the entry relating to disease D8 (primary carcinoma of the lung, etc.) for sub-paragraph (b) there shall be substituted the following sub-paragraph—

"(b) unilateral or bilateral diffuse pleural thickening extending to a thickness of 5mm or more at any point within the area affected as measured by a plain chest radiograph (not being a computerised tomography scan or other form of imaging) which—

(i) in the case of unilateral diffuse pleural thickening, covers 50% or more of the area of the chest wall of the lung affected; or

(ii) in the case of bilateral diffuse pleural thickening, covers 25% or more of the combined area of the chest wall of both lungs.".

(4) In column 1 for the entry relating to disease D9 (bilateral diffuse pleural thickening) there shall be substituted the following entry—

"**D9.** Unilateral or bilateral diffuse pleural thickening extending to a thickness of 5mm or more at any point within the area affected as measured by a plain chest radiograph (not being a computerised tomography scan or other form of imaging) which—

(i) in the case of unilateral diffuse pleural thickening, covers 50% or more of the area of the chest wall of the lung affected; or

(ii) in the case of bilateral diffuse pleural thickening, covers 25% or more of the combined area of the chest wall of both lungs.".

(5) For the entry relating to disease D12 (chronic bronchitis and emphysema) there shall be substituted the following entry—

"**D12.** Except in the circumstances specified in regulation 2(d)— (a) chronic bronchitis; or (b) emphysema; or (c) both, where there is accompanying evidence of a forced expiratory volume in one second (measured from the position of maximum inspiration with the claimant making maximum effort) which is— (i) at least one litre below the mean value predicted in accordance with "Lung Function: Assessment and Application in Medicine" by J.E. Cotes, (5th ed., 1994) published at Oxford by Blackwell Scientific Publications Limited (ISBN 0–632–03926–9) for a person of the claimant's age, height and sex; or (ii) less than one litre.	Exposure to coal dust by reason of working underground in a coal mine for a period or periods amounting in aggregate to at least 20 years (whether before or after 5th July 1948) and any such period or periods shall include a period or periods of incapacity while engaged in such an occupation.

A2–325A Add: The Staffordshire (Coroners) Order 1997, S.I. 1997 No. 492.

The Staffordshire (Coroners) Order 1997

(1997 No. 492)

1.—(1) This Order may be cited as the Staffordshire (Coroners) Order 1997 and shall come into force on 1st April 1997.

(2) In this Order "the 1988 Act" means the Coroners Act 1988.

2.—(1) There shall be a single coroner's district, called the Stoke-on-Trent and North Staffordshire Coroner's District, for the County of Stoke-on-Trent (which county comes into existence on 1st April 1997 by virtue of article 3(2) of the Staffordshire (City of Stoke-on-Trent) (Structural and Boundary Changes) Order 1995 and for so much of the County of Staffordshire as is not included in the South Staffordshire Coroner's District.

(2) The Council of the City of Stoke-on-Trent shall be the relevant council within the meaning of section 1(1A) of the 1988 Act for the coroner's district constituted by paragraph (1) above.

(3) The person who, at 31st March 1997, is the coroner for the existing North Staffordshire Coroner's District shall be deemed on 1st April 1997 to be appointed coroner for the coroner's district constituted by paragraph (1) above.

(4) Any agreement between the person to whom paragraph (3) applies and Staffordshire County Council (as the relevant council for the purposes of section 1 of the 1988 Act prior to 1st April 1997) as to his salary and pension as a coroner shall be deemed on and after 1st April 1997 to have effect as if originally made between him and the Stoke-on-Trent City Council.

(5) Any person who, at 31st March 1997, is a deputy or assistant deputy coroner for the existing North Staffordshire Coroner's District shall be deemed on 1st April 1997 to be appointed deputy or, as the case may be, assistant deputy coroner for the coroner's district constituted by paragraph (1) above.

3.—(1) On 1st April 1997, any process issued, order made, direction given, inquest begun or other thing done by or to the coroner for the existing North Staffordshire Coroner's District shall be deemed to have been issued, made, given, begun or done by or to the coroner for the coroner's district constituted by article 2(1) above.

(2) All documents, exhibits, registers and other things in the custody of the coroner for the existing North Staffordshire Coroner's District in connection with inquests or post-mortem investigations shall be transferred to the coroner for the coroner's district constituted by article 2(1) above.

(3) In this article "coroner" includes any deputy coroner or assistant deputy coroner.

A2–325B Add: The Wiltshire (Coroners) Order 1997, S.I. 1997 No. 493.

The Wiltshire (Coroners) Order 1997

(1997 No. 493)

1. This Order may be cited as the Wiltshire (Coroners) Order 1997 and shall come into force on 1st April 1997.

2.—(1) There shall be a single coroner's district, called the Wiltshire and Thamesdown Coroner's District, for the Counties of Wiltshire and Thamesdown (which county comes into existence on 1st April 1997 by virtue of article 8(2) of the Wiltshire (Borough of Thamesdown) (Structural Change) Order 1995.

(2) The Council of the County of Wiltshire shall be the relevant council within the meaning of section 1(1A) of the Coroners Act 1988 for the coroner's district constituted by paragraph (1) above.

(3) The person who, at 31st March 1997, is the coroner for the County of Wiltshire shall be deemed on 1st April 1997 to be appointed coroner for the coroner's district constituted by paragraph (1) above.

(4) Any person who, at 31st March 1997, is a deputy or assistant deputy coroner for the County of Wiltshire shall be deemed on 1st April 1997 to be appointed deputy or, as the case may be, assistant deputy coroner for the coroner's district constituted by paragraph (1) above.

3.—(1) On 1st April 1997, any process issued, order made, direction given, inquest begun or other thing done by or to the coroner for the County of Wiltshire shall be deemed to have been issued, made, given, begun or done by or to the coroner for the coroner's district constituted by article 2(1) above.

(2) All documents, exhibits, registers and other things in the custody of the coroner for the County of Wiltshire in connection with inquests or post-mortem investigations shall be transferred to the coroner for the coroner's district constituted by article 2(1) above.

(3) In this article "coroner" includes any deputy coroner or assistant deputy coroner.

Add: The York and North Yorkshire (Coroners) Order 1996, S.I. 1996 No. 659. **A2–325C**

The York and North Yorkshire (Coroners) Order 1996

(1996 No. 659)

1.—(1) This Order may be cited as the York and North Yorkshire (Coroners) Order 1996.

(2) In this Order "the 1988 Act" means the Coroners Act 1988.

2. Without prejudice to any order made under section 4(2) of the 1988 Act after the coming into force of this Order, on 1st April 1996—

(a) there shall be added to the Claro Coroner's District of the County of North Yorkshire the following parishes of the District of Selby, namely, Barlby, Cliffe, Escrick, Hemingbrough, Kelfield, North Duffield, Riccall, Skipwith, Stillingfleet and Thorganby; and

(b) there shall be added to the Scarborough and Ryedale Coroner's District of that County the following parishes of—

  (i) the District of Hambleton, namely, Aldwark, Alne, Brafferton, Brandsby cum Stearsby, Crayke, Dalby cum Skewsby, Easingwold, Farlington, Flawith, Helperby, Huby, Linton on Ouse, Marton cum Moxby, Myton on Swale, Newton on Ouse, Overton, Raskelf, Shipton by Beningbrough, Stillington, Sutton on Forest, Tholthorpe, Thormanby, Tollerton, Whenby and Youlton; and

  (ii) the District of Ryedale, namely, Barton le Willows, Buttercrambe with Bossall, Claxton, Crambe, Flaxton, Foston, Gate Helmsley, Harton, Lillings Ambo, Sand Hutton, Sheriff Hutton with Cornbrough, Stittenham, Thornton le Clay, Upper Helmsley and Warthill.

3.—(1) The person who, at 31st March 1996, is the coroner for the existing York Coroner's District of the County of North Yorkshire by virtue of having been appointed for or assigned to that district shall be deemed on 1st April 1996 to be appointed coroner for the County of York (which comes into existence on 1st April 1996 by virtue of the North Yorkshire (District of York) (Structural and Boundary Changes) Order 1995).

(2) Any agreement between the person to whom paragraph (1) applies and North Yorkshire County Council (as the relevant council for the purposes of section 1 of the 1988 Act prior to 1st April 1996) as to his salary and pension as a coroner shall be deemed on and after 1st April 1996 to have effect as if originally made between him and York District Council.

(3) Any person who, at 31st March 1996, is a deputy or assistant deputy coroner for the existing York Coroner's District shall be deemed on 1st April 1996 to be appointed deputy or, as the case may be, assistant deputy coroner for the County of York.

4.—(1) On 1st April 1996, any process issued, order made, direction given, inquest begun or other thing done by or to the coroner for the existing York Coroner's District of the County of North Yorkshire shall be deemed to have been issued, made, given, begun or done by or to the coroner for the County of York.

(2) All documents, exhibits, registers and other things in the custody of the coroner appointed for or assigned to the existing York Coroner's District of the County of North Yorkshire in connection with inquests or post-mortem examinations shall be transferred to the coroner for the County of York.

(3) In this article "coroner" includes any deputy coroner or assistant deputy coroner.

Appendix 5

SCHEDULE OF FEES AND ALLOWANCES

An updated Schedule was issued by the Secretary of State on May 9, 1995. The text is the same as that in Appendix 5 (with some additions, indicated below), and therefore the current figures are shown below using the same numbering.

(1) Jurors and ordinary witnesses

(a) *Subsistence allowance*

(i) up to 5 hours	£2.10
(ii) 5–10 hours	£4.25
(iii) over 10 hours	£9.30

(b) *Overnight allowance*

(i) within 5 miles of Charing Cross	£65.80
(ii) elsewhere	£63.15

(c) *Financial loss*

(i) period of loss not exceeding 4 hours	£22.40
(ii) period of loss exceeding 4 hours	£44.80

(2) Professional witnesses

Professional witness allowance

EITHER	
(a) compensation (no replacement)	
(i) absence up to 2 hours	£52.20
(ii) absence 2–4 hours	£78.30
(iii) absence 4–6 hours	£117.40
(iv) absence over 6 hours	£156.50
OR	
(b) cost of replacement	
(i) absence up to 4 hours	£78.30
(ii) absence over 4 hours	£156.50
(c) Overnight allowance	
(i) within 5 miles of Charing Cross	£59.90
(ii) elsewhere	£54.55

(3) Expert witness

(b) *Overnight allowance*

As for Professional witness, above.

(4) Post-mortem fees

(a) ordinary examination	£68.00
(b) examination including additional skills	£190.20

(c) allowances for travelling to or from examination: these now depend on motor car engine capacity, and the mileage, as shown below (rates in pence per mile):

	Up to 5000 miles	Over 5000 miles
Up to 1500cc	35.7	17.0
1500cc–2000cc	40.0	21.0
Over 2000cc	43.0	27.0

(5) Travelling allowances for all jurors and witnesses

(c) allowances for travelling to or from inquest by private conveyance: these now depend, for cars as well as motor cycles, on engine capacity as well as mileage, as shown below (rates in pence per mile):

(i) Motor cycles	
(a) public transport rate	23.8
(b) standard rate	25.4
(ii) Motor cars	
(a) public transport rate	23.8
(b) standard rate:	36.0

Appendix 6

TREASURE ACT 1996: CODE OF PRACTICE

F. Secretary of State's Power to Disclaim Objects

45. Under Section 6 of the Act the Secretary of State has the power to disclaim objects that have been submitted as potential treasure. Since it is anticipated that museums will not wish to acquire all of the objects that will qualify as treasure, this provision means that it will not normally be necessary to hold treasure inquests in such cases. **A6–01**

46. Although the Secretary of State will be able to use this power at any stage once a find of potential treasure has been reported to the coroner, the normal procedure will be as follows. All finds of treasure must to be reported to the coroner. The coroner will then seek advice either from the local museum or local authority archaeological officer or archaeological unit or from the national museum, in accordance with the arrangements that have been agreed for each coroner's district (see paragraphs 38–41 [not reproduced here]). The local museum or archaeological officer and the national museum should agree whether to advise the Secretary of State that the object should be disclaimed; in some cases it may be necessary for the object to be delivered to the national museum for further study and it is noted in paragraph 51 that the national museum can also provide specialist conservation or metallurgical analysis. The local museum or archaeological officer and the national museum will also consult any other museums registered with the Museums and Galleries Commission that they believe may have a potential interest in acquiring the find. If as a result of this process of consultation, no museum wishes to acquire the object(s), then the national museum will advise the Secretary of State that the Crown's interest in the find should be disclaimed, and will inform the coroner. The coroner will not then need to proceed with an inquest and will take the steps set out in paragraph 47. If information about the find has not already been passed on to the appropriate Sites and Monuments Record (see list in Appendix 3 [not reproduced here]), then it will be done at this stage (see paragraph 39 [not reproduced here]). Only a complete find (for example, a complete coin hoard) may be disclaimed in this way; if a museum wishes to acquire any objects from a find, then the whole find will need to be considered at a treasure inquest.

47. Any objects disclaimed in this way will be treated as though they had never been treasure and will be returned by the coroner. The coroner will give notification to the occupier and the landowner (if different) that he intends to return them to the finder not less than 28 days after the date of his notification unless he receives an objection from either of them. If the coroner receives such an objection, the find will be retained by the coroner, or by the body to whom he has entrusted it, pending the resolution of the dispute between the parties. The coroner does not have the power to make a legal determination as to title as between the occupier, the landowner and the finder, and this question will, if necessary, need to be resolved in the courts. **A6–02**

48. It is recommended that a record of the coroner's findings and documentation relating to the disposal of the object should be kept with it. The person to whom objects have been returned in this way will be free to dispose of them as he wishes. However, all such objects will require an export licence from the Department of National Heritage if they are to be exported abroad. Application forms for export licences may be obtained from the Cultural Property Unit of the Department of National Heritage (0171 211 6000).

A6–03 **49.** The procedure outlined in paragraphs 46–48 may also be followed in the case of objects, such as those from archaeological excavations, where no reward is payable because the finder has waived his rights to a reward, provided that this is done in accordance with a pre-existing agreement between the parties concerned and provided that the Secretary of State is satisfied with the arrangements for their disposal. Such finds should also be reported to the coroner in the normal way and the coroner should be informed of the outcome. (See also paragraph 76.)

G. PROCEDURE WHEN A FIND HAS BEEN REPORTED TO THE CORONER; TREASURE INQUESTS

A6–04 **50.** Detailed guidelines on the procedure to be followed by coroners in treasure inquests will be set out in a Home Office Circular. This section of the Code is intended to summarise the main points insofar as they affect those who are likely to have an interest in treasure inquests (finders, occupiers, landowners, museums, etc.).

51. The coroner will hold an inquest on any find that has been reported to him and that he has reasonable grounds for believing to be treasure, except where the find has been disclaimed by the Secretary of State. On the other hand, it is expected that all those finds that no museum wishes to acquire will already have been disclaimed under the procedure laid down in paragraph 46, so it will effectively only be necessary to hold inquests on those finds that a museum wishes to acquire. A report on the find will be prepared for the coroner by national and local archaeologists in conjunction, as appropriate (see paragraph 41).[1] The coroner is required by the Act to inform the national museum if he intends to hold an inquest. In addition, the national museum will be able to provide specialist conservation and analytical facilities. Where necessary the coroner will make arrangements for the object to be delivered to the national museum. (However, the coroner may ask the national museum to make arrangements regarding the delivery of fragile objects.)

A6–05 **52.** The body that is providing advice to the coroner in accordance with paragraph 51 will give the coroner a report giving brief details of the objects together with an assessment as to whether they fall within the definition of treasure and, if so, on what grounds. The report will not contain a valuation of the objects.

53. In the case of objects other than coins, it may be necessary to obtain a scientific analysis, wherever possible without sampling, of one or more objects from the find in order to determine whether they fall within the definition of treasure under the Act. It will not normally be necessary to obtain an analysis of the metal content of coins. In some cases it may also be necessary to clean the objects so that they can be identified (see Appendix 5, section 6 [not reproduced here]).

54. The coroner will have the duty of notifying the finder, the occupier and the owner of the land where the find was made of the place and date when he intends to hold an inquest. These persons will be given an opportunity to examine witnesses at the inquest and may, according to the coroner's discretion, be represented at the inquest. Since it may not always be straightforward for the coroner to discover the identity of the landowner, the Act requires the coroner to ask the finder or the occupier who the landowner is and the coroner will then take reasonable steps to ensure that he is informed.

---

[1] In the case of finds from Wales, the coroner will normally ask for a report from the National Museums & Galleries of Wales.

55. The inquest will be held without a jury unless the coroner, at his discretion, decides otherwise. In some cases the Crown and/or the national museum and/or the local museum or local archaeological officer (as identified in paragraph 51) may wish to be represented at the inquest. The recommendation in paragraph 43 [not reproduced here] about the desirability of keeping find-spots confidential applies. **A6–06**

56. If an object is found not to be treasure as a result of an inquest, then it will be returned by the coroner according to the principles set out on the return of objects that have been disclaimed in paragraph 47. The recommendation that relevant documentation be kept with the object and the conditions regarding the export of such objects in paragraph 48 also apply. The coroner will be informed by the Department of National Heritage about the decision taken by the Secretary of State in relation to the objects with which he has been concerned.

57. If a find is declared treasure and if the coroner is advised that a museum may wish to acquire either the whole find or an object from it, the coroner shall arrange for the find to be delivered to the national museum so that it can be valued by the Treasure Valuation Committee. (However, the coroner may ask the national museum to make arrangements regarding the delivery of fragile objects.) **A6–07**

58. The decision of the inquest will be subject to the jurisdiction of the courts by way of judicial review. In certain circumstances coroners' inquests may also be reviewed under section 13 of the Coroner's Act 1988.

59. The coroner or the body into whose care a find has been entrusted will take reasonable steps to ensure its safe custody and, in the event of an object being lost or damaged, except by the negligence of the party concerned, the Secretary of State may make an *ex gratia* payment to the person who would have been entitled to the reward under the guidelines contained in paragraphs 66–80 of this code, subject to a lower limit of £100.

H. ACQUISITION OF TREASURE

60. The current practice is that objects that are declared treasure trove are offered in the first instance by the Secretary of State to the national museum and that, if the national museum does not wish to acquire the objects, it offers them to other museums. This system will continue (subject to a review after three years: see paragraph 84 [not reproduced here]), but the following procedures and principles will be followed by the national museum in dealing with finds of treasure: **A6–08**

(1) The Museum of London will have the first right to acquire any finds of treasure made within the franchise enjoyed by the Corporation of London. Bristol Museums and Art Gallery will enjoy a similar right in respect of any finds of treasure made within any franchise that may be held by the City of Bristol.

(2) Finds of national importance should be kept intact and will normally be acquired by the national museum. In England, it is expected that only a small proportion of finds of treasure will normally be classed as being of national importance. The national museum will consult the local registered museum[2] over such finds. In the event that a find of regional or local interest cannot be acquired by the local registered museum or by another registered museum, the national museum may then consider acquiring it.

(3) In the case of other finds not of national importance there may also be good reasons both academically and archaeologically for keeping them intact. If the local registered museum wishes to acquire such a find intact, then it will have the opportunity to do so; if the local museum does not wish to acquire the find, it

[2] This museum will already have been identified under the procedure outlined in paragraphs 38–41 and 46 [not reproduced here].

may be offered to another registered museum in the United Kingdom with a relevant interest in the objects contained in the find. When considering to which local registered museum a find will be offered, account will be taken of the collecting areas and collecting policies of any interested local museums. The documentation relating to the find will be copied to the museum that acquires it.

(4) If no museum wishes to acquire the find intact, then one or more of the museums listed in (2) above may wish to select some of the objects from the find for their collections by mutual agreement. Those objects that are not required by museums will be returned by the coroner according to the principles laid down in paragraph 47. The documentation relating to the whole find will be copied to each museum that acquires some objects from the find.

(5) There is a presumption that objects of treasure found during the course of archaeological excavations will be kept with the rest of the archaeological archive.

(6) A find from consecrated land that would have qualified as treasure trove under the common law of treasure trove, and which will therefore fall outside the scope of the order described in paragraph 16 [not reproduced here], will be offered to a local church museum (if there is one) if the national museum does not wish to acquire it.

(7) If finders and anyone else with an interest in the find wish to waive their right to a reward on condition that the find is deposited in a particular registered museum, their wishes will be taken into account.

(8) The references to "registered" museums above are to museums with registration from the Museums and Galleries Commission.

(9) The Department of National Heritage's review of museum policy, *Treasures in Trust*, was based on the premise that "a museum's collections are to be held on behalf of the public as inalienable cultural assets" (3.2) and this applies to acquisitions of treasure. Any museum that acquires treasure may only dispose of it in accordance with the registration guidelines of the Museums and Galleries Commission (paragraph 4.2.5) (or its successor), and in accordance with any conditions on disposal imposed by any grant-awarding bodies that may have assisted in the acquisition of the object.

(10) It is expected that museums that acquire finds of treasure will generally wish to place them on exhibition. However, where finds of treasure are not on exhibition, finders and any other interested members of the public will have access to them on request, in accordance with the Museums and Galleries Commission's registration guidelines.

I. VALUATION OF TREASURE

A6–09 **61.** The Government strongly reaffirms the principle behind the establishment of the Treasure Trove Reviewing Committee, which was established in 1977 to provide independent scrutiny of valuations of finds of treasure, in the belief that it has worked very well. The Committee will therefore be retained; but it will be renamed the Treasure Valuation Committee in order to reflect more accurately its role. Its terms of reference will be to recommend to the Secretary of State valuations for the items brought before it which correspond as closely as possible, taking account of all relevant factors, to what may be paid for the object(s) in a sale on the open market between a willing seller and a willing buyer; and to provide advice to the Secretary of State in cases where there may be grounds for either no reward to be paid to the finder, or for a reduced reward to be paid, or where there is a dispute as to the apportionment of the reward between the finder and the occupier/owner of the land or between the occupier and a person having a superior interest (see paragraphs 64 and 71).

62. However, the Government recognises that it is important not just that the valuations agreed by the Committee should be fair but that they should be seen to be fair. Therefore, in order to ensure the widest possible confidence in treasure valuations, the Committee will commission reports from independent experts drawn from the trade on all finds that come before it, and the reports submitted by the national museums will cease to contain valuations but will simply contain a description of the objects. In most cases of treasure the valuations will be straightforward and it will be sufficient for the Committee to commission a single valuation, but the Committee will have the discretion to commission more than one valuation where it deems it to be desirable. All interested parties (finders, occupiers and landowners, if eligible for rewards, and any museum that intends to acquire objects from the find) will be given the opportunity to comment on these valuations and on the reports of the national museums before the Committee reaches its decision; in addition, finders and occupiers and landowners; if eligible for rewards, will continue to have the right to submit their own evidence to the Committee. Such evidence may be in the form of valuations commissioned by these parties.

63. It is important to bear in mind that a finder who fails to report a find of treasure in contravention of section 8 of the Act and sells it to a dealer is, besides committing an offence, likely also to obtain a much lower price for it than if he had reported it in the proper way. Reporting a find of treasure in accordance with the requirements of the Act is the best guarantee of receiving a fair reward. **A6–10**

64. In addition, the Secretary of State may request the Treasure Valuation Committee to investigate the circumstances where there may be any grounds for the abatement of the reward under the terms of paragraphs 79 and 80 and to make a recommendation.

65. Should an interested party (as defined in paragraph 62) be dissatisfied with the Committee's recommendation, that party will have the right to make representations to the Secretary of State before a decision is made. The Secretary of State will normally allow one month after the finder (or the occupier or landowner) has been notified of the Committee's recommendation to allow any representation to be made before making the order. The Secretary of State's decision will be subject to the jurisdiction of the courts by way of judicial review. Any claim of maladministration can be investigated by the Parliamentary Commissioner for Administration.

J. REWARDS

I. Objectives

66. These guidelines replace the current practice in the payment of rewards for treasure trove, which was most recently re-stated in the *Report of a Review of Ex Gratia Awards to Finders of Treasure Trove* (H.M. Treasury, 1988). The paramount objective in the payment of rewards for finds of treasure is to encourage the reporting of finds and to ensure that there are adequate incentives to finders while at the same time discouraging wrong behaviour. The Department of National Heritage will pay the reward to the person entitled to it according to the provisions in these guidelines. The Department will only make such payment after having received an equivalent sum of money from the museum or museums which wish to acquire the objects. **A6–11**

II. Guidelines for the payment of rewards where the finder is searching for artefacts

67. Where the finder has a valid permission from the occupier to be on the land where he made his find in order to search for and remove artefacts, he will receive the reward in full. The burden of proof as to whether he has permission will rest with the finder. **A6–12**

68. If it is established that the permission to enter the land was subject to the finder and occupier and/or the owner agreeing to share any reward, the Secretary of State will be prepared to apportion the reward with reference to the agreement. If there is a dispute as to the terms of such an agreement, the Secretary of State will determine what is appropriate. Where permission to enter land in order to search for treasure has been established, the burden of proving that it was subject to an agreement to share the proceeds of the reward will be with the occupier or the owner (where different).

69. There may be occasions where an occupier for the time being, because of the extent and nature of his interest in the land, did not have the capacity to give permission and should not have done so; for example, an agricultural tenant may be prohibited from authorising a treasure search under the terms of his tenancy. It is not thought appropriate to abate the finder's reward unless it appears to the Secretary of State that the finder was aware, or could reasonably have established, that the person who granted consent to enter into the land had no authority to do so. Where the Secretary of State does abate the finder's reward, the balance of the abated reward will be paid to the person who would have been entitled to give permission to enter the land to search for treasure (usually the owner).

A6–13 **70.** Following from this, there may also be occasions where an occupier for the time being, because of the extent and nature of his interest in the land, would be liable to a person having a superior interest in the land for the proceeds of the sale of any object found on the land and the Secretary of State intends to give effect to this in making the reward. If there is a dispute as to how a reward should be apportioned between the occupier of the land and the person having the superior interest (usually the owner), the Secretary of State will determine what is appropriate.

71. Whenever there is a dispute as to whether a reward should be abated or as to how it should be apportioned, the Secretary of State will have regard to any representations made by the parties and may ask for advice from the Treasure Valuation Committee.

72. If there is more than one finder, that part of the reward to which they are entitled will be divided equally between them except where there is an agreement to the contrary.

73. If a finder does not remove the whole of a find from the ground but reports it, thus affording the opportunity for the archaeological excavation of the remainder of the find, the original finder will normally be eligible for a reward for the whole find and not just that part which he himself had removed from the ground, although the Secretary of State will need to examine the individual circumstances of each case.

A6–14 **74.** Finders may expect to receive no rewards at all or abated rewards under the following circumstances:

- (i) where the finder has committed an offence under section 8 of the Act by failing to report treasure within 14 days of making the find or within 14 days of believing or of having reasonable grounds for believing that the find was treasure, without a reasonable excuse;
- (ii) where the finder has committed an offence under section 42 of the 1979 Ancient Monuments and Archaeological Areas Act (unauthorised use of a metal detector on a protected place) (see paragraph 29 [not reproduced here]);
- (iii) where there is evidence of illegal activity in relation to a find whether or not a prosecution has been mounted;
- (iv) where all the relevant circumstances surrounding a find, including the find-spot, were not reported;
- (v) where there is evidence that only part of a find has been handed in;
- (vi) where there are reasonable grounds for believing that a find was made elsewhere than on the alleged site;

(vii) where there are reasonable grounds for believing that the finder was trespassing[3] ;

(viii) where significant damage has been done deliberately or recklessly either to the actual object, or to a surrounding monument or to the archaeological deposits making up the contexts which may explain the circumstances in which the object became buried or concealed, when the object was removed from the place where it was found;

(ix) where there are other factors that the Secretary of State thinks it appropriate to take into account in individual cases.

It will be within the discretion of the Secretary of State to decide by how much the reward to the finder is to be abated in such circumstances or whether no reward will be payable at all to the finder.

75. In such circumstances the occupier or the landowner will be eligible for the whole of the balance of the reward in such proportion as the Secretary of State may determine, according to the principles laid down in paragraph 69, provided that there is no evidence that they have been a party to wrong behaviour on the part of the finder. The museum that acquires the find will only have to pay that part of the reward that is actually payable.

76. Rewards will not normally be payable when the find is made by an archaeologist. This will not affect any interest that the occupier or the landowner may have in any reward. (See also paragraph 49 [not reproduced here].)

III. Guidelines for the payment of rewards where the finder was not searching for artefacts

77. Where the finder, who has not been searching for artefacts, makes a chance find and where he clearly has permission to be where he made his find and where he has reported his find according to the law, then the reward will be divided in whatever proportions the Secretary of State thinks fit, taking account of the circumstances of each case. In most cases the finder may expect to receive half of the reward; that part of the reward for which the occupier and the landowner may be eligible will be divided between them according to the principles laid down in paragraph 69. **A6–15**

78. Where the finder has not been searching for artefacts and there are reasonable grounds for believing that the finder did not have permission to be where he made the find, then it may be appropriate for the reward to be divided between the finder, the occupier and the landowner, the Secretary of State being able to use discretion according to the individual circumstances of the case.

IV. Amount of abatement

79. Decisions about the level of rewards in individual cases will be taken in the light of the particular circumstances of each case and in making a decision the Secretary of State shall be guided by the recommendations of the Treasure Valuation Committee. In making its recommendations, the Committee shall seek to find a balance between the objective of those rewards to encourage the prompt and proper reporting of finds and the need for those rewards not themselves to provide an incentive for illegal or improper behaviour. The Committee shall also take account of the archaeological and historical significance of the effect of illegal or improper behaviour involved in the specific **A6–16**

[3] As regards finds made on the foreshore (that is the land between mean high water and mean low water), the Crown Estate confirms that a finder on Crown Estate foreshore will ordinarily be treated as being on the land with permission, that is, not trespassing, but this implied permission does not include permission to search. (Just over half of the foreshore on the coast of England, Wales and Northern Ireland is Crown land.)

circumstances of a particular case. In such cases the interested parties will have the opportunity to submit evidence to the Committee. The Secretary of State will notify the parties concerned of the decision, giving such reasons as may be necessary.

80. The Secretary of State's decision will be subject to the jurisdiction of the courts by way of judicial review. Any claim of maladministration can be investigated by the Parliamentary Commissioner for Administration.